PACE
TO
PEACE

Finding Inner Rest in a World of Unrest

Edward Hersh

Carpenter's Son Publishing

Published by Carpenter's Son Publishing, Franklin, Tennessee

Edited by Ann Tatlock

Cover Design and Interior Design by Suzanne Lawing

Illustrations by Maria Tomassetti and Stephanie Hersh

Printed in the United States of America

978-1-954437-61-6

Contents

Preface 7

Introduction 9

Part 1: Prepare the Heart

Chapter 1   Housing Peace in the Heart 19

Chapter 2   Knowing Is Not Enough. 33

Chapter 3   Trade the Will for the Well. 47

Part 2: Accept Our Broken Heart Condition

Chapter 4   Spiritual Laws that Govern Life. 61

Chapter 5   Bitter Root Judgments 69

Chapter 6   Emotional Trunk. 83

Chapter 7   Identity and Shame 95

Chapter 8   Trauma 121

Part 3: Cooperate With God in Surrender

Chapter 9   Give Away the House 135

Chapter 10   Clean Up the House 151

Chapter 11   Care for the Neighborhood 173

Part 4: Engage Inner Change as a Lifestyle

Chapter 12   Remove Blockages to Peace 189

Chapter 13   Garden the Soul. 207

Chapter 14   Lead with Transformational Living 223

Chapter 15   Choose God Daily. 235

Chapter 16   God Is Altogether Good. 251

Chapter 17   Apply Truth 271

Chapter 18   PACE to Finish Line – Conclusions 285

Appendix A   The Cycle of Defeat. 289

Appendix B   A Sample Prayer of Forgiveness 291

Appendix C   Emotions and Misbeliefs (Lies). 293

Appendix D   Sample Inner Vows 297

Bibliography   299

About the Author   305

Invitation   307

Questions For Each Chapter To Help Apply 309

Preface

Change is not our enemy. There is no need to fear change, although there is plenty to fear when we refuse godly change. There will never be another day exactly like today. This reality makes change a built-in factor of tomorrow and every day in the future. Since change is unavoidable, we must learn how to make it our friend. For better or for worse, our reality is shaped by how well we manage change. Today's change creates tomorrow's reality.

God never changes, but for mankind to experience God in greater measures, change is needed on man's part. My hope is that this book helps the reader pace to a deeper level of peace in the transforming power of the gospel of Jesus Christ. Lasting peace of mind and heart is only possible through pursuit of God. The way to Father God is through a personal relationship with Jesus Christ whom the Bible calls the "Prince of Peace" (Isaiah 9:6). Some reading this, like myself, believed in Jesus for the forgiveness of their sin as a child. I was water baptized at age twelve. Most of my life I have been in churches that believe in the Holy Spirit baptism, and have had my own empowering encounters with the Holy Spirit. I have ministered to others for receiving their own encounters with God in these ways. But it was about twenty-five years ago that I began seeing a significant area of lack in the Body of Christ as a whole.

The last twenty-five years have been a journey for me of growing in the truths of transformation and sanctification. In the mid-1990s, I encountered a ministry called Elijah House founded by John and Paula Sandford. Applying their teaching of what is sometimes called "inner healing" brought tremendous healing in my heart and inspired me to answer a call of God to pursue formal training in counseling to be equipped to help others find greater freedom in Christ. I completed a master's degree program at Regent University, and then earned a doctorate at Trinity School of the Bible and Theological Seminary. Through self-study I also discovered many healing prayer ministries similar to Elijah House that are all based on the same Scriptures, but use slightly different terminology for how their model is practiced.

Over the years I have developed my own tools from studying the Scriptures and incorporating ideas gleaned from various resources. I consider myself a continuous learner. My approach to the counseling and teaching ministry I do is eclectic. In terms of content, there is nothing new under the sun. But in terms of watching how the Son of God works his healing in peoples' lives, it is always unique to the individual. This book is a sort of summary of these years of God working in my own life and the lives of those I serve.

Inner person change may not be at the top of most people's list of the most important things in life, but for the serious follower of Jesus, it's the key to becoming more like him. More of Jesus means more peace, at a pace more rewarding and less burdensome. There is no time to waste. Let's dive in, and allow his pace to become our peace.

Introduction

This book is a tool to facilitate transformation of the inner person. Why is inner peace only possible through constant change? The answer will become apparent as you read, study, and apply the truth found here. We will explore themes discussed in the Bible, especially the book of Hebrews that directly connects our relationship with God and the quality of the inner rest of our souls (see Hebrews 12:14-15, 3:1-12). Increasing the quality of our relationship with God requires constant realignment of our thoughts, actions, and patterns of behavior (Romans 12:1-2). Transformation and sanctification are processes of consistently reordering our old attitudes, beliefs, and standards of living to align with God's.

"Pursue peace with all men, and the sanctification without which no one will see the Lord. See to it that no one comes short of the grace of God; that no root of bitterness springing up causes trouble, and by it many be defiled" (Hebrews 12:14-15 NASB).

Looking at these verses in context of the book of Hebrews from the beginning of the chapter to the point where they appear, the sanctification of our soul emerges as a very dominant theme. Faith is defined in the previous chapter, Chapter 11, in the passage best known for introducing the "heroes of faith." Chapter 12 offers specifics of how faith is lived out.

First, Jesus is the "founder" AND "perfecter" of our faith (see Hebrews 12:2, ESV). The Passion Translation (TPT) expresses it as, "Jesus who birthed faith within us and who leads us forward into faith's perfection"—that is, completion. There is a beginning and a completion to faith in Christ. Believing in Jesus at a conversion experience begins a process of completing faith's work the remainder of our lives.

Secondly, verses 4-11 speak of growing, as children grow in their Father's (parents') care. Growth involves change and stretching of what is, into what it needs to become. The growth process requires discipline. A commitment to this kind of change brings about joy and peace.

Now to verses 14-15, quoted above. Sanctification is explicitly mentioned "without which no one will see the Lord" (Hebrews 12:14). Without completion of faith in Jesus through the sanctification process (change and growth through discipline toward holiness), we have no faith at all. This ongoing change is to be pursued, intentionally sought, and not merely expected to happen on its own. Moreover, this process is intrinsically linked back to our conversion to faith in Christ, and forward to establishing the conditions for our inner peace.

The phrase "pursue peace with all men" is obviously an exhortation to relate to people on friendly terms whenever possible. But a deeper meaning struck me as I did a word study on the use of the word peace in the Bible.

Peace is not merely the absence of conflict. It is not merely a feeling of self-satisfaction, contentment, security, or harmony with external worldly circumstances. Webster's 1828 dictionary explains the definition of peace as, "a state of quiet or tranquility; freedom from disturbance or agitation." The Bible uses the term *peace* most often as a way to describe our inner (heart) condition before Almighty God. Defining peace in the *Lexham Theological Wordbook*, J. Lookadoo points out, "In the biblical writings, peace is the wholeness that comes as a result of alignment with God's creative and redemptive purposes.... Peace occurs not only in interpersonal relationships, but also in ethnic and political relationships. Peace also carries a cosmic connotation, in which all aspects of creation, both human and non-human, should exist in harmony with each other. Peace is thus the ideal of creation that God's redemptive activity seeks to restore…. The flourishing existence of creation described in Gen 1–2 shapes how peace is understood throughout the rest of the Bible. Peace involves well-being…. Ultimately peace comes as a result of Jesus' work and thus is a gift given by God. Ephesians describes Christ creating a new humanity by healing the divisions between Jews and Gentiles and making peace (*eirēnē*) between them (Eph 2:14–15)—and by being 'our peace (*eirēnē*)'"[1]

God's purposes and plans for peace are far greater than our personal experiences of escaping the feelings of unrest inside. However, our inner life is very important to God. So important that he commands complete surrender of our ways of thinking, feeling, and behaving in exchange for his. The psalmist reflects, "Those who love Your law have great peace, and nothing causes them to stumble" (Psalm 119:165 NASB). God's ways are superior to human ways. We are wise to accept this truth, "How blessed is the man who finds wisdom, and the man who gains understanding. Her ways are pleasant ways, and all her paths are peace" (Proverbs 3:13,17 NASB).

Jesus himself had some things to say about peace. Jesus didn't come into the world to chase away conflict (see Matthew 10:24). He came to deliver us from enslavement to conflict. First, the conflict that exists within our own soul, and the conflict that puts us at war (sometimes literally) with people around us. Without Christ, conflict is inevitable within, but with and through Christ conflict is, was, and will be annihilated. Since the first sin of mankind, conflict within and conflict without (our environment) are built into the default nature of every

---

1 D. Mangum, D. R. Brown, R. Klippenstein, and R. Hurst, eds. *Lexham Theological Wordbook*. Bellingham, WA: Lexham Press, 2014. Digital Logos Edition.

human being. Putting our faith and trust in Jesus means we are yielding to his power to remove the grip of unrest in lost parts of our souls.

At the root of conflict is bitterness. Bitterness is created by the seeds of failed expectations, disappointments, regret, hurt, or offense. Roots of bitterness are specifically mentioned in these verses in Hebrews as destructive anti-growth agents. Bitter roots are weeds that will "defile" (reduce the productivity of the garden of our hearts). Bitter roots can take the form of ill-willed thoughts, envy, jealousy, malice, slander, and the like. The critical, condemning thoughts and opinions turn into blame, resentment, hatred and even sometimes revenge. Our tendency to want to rule our own fate causes our failure to trust God to work all circumstances for good. God's justice demands that only he can sit on the throne as Judge. Our demands to think and act as Judge create conflict. The rebellion against God at the core of this conflict is why the "Prince of Peace," Messiah Jesus, came to this earth (see Isaiah 9:6).

This goes to the heart of the gospel message. Luke records Jesus as saying, "For the Son of Man has come to seek and to save that which was lost" (Luke 19:10 NKJV). Until recently, like most Christians, I thought of "lost" souls coming to faith in Jesus in a conversion experience as the full extent of interpreting the meaning of this statement in Luke 19.

However, God is challenging me with a deeper understanding. The inner peace stolen by the enemy of our soul with the entry of sin into the world is part of the loss that Jesus came to redeem. Through the transformation and sanctification process, the seeking and saving of the losses in our lives continues. Faith in Jesus makes us whole. All the broken parts of our soul still touched by the losses are being brought together into the wholeness God intends for us from the beginning. Sanctification is God's divine plan. Being made whole through holiness (set apart on the inside) yields the fruit of increasingly greater degrees of outwardly "holy" behavior. Becoming completely at peace with God's plan in our innermost being begins at conversion and is fulfilled through and through a lifelong PACE. I call this a PACE, as each letter in the word corresponds to one of the four parts of this book; Prepare, Accept, Cooperate, and Engage (described below);.

I grew up in the Christian church thinking the "salvation of souls" refers merely to the conversion of souls. However, the term salvation includes sanctification as well. It includes Jesus completing the faith he has begun. It includes the discipline of growing the faith into maturity. It includes the inner peace Hebrews calls the "peaceful fruit of righteousness" (see Hebrews 12:11).

The "harvest" of souls includes all of the above. Let's be clear that believing in Jesus is not just a decision of the mind to repent (turn around) from one way of life to another. It is a radical surrender to a process of heart transformation as well. For a Christian, seeking the sanctification of our soul is not an option. Responding to God and allowing him to change our heart from the inside out will yield greater degrees of inner peace. Inner peace can be a gauge for measuring our progress. The more we surrender to God, the more peace we will have in our soul.

Inner change is difficult, but we can be at peace with the uncertainty change brings when we are trusting God through our faith in Jesus. An inner peace and assurance of what Jesus has accomplished for us, AND what he continues to empower us to do, is foundational for facing the challenges of life. It's all about his power, not ours.

In summary, I offer my paraphrase of the Hebrews 12:14-15 verses quoted at the beginning. "Pursue inner peace through reconciliation with God, for yourself, and seek this condition for every person you know. Practice surrendering your heart to God for the purpose of a holy being, until the day you see Jesus face to face. Make sure you are living the fullest of God's purposes for your life by rooting out any bitterness that remains—i.e., admitting your critical judgments, surrendering all judgments to God, and releasing all demands for justice so your relationships (with God, others, and self) can be made whole." This book is a tool to help guide and encourage you on the journey.

In Hebrews 3, God gives us a picture of what it takes to "enter his rest" and find lasting peace for our souls. The example of the people of Israel in the Old Testament shows us how a lack of belief in God's ways will rob us from the blessings of soul rest. The author of Hebrews says,

> And to whom did He swear that they would not enter His rest, but to those who were disobedient? So we see that they were not able to enter because of unbelief. Therefore, let us fear if, while a promise remains of entering His rest, any one of you may seem to have come short of it. For indeed we have had good news preached to us, just as they also; but the word they heard did not profit them, because it was not united by faith in those who heard. For we who have believed enter that rest. (Hebrews 3:18-4:3 NASB)

The Israelites had a history of following God for a while and then falling away, ending up outside the boundaries of peaceful existence. Sometimes when they disobeyed God, their enemies physically plundered their communities. A spiritual parallel in the verses above shows us that our beliefs (and views of God) govern the level of rest in our souls. Surrendering our hearts to God through faith in Jesus in ever increasing measure increases the pace to peace in our hearts.

Four Parts to P-A-C-E

P-repare the Heart

A-ccept Our Broken Heart Condition

C-ooperate with God through Surrender

E-ngage Inner Change as a Lifestyle

The journey through this book begins in Part One with preparing the heart. Recognizing what makes us "tick" (so to speak) is critical to making any kind of positive directional changes. Our heart is like a house. The center of all activities for a farm is the farmhouse. The farmer eats, rests, plays, plans, and finds shelter in the farmhouse. When the farmhouse functions well to meet the needs of the farmer, the foundation for the success of the mission of the farm is secure.

Part Two of this book is about accepting our broken-down heart condition. Without God, our farmhouse and therefore our entire farm is in disrepair and cannot be fixed on its own. Self-honesty about the true condition of our heart is key to taking first steps toward positive change.

The humility to continue taking steps toward God is essential to grow out of our brokenness.

Part Three walks through cooperating with God to restore our heart so it can thrive once again. Surrender is a key. Gaining something new requires giving up the old. That's easier said than done when it comes to old (familiar) patterns of thought and behavior. We must become "wholly" dissatisfied with our own ways to gain satisfaction with God's "holy" ways (see Proverbs 14:11-12).

Part Four deals with engaging transformational growth as a lifestyle. Changing to be a better person is great, but God's purposes are far beyond our imaginations and expectations. The only way to discover God's greater purposes is to embrace inner change by drawing ever closer to God. This includes nurturing a healthy discontent with how far we've already come. The moment a farmer becomes too content with his farm's productivity, conditions out of his control (e.g., severe weather, pests, economy, thieves) will push things in a declining direction. We must remain vigilant in fighting our broken world's declining tendencies. We must embrace our need for constant change from the inside out.

I provide some practical tools along the way and in the appendices. Also in the back of the book are a group of questions for each chapter. The questions are designed to help the pace reader on their own journey to peace. I encourage writing out the answers for each chapter before going on to the next chapter.

Inner life change begins with a better understanding of our inner life. So let's get started.

Part 1

Prepare the Heart

Watch over your heart with all diligence,
For from it flow the springs of life. Proverbs 4:23 (NASB)

"Now why do you call Me, 'Lord, Lord,' and do not do what I say?
Everyone who comes to Me and hears My words and acts on them, I will
show you whom he is like: he is like a man building a house, who dug deep
and laid a foundation on the rock; and when there was a flood, the river
burst against that house and yet it could not shake it, because it had been
well built. But the one who has heard and has not acted accordingly is like
a man who built a house on the ground without a foundation; and the
river burst against it and it immediately collapsed, and the ruin of that
house was great." Luke 6:46-49 (NASB)

Planning and preparation are a big part of life. Good meals are preceded by securing the necessary ingredients, orderly putting the substances together, and cooking with correct heat and timing. In recent

decades, "instant" dinners have tried to short circuit the process, but imitation (instant) meals never taste as good as cooking from scratch. Building a house takes even more preparation. As we see in Luke 6:46-49, building a house worth living in requires preparing a firm foundation. Even before the foundation is built, much planning and preparation is necessary (i.e., structure schematics, digging dirt, pouring footers, laying blocks, etc.). Jesus teaches us an essential lesson with this illustration. To be a Christ-follower, we cannot just say "Lord" with our mouth, but we must continuously think and act on truth, day by day, moment by moment, like building blocks for a secure foundation. Believing and acting on truth to demonstrate our commitment to Jesus as Lord is easier said than done. It takes great intentionality; hence, I devote the first three chapters of this book to it.

Chapter 1

Housing Peace in the Heart

Even with a secure foundation in place, a house cannot be built without a great amount of preparation. Building a house from scratch requires planning precise details in order for everything to fit properly and work smoothly. Effort is needed to make it a secure shelter. Life's journey is a process with many parallels to the building and rebuilding of a house. For our soul to be at rest, we must pay attention to some important details.

House Reconstruction

My wife and I have owned a number of homes over the years. Most were older than I was, and it seemed like something fell into disrepair frequently, and at the most inopportune times. I have come to understand many spiritual lessons through my experiences of owning and living in a house.

Coming to faith in Jesus in a conversion experience is like transferring the deed of a property to God's ownership. Our physical, mental, and emotional being is no longer our own, but we have been bought with the price of the blood of Jesus (1 Corinthians 6:20).

At conversion, the Holy Spirit awakens our dead personal spirit, and comes to live inside our bodies (Romans 8:9-11). Then the fun begins. The processes of transformation and sanctification become our destiny. They are illustrated well by property ownership. A number of places in the Bible speak of our body as a tent, temple, dwelling, or house. Anyone who has lived in a particular house for a length of time knows that houses can take a lot of work to maintain. Although houses are viewed as an asset on a financial balance sheet, tax collectors have come up with a method of depreciating their value over time because repairs and improvements are so large and expensive. The older the house, the more surprises that may be found when trying to fix something. Chipped paint may lead to broken plaster which may lead to finding a plumbing leak which leads to rotten floorboards, and so on. For this illustration, when we "sell out" to God, he buys us "as is." Now the repairs are in his control and on his terms and in his timing. Methods of restoration, tools and materials used, floor plans, space utilization, landscaping, outside buildings, etc. are all changed how and when the Owner decides.

In the Bible, the ancient Israelites are spoken of as a "house," where God dwells among his people. In addition to a community meaning of "house," since the coming of Jesus to the earth, the Bible also refers to an individual's heart as being a "house" for the Holy Spirit to dwell within. What an incredible thought: "My heart is a house for God to dwell in!" God's goal is to create a place of peace for his presence to abide.

As individuals and as a community, the verses below indicate God's people sometimes have a hard time maintaining their devotion to God. God is faithful to grant them peace in their hearts when they remain faithful. Christ Jesus' temptation and suffering now provides full access to Father God and a way for our "house" to be made alive in him. See the second chapter of the book of Hebrews for an introduction to the following quote.

> Therefore, holy brothers and sisters, who share in the heavenly calling, fix your thoughts on Jesus, whom we acknowledge as our apostle and high priest. He was faithful to the one who ap-

pointed him, just as Moses was faithful in all God's house. Jesus has been found worthy of greater honor than Moses, just as the builder of a house has greater honor than the house itself. For every house is built by someone, but God is the builder of everything. "Moses was faithful as a servant in all God's house," bearing witness to what would be spoken by God in the future. But Christ is faithful as the Son over God's house. And we are his house, if indeed we hold firmly to our confidence and the hope in which we glory.

So, as the Holy Spirit says:

"Today, if you hear his voice,
    do not harden your hearts
as you did in the rebellion,
    during the time of testing in the wilderness,
where your ancestors tested and tried me,
    though for forty years they saw what I did.
That is why I was angry with that generation;
    I said, 'Their hearts are always going astray,
and they have not known my ways.'
    So I declared on oath in my anger,
'They shall never enter my rest.'

See to it, brothers and sisters, that none of you has a sinful, unbelieving heart that turns away from the living God." (Hebrews 3:1-12 NIV)

A heart turned toward God finds peace. A heart turned away from God has no rest. A believing heart turns toward God. An unbelieving heart turns away. Belief in God empowers peace. Unbelief destroys any opportunity for us to experience peace in our body, mind, soul, and spirit. At conversion, believing in Jesus begins a process whereby more and more measures of faith and trust (belief) is placed in Father God for our identity, provision, and protection. We are still prone to complaining and blaming like the people of God described above, but now we have Jesus as "the Way, the Truth, and the Life" (see John 14).

This process of change requires altering our former beliefs. Our beliefs must be brought into alignment with God's "beliefs." This is done through surrendering possession of our house to God. God now owns our heart, and we must cooperate with the reconstruction he wants to do. God may want to tear down a wall to make more space in a room. We build walls of self-protection in our hearts that often damage our relationships. God may want to strip old paint off the door frames of another room to expose the original wood. We often make surface excuses to hide our imperfect perceptions, and thus we mask who God originally intended us to be. God may just want to clean the junk out of some dark closets. We hide things in places that become dark holes of disappointment and depression. Just about any task of house renovation and maintenance can be likened to alterations in the human heart.

The more remaking and remodeling, the more useful and beautiful the living space of the house becomes. The more heart-change in the right direction, the more peace and rest that follows. Room by room, corner by corner, piece by piece our heart is changed into a place of beauty and productivity. A house foundation that is shored up and strengthened, will bear the weight of upward expansion, and also be better prepared for storms ahead (see the story Jesus told in Matthew 7:24-27). Storms of life are inevitable and may take the form of relationship or business breakups, unemployment, pandemics, health problems, or some kind of injustice. A heart transformed into greater wholeness has greater capacity, resilience, and forbearance for these kinds of troubles.

Some may find this difficult to believe, but one of the best ways to discover where our heart needs transformational healing and reconstruction is to allow ourselves to feel the pain of our inner hurts. Just as a house may look a bit messy from demolition work before reconstruction can begin, cleaning up the messes in our lives is somewhat necessary before beauty is restored. I can speak from my own experience that every corner cleaned up is one more step to sweeter rest of soul. Hopefully this does not scare you away from reading on. This book is my attempt to help the reader find, to the greatest degree possible, meaning and purpose through the God-ordained process of transformation from the inside out.

The Bible records Jesus as saying, "Therefore everyone who hears these words of mine and puts them into practice is like a wise man who built his house on the rock. The rain came down, the streams rose, and the winds blew and beat against that house; yet it did not fall, because it had its foundation on the rock. But everyone who hears these words of mine and does not put them into practice is like a foolish man who built his house on sand. The rain came down, the streams rose, and the winds blew and beat against that house, and it fell with a great crash" (Matthew 7:24-27 NIV).

Our whole life is a building and rebuilding (reconstructing) process. As transforming and sanctifying revelation comes from God, we are to apply his orders. We make his plans fit into the new structure (house) he is re-creating. Yielding to his design all through the process is the only way to ensure a firm standing.

The house reconstruction illustration shows how continually practicing transformation from the inside out is the only way to a firm foundation for meaning and purpose in life, and being productive as a person (see Matthew 7:15-27). In the verses just prior to the ones quoted above and all through Christ's teaching he illustrates heart re-creation by talking about "fruit" (behavior). The kind of house a person maintains reveals the inside heart condition and is evidenced by a person's behavior. Let's look now at heart re-creation.

Heart Re-creation

The wisdom of the Bible is unmatched as a source of refuge and inner strength. A verse in Proverbs states a very significant key to a healthy life. "Above all else guard your heart, for everything you do flows from it" (Proverbs 4:23 NIV).

The *Cornerstone Biblical Commentary* says, "Heart is a word that Proverbs uses to describe the entire internal life of a person. It is an internal reflection of the person." The heart of a person is the core inner self. The Hebrew word used in the text is a combination of inclination, disposition, determination, courage, will, intention, attention, consideration, and reason. The heart determines and reflects values, attitudes, and motivations. Who we are as a person (identity) is determined by our heart.

Our physical heart pumps our blood to the parts of the body needing to function from the life the blood carries. So too our soul-heart carries the contents of our inner self to the whole being. If we eat proper foods and our systems are functioning properly, the blood does its job of nourishing toward health. If the blood becomes tainted or systems aren't properly working, our body suffers. But if the heart itself is bad, everything falls apart. A bad heart gives us no chance for good health (physically, mentally, or spiritually speaking). More on this can be explored in materials by Dr. Caroline Leaf, Dr. Daniel Amen, and Dr. Timothy Jennings. For example, Dr. Jennings has a book titled *The God-Shaped Heart*.

The Psalms are filled with many deep-felt emotional expressions of the heart. One example is when King David recognized his deep need for heart re-creation after a particularly huge blunder. Part of Psalm 51 reads,

Behold, I was brought forth in iniquity,
And in sin my mother conceived me.
Behold, You desire truth in the innermost being,
And in the hidden part You will make me know wisdom..
Purify me with hyssop, and I shall be clean;
Wash me, and I will be whiter than snow.
Make me to hear joy and gladness,
Let the bones which You have broken rejoice.
Hide Your face from my sins
And blot out all my iniquities.
Create in me a clean heart, O God,

And renew a steadfast spirit within me.
 Do not cast me away from Your presence,
And do not take Your Holy Spirit from me.
 Restore to me the joy of Your salvation,
And sustain me with a willing spirit. (Psalm 51:5-12 NASB)

David recognized his need for his heart to be cleansed. Because of the original sin of Adam and Eve, we all inherit guilt (dirty heart) as persons born into the human race. Our tendency toward sin takes us in a direction of disconnecting from God. But true meaning and purpose in life can only come through connection with God. For connection with God, a dirty heart must be exchanged for the clean heart God desires to give us through a transformational cleansing. David acknowledges that only God can do this kind of cleansing, and is an example for us in pursuing transformation of our inner being.

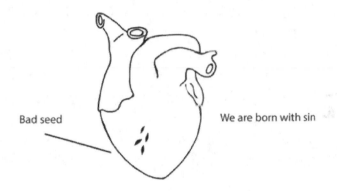

Bad seed

We are born with sin

Jesus focuses much of his teaching on the heart. To follow Jesus, we must examine our heart and respond to him with our heart. He uses the illustration of fruit (thoughts, affections, and behaviors) growing on a tree. "You'll never find choice fruit hanging on a bad, unhealthy tree. And rotten fruit doesn't hang on a good, healthy tree. Every tree will be revealed by the quality of fruit that it produces. Figs or grapes will never be picked off thorn trees. People are known in this same way. Out of the virtue stored in their hearts, good and upright people will produce good fruit. But out of the evil hidden in their hearts, evil ones will produce what is evil. For the overflow of what has been stored in your heart will be seen by your fruit and will be heard in your words" (Luke 6:43-46 TPT).

Although the word *soul* may have many different connotations in readers' minds, I use the word heart almost synonymously with soul. The soul is the intersection of the physical and spiritual realities in a human body (explained in a later chapter). In viewing the human makeup as a house (from the external view), we have a heart (inner habitation of the dwelling) that determines the house's identity. In viewing our heart from inside the house (internal view), we *are* the heart that no one else sees (Proverbs 14:10). We have a house (physical body), and are a house (spiritual inhabitant). We *have* a heart (physical organ), and are the heart (living soul). Both the house and the heart are a physical structure and a spiritual application of reality.

There is an external surface to the house that the outside world can see, but the real house is what's inside. The heart represents the internal atmosphere of what really goes on in the house. The house is not a house if it has no inhabitant(s) to house. In turn, the inhabitants cannot be sheltered (housed) by a house, if they have no house to house them. The human being is both the house and inhabitant together. The body is dead without the heart, and the heart cannot exist without a body.

Flow of Life

Our physical body needs a house (shelter) to protect us from the harsher elements of nature such as extreme hot or cold weather. Besides shelter, the body has another basic need for existence. The body needs water and food to sustain life. In later chapters we will discuss more on spiritual bread and the "living water' that Jesus provides. For now, the picture of a water pump helps us see how a physical house (and the entire property) needs a water source to thrive. Not only humans but also the animals living on a property need water. The plant life needs water. Animals and plants supply the food source for the human body. Even the most well-equipped house or farm cannot function without a connection to, and dependence on, a source of water. The water source is sometimes a spring, or water is pumped from a well. When the pump malfunctions, there is no water. When water is clean and plentiful, life is abundant.

Our physical heart is a pump. When the pump stops, life stops. When the pump functions well, life thrives. The body needs a constant stream of blood flow for existence. Spiritually speaking, the heart maintains the flow that sustains life.

Guarding the Heart

Now that we see the significance of our heart (inner person), let's look at the wisdom of "guarding" spoken of in the Proverbs. Although defense may be the primary way we see the word *guard*, we can consider offensive connotations as well. Pollutants make water undrinkable and poisons the bloodstream which can shut down our bodily organs. So too our heart can be poisoned by things like pornography, illegal drugs, other addictive things, and people with bad behavior, attitudes, or ideals. Guarding against bad influencers of our body, mind, soul, and spirit goes a long way to keeping us on track for wholeness as a person.

Guarding our heart also involves an offensive strategy. If a glass is half full of contaminated water, guarding against contamination will not make it more drinkable. We must go on the offense to rid the glass of the bad water and begin replacing it with pure water. So too our hearts must be intentionally drained of the bad influencers already present, and filled with good influencers. Another picture of how this works is the refinement process for precious metals. Purifying requires intentionally applying heat to burn away the impurities so the good qualities shine brighter.

Psychiatrist Daniel Amen describes our Automatic Negative Thoughts as ANTS. Amen's articles and books describe how this acronym came to him after finding an ant-infested kitchen in his home. The infestation was like the images of brains of his anxiety- and depression-ridden patients who had one negative thought after another stealing their happiness and contentment in life. Getting rid of ANTS means we must be actively resistant to complaining, blaming, and justifying. We must avoid the progression of making false assumptions, envisioning wrongful perceptions (beliefs), drawing inaccurate conclusions, forming harmful opinions, and allowing bitter, condemning judgments to take root in our hearts.

The Bible tells us, "Therefore, rid yourselves of all malice and all deceit, hypocrisy, envy, and slander of every kind. Like newborn babies, crave pure spiritual milk, so that by it you may grow up in your salvation, now that you have tasted that the Lord is good" (1 Peter 2:1-2 NIV). The best source of "pure spiritual milk" is the Bible. The more we influence our hearts with God's Word, the less worldly influences have a chance to take hold. The Bible (as our "sword") is the best offensive weapon we have against the enemy of our soul.

Another Bible reference important to mention is this, "Do not be anxious about anything, but in every situation, by prayer and petition, with thanksgiving, present your requests to God. And the peace of God, which transcends all understanding, will guard your hearts and your minds in Christ Jesus" (Philippians 4:6-7 NIV). Peace that only God can give, not mere human understanding, is the most secure way of guarding our hearts and minds. Asking God for his peace, and placing our complete trust in his willingness and ability to grant his peace (through salvation and sanctification in Jesus), is the surest path to peace.

Into the Light

A significant connection that most houses have to the outside world is an electrical panel box. In the last century electricity has become the means by which we provide light in the darkness, run our power tools for (re)construction, preserve our foods with refrigeration, recharge our batteries that run our phones and appliances, and so on.

As a living soul our house is in need of a power source to run electricity throughout the house to power all that needs powered up. Our heart is like a panel box for the house. As the container for the spiritual part of our being, it is the center for transforming the outside power from the power grid into a usable source of power within.

The community in which I live is home to the original Amish settlement in the USA. The Amish are known for their simple ways of living and doing without electricity. The Amish do not connect to the power grid fed by the utility company. They choose instead to generate their own power in order to remain self-sufficient. I see this as a picture of what our life is like before converting to Christ. Whatever "power" we have to function isn't coming from connection with God. When we believe in Jesus and start relying on God's power, it is like connecting our house to the power grid instead of relying on our own strength for salvation.

Again, connecting to God in this way is an ever-deepening commitment to his reconstruction process. Our heart is being transformed so that he can bring light to the dark spots (see 1 Peter 2:9). Our broken world creates dark spots in the form of burdens, brokenness, hurts, wounds, traumas, and injustices. They may be hidden in dark closets, fixtures that need to be replaced, entire rooms that haven't yet been renovated, or even basement foundational issues never discovered before part of the house is caving in.

Our houses are vulnerable to many issues that could shape the condition we are in at any given time. Environmental and construction influences (e.g., foundation flaws), damage caused by storms or pests (e.g., tornado or termites), system breakdowns (e.g., heating or A/C), abuse (e.g., misusing equipment), clutter, and normal wear and tear. In our personal lives, these may translate into family of origin issues, generational sins, other background turbulence, abuses, health issues, financial concerns, relational difficulties, and other negative influenc-

Our heart is like a
broken down house
in need of restoration.

"I dwell *on* a high and holy place,
And *also* with the contrite and lowly of spirit,
In order to revive the spirit of the lowly
And to revive the heart of the contrite." Isaiah 57:15

ers. Before we realize it, loss conditions create hard, "stony" hearts hiding in denial and numb emotions.

A prophetic word spoken through Ezekiel in ancient Israel gives us a picture of what it is like for God to call a people (both individually and corporately) out of ungodliness to godliness.

"For I will take you from the nations, gather you from all the lands and bring you into your own land. Then I will sprinkle clean water on you, and you will be clean; I will cleanse you from all your filthiness and from all your idols. Moreover, I will give you a new heart and put a new spirit within you; and I will remove the heart of stone from your flesh and give you a heart of flesh" (Ezekiel 36:24-26 NASB). As noted above, Jesus is the one who revives and re-creates our hearts. He washes us clean, empowers us with his Spirit, and makes us pliable and receptive to the ongoing process of transformation.

Our house (heart) must be seen as a combination of dark and light together. It is a common misconception to think of our house (heart) as one unit of either all light or all dark. A house has many rooms. Each of us is one person with many natural elements (natures). What we are like inside has many components. Dark spots remain because sin still remains in parts of our heart even after being born again. Transformation and sanctification are needed to have the unsurrendered dark spots surrendered to Jesus for him to bring light to those areas. As the nature of Jesus transforms those areas, we take on his nature in those areas. As the Bible tells us in the verses quoted earlier from Luke 6:43-46, our behavior (good fruit) changes accordingly. Bad behavior (bad fruit) points to a dark spot (bad root) in the heart. Good behavior (good fruit) is produced more and more as we allow Jesus to turn the dark into light.

For those who may think I am contradicting verses in the Bible that speak of Jesus cleansing our heart of sin, I hope you can see in the rest of this book how cleansing of sin is a process, and not merely a one-time event. The one-time event (justification is the theological term) is a legal transaction. We sign the contract and sell our house to Jesus. As Jesus takes possession of our house, the renovations continue (sanctification is the theological term). So we are saved, and being saved, at the same time.

Phrases like "all things have become new" (2 Corinthians 5:17), and our sins shall be washed away as "whiter than snow" (Psalm 51:7), must be viewed in context of reconstruction and re-creation. We are made new and being made new. We are washed clean, and being washed clean. If the being made new and washing clean does not continue, the dark spots remain, and the bad fruit cannot be changed to good fruit.

There is no dark spot too dark for Jesus to heal. Even if part or all of our house is burned to ashes, Isaiah the prophet gives us a picture of what happens. Speaking of what Jesus gives us in salvation, among many other things, he gives us, "a crown of beauty instead of ashes"

(Isaiah 61:3 CSB). Jesus can even work with the ashes (failures, disasters, messes, garbage) of our lives to turn our house into a welcoming place for God's presence to dwell. Every dark spot removed is a miracle. To God be the glory!

Chapter 2

Knowing Is Not Enough

Reconstruction of our houses and re-creation of our hearts are not accomplished merely by knowing of our need for reconstruction and re-creation. Makeovers take a tremendous amount of work in developing and executing plans, and overcoming obstacles that get in the way.

Knowing about transformation is not the same thing as submitting to the process of change. Revelation does not automatically translate to revolution. Some things we know we should stop doing, we do. And some things we know we should start doing, we do not do. Having knowledge, for example, that eating processed foods and consuming a lot of sugar is bad for our health, doesn't automatically translate into nutritious cooking and refraining from too many desserts. Knowing the value of physical exercise doesn't make it an intentional regular regiment. Knowing it's wrong to slander another person doesn't guarantee an offended person will not speak unkind words to others about their offender. Knowing that bitterness and resentment cause destruction of body and soul doesn't mean we will choose to surrender condemning judgments to God for forgiveness. Having knowledge of right doesn't always keep us out of wrong.

Without going into a deep discussion of the brain science be-hind this truth, let's look at a brief explanation. Psychiatrist Timothy Jennings has some great explanations in his books *The God-Shaped Brain* and *The God-Shaped Heart*. Dr. Jennings uses computer func-tion to illustrate how the mind, heart, and brain operate in the human being. As a former Information Technology (IT) professional myself, and now as a counselor, I see the value of making these terms clear in our understanding. Let me say too that no illustration is a perfect match to reality. God created people. Man created computers. In no way am I suggesting that computer engineering comes anywhere close to God's ways and workings.

The human brain and the physical aspects of the nervous system are like the hardware components of the computer. The human mind (cognitive functioning) can be likened to the software programs that run the various applications that process the data. The human heart is likened to the core operating system (OS) of the computer. The OS is a form of software also, but it must interface with both the hardware and the application software running on top of it. The heart (operat-ing system) of a person is essential to the integrity of function of the whole person. Without the operating system between the hardware and the applications, each could not function.

To illustrate a bit further, the mind can be thought of as our will-power, intellect, consciousness, senses, and sensory feelings. The heart can be thought of as the personal spirit, deeper feelings and emotions, creativity, curiosity, imagination, intuition, masculinity or femininity, spontaneity, gifts, and talents. Our heart is our core identity. Our heart defines who we are as a person. Our heart performs the operations connecting the physical bodily systems with the mind's cognitive in-terpretations of the external world. The external world environment is the data. The data spring from environmental conditions, flow through the mind into the heart, and on to memory storage in the brain. The data stored in memory also flow the other direction out of the brain through the heart and mind and become forms of interactions with the external environment. These exchanges create the reality of our world. Our speech and actions are a direct result of our thinking and memory processing.

Heart Over Mind

One of the reasons the teachings of Jesus focused on the heart is to help people understand that their internal condition determines their speech and behavior. In fact, he pointed out on many occasions how mere knowledge of the law (rules), without a compassionate heart, actually keeps people in physical and spiritual poverty. An example of this is when he healed people on the Sabbath (see Luke 13:10-17).

Mark's Gospel records the words of Jesus, "'Are you so lacking in understanding also? Do you not understand that whatever goes into the man from outside cannot defile him, because it does not go into his heart, but into his stomach, and is eliminated?' (*Thus He* declared all foods clean.) And He was saying, 'That which proceeds out of the man, that is what defiles the man. For from within, out of the heart of men, proceed the evil thoughts, fornications, thefts, murders, adulteries, deeds of coveting *and* wickedness, as well as deceit, sensuality, envy, slander, pride *and* foolishness. All these evil things proceed from within and defile the man'" (Mark 7:18-23 NASB).

Luke's Gospel makes the point that good things also originate in the heart. "The good man out of the good treasure of his heart brings forth what is good; and the evil *man* out of the evil treasure brings forth what is evil; for his mouth speaks from that which fills his heart" (Luke 6:45 NASB). This is not speaking of two different people, but the same person with both dark and light within. The dark (bad root) generates bad fruit. The light (good root) generates good fruit.

The writer of Proverbs says, "As in water face *reflects* face, so a man's heart reveals the man" (Proverbs 27:19 NJKV). The data coming out of a computer merely reveals what was put in and how it was processed. So too the speech and actions of a person reveals their background, core beliefs, and worldview. A person's life experiences from day one

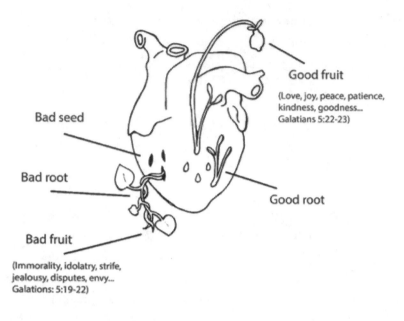

Good fruit

(Love, joy, peace, patience, kindness, goodness... Galatians 5:22-23)

Bad seed

Bad root

Good root

Bad fruit

(Immorality, idolatry, strife, jealousy, disputes, envy... Galations: 5:19-22)

are the data going in. How the person responds to his world in the present is determined by the sum total of past experiences (i.e., previous processing by the mind and heart). Hence, the processing we do in our heart determines both who we are and who we are becoming. That's why the Proverb says, "Watch over your heart with all diligence, For from it *flow* the springs of life" (Proverbs 4:23 NASB).

A person may be super intelligent, or be trained in the best schools and practices, and still engage in behaviors that destroy his life. As any counselor can validate, I see this pattern in well-intentioned persons many times. A person cannot usually kick a bad habit or addiction with mere knowledge of its destructive power.

Redemption Through the Heart

God created man with a heart that reflected his Creator to perfection. The Creator's image has a unique stamp in every individual's heart since the beginning of time. That is the good part of a person's heart. But with the first man, Adam and Eve, the virus of sin introduced a bad part into the heart. The virus implanted a stamp that also broke the heart of every individual since the beginning of time. Our fractured hearts must reckon not only with the good, but also the bad parts as well. All sorts of data processing failures make us vulnerable to bad data going in (believing lies), and bad data coming out (filtered perceptions, distorted thinking, false assumptions, corrupted opinions, bad decisions, and condemning judgments). These lead to bad behaviors. This brokenness is automatic and only has one reliable solution.

The solution is Jesus Christ. Jesus is the only way to fix the inherently broken parts of our hearts. He came to earth about 2,000 years ago to reveal God in the form of a human. Believing in Jesus begins a reprogramming of our operating system. We are a new creation (2 Corinthians 5:17). As we surrender and assimilate to the recoding in our heart, our mind is renewed (see Romans 12:1-2) to respond to life more in keeping with our original design. In our original whole condition, we live in the Truth (God's reality). The more we can operate in truth (in sync with original design), the freer we are to become the person we were created to be.

However, merely knowing about the virus, and knowing that Jesus removes it, remains as data in a memory bank unless further action is taken. Question--Why is knowing the truth not enough? Answer--Because knowing doesn't automatically translate into obedience. Faith in Christ is demonstrated by practicing Christ's teaching (truth), not merely understanding the concepts. God is a personal God, not a concept. Truth is found through relationship (with God), not religion (knowledge about God). Jesus makes this clear in the following two verses: "Jesus told the people who had faith in him, 'If you keep on obeying what I have said, you truly are my disciples. You will know the truth, and the truth will set you free'" (John 8:31-32; CEV). Many people quote the second verse without the conditional first verse, and their interpretation becomes the exact opposite of the truth. Increasing one's knowledge of the concepts of Christ's teaching, without fully engaging, applying, and practicing the concepts, is a little like trying to run an app designed for an Android device on an Apple device. The software may be designed to perfection, but if it isn't run on the OS it's designed for, it is practically worthless.

It's Nothing Short of Miraculous

Learning godly principles without applying them may set us up for deceiving ourselves into thinking we are someone or something we are not. You may have heard it said, "Knowledge puffs up, but love builds up." Love is an action that demonstrates care for another person above self. Knowledge (without application) tends to pump up the self, in preference to, or exclusion of, desires and needs of others. Thinking too highly (or too lowly) of ourselves sets us up for much frustration and discord in our relationships with other people.

I could share many examples from my own life and the lives of those I've ministered to, where not following God's instructions (not applying Christ's teaching) has caused great loss. Some of these may be like the following. We are offended by a friend's unkind words, so we respond with sassy words in return. A co-worker stretches the truth about their accomplishments to make our accomplishments less significant, so we say or do things to make them look bad in the presence of their boss. A roommate doesn't stop doing something that annoys you (after you've told them to stop several times), so you start intentionally doing something to your roommate that you know annoys them. We may know about forbearance and forgiveness, in situations, but following through with the right actions can be a challenge.

A miracle by definition is a supernatural intervention. If we choose to rely on our strength and willpower (natural realm), we can miss the everyday miracles (supernatural realm) God desires for us to participate in. We will see more about willpower in the next chapter.

In my own life, I have been forced to reckon with this through limited physical eyesight. Due to an injury at birth, both of my optic nerves were damaged to the extent of legal blindness. One major limitation is not seeing well enough to obtain a driver's license. This puts me in situations of need for transportation. Print material, signage, videos, and other visual content are often inaccessible, so alternative formats are necessary to obtain information. I have learned that God's provision comes in an unexpected means of travel or in computer software that enlarges the screen for readability. Sometimes too, by allowing drivers to give me a ride, they share in God's blessing for helping someone in need. If I were to demand from God 20/20 visual acuity (normal) eyesight, I would miss opportunities for God to meet my needs in unconventional, and often miraculous, ways. The loss created by damaged vision is overcome by believing and applying the truth that "my God will supply all your needs according to His riches in glory in Christ Jesus" (Philippians 4:19 NASB).

Jesus performed many physical healings when he was on earth, and still does today as well. The ones recorded in the Bible almost always have a spiritual application associated with them. One of my personal favorites is in John 9 where Jesus restored a blind man's sight and then exclaimed, "For judgment I came into this world, so that those who do not see may see, and that those who see may become blind" (John 9:39 NASB). Again, God's reality is not born out of what we know and see, but through becoming "blind" to what we know and see, so that we can see into a spiritual reality.

The miracle of forgiveness is another example of applying Christ's teaching to know the truth that sets one free. True forgiveness occurs in the heart as defined by Jesus (see Matthew 18:35). As noted above, sin implanted a virus in the heart that can only be removed through the salvation power of Jesus. Our natural tendency to hold bitterness, resentment, and blame causes sin at the heart level, not just with our actions. This is evidenced by the verses quoted earlier from Mark 7:18-23. Since sin is at the heart level, repentance must be at the heart level. Repenting of the ill-gotten attitudes, lie-based beliefs, assumptions, conclusions, decisions, and condemning judgments that caused our sinful reactions, releases the miracle to be possible. Surrendering to God the right to be Judge puts the heart in position to once again operate as originally designed. Forgiving from the heart is not a decision based on mental faculties (knowledge) alone, but depends on a decision to cooperate with God's decisions for justice in the offensive situation. We will look at forgiveness in more detail later.

Applying Christ's teaching to everything we experience in life keeps us in the truth. Seeing God in truth, seeing ourselves in truth, and seeing other people in truth keeps our immune system strong. A healthy immune system is the best way to stay free of the virus of sin that would aim to keep us sick. Again, building and guarding our spiritual immune system is vital. Time alone in God's presence is similar to running a good anti-virus software protection for the computer's core functions. Keeping to regular times of rest and soul downtime also serves as an intentional "reboot," to clear the clogs and unnecessary background processing that overload the system.

When things are not going well, instead of trying too hard to figure out what is going wrong, it is far better to focus on applying God's instructions and ways of operation more closely. God wants us to trust him, which is sometimes not accompanied by understanding. Numerous illustrations in the Bible show this truth. For example, Martha may still have been trying to figure out why Jesus didn't show up earlier when he knew Lazarus was sick and needed healing. "Lord, if You had been here, my brother would not have died," she said (John 11:21). Jesus knew the outcome of his visit and invited the family to participate in the miracle. "So Jesus, again being deeply moved within, came to the tomb. Now it was a cave, and a stone was lying against it. Jesus said, 'Remove the stone'" (John 11:38-39 NASB). If the power of God could put breath back into the body of a dead man, he certainly could have moved a rock and unwrapped the grave clothes (as he also asked bystanders to do moments later). Getting them to remove the stone also illustrates how God invites our participation into the process of healing and restoration. Martha's natural, knowledge-based response was, "Lord, by this time there will be a stench, for he has been *dead* four days" (v. 39). Again, trying to figure out how this was going to work was not helping the situation. Jesus raising Lazarus from the dead has much to teach us (both literally and metaphorically) about following God into recovery and transformational living. I encourage reading the entire story in John 11 with this in mind.

Core Subconscious Beliefs

When life hurts, where do we turn? To whom do we look for healing? Transformational healing requires turning our attention to God, and through communication with him, changing our perspective on the past, and gaining new hope for the journey ahead. In our computer illustration it's like allowing God to update our operating system to correct the flaws, strengthen the security against more viruses, and enhance features for smoother operation. I describe here a few important considerations.

As noted above, to receive healing from God, cognitive insight is not enough. Although the part of the human being we can see (physical) is most obvious, the unseen part (non-physical or inner being) is more dominant, thus very real. *The Body Keeps the Score: Brain, Mind, and Body in the Healing of Trauma* by psychiatrist Bessel van der Kolk explains in simple language how our emotional brain limits our rational brain. Exploring our deepest feelings, desires, and core beliefs about our world must be part of the healing process. We will look at this more later, too.

Next, our heart is broken because our world is broken. Since the first human sinned, the Bible explains how we each fall short of the original design God has for our lives. As we grow from childhood into adulthood, our hurts and wounds magnify our pain. The broken things in our past create more brokenness and sometimes the real source of pain becomes hard to uncover.

Also, we must acknowledge that there are no exceptions. We all need healing to become a whole person. In the physical world, every child gets, at the very least, banged knees, splinters, or broken skin that is vulnerable to infection and disease. If time passes before the wound is discovered by a caretaker, it may have to be reopened and cleaned out for it to heal properly. Though emotional hurts and wounds may not be visible, they are real, and the passing of time makes them worse. Insensitivities, neglects, mistreatments, rejection, losses, and shame (self-inflicted or by others) does not go away on its own. It often requires a process to dislodge and remain free of setbacks.

For some, pain may be caused (or complicated) by trauma, violence, gross injustice, abuse, or severe neglect. But common to us all are hurts caused by things like illnesses, injuries, broken relationships, family breakups, bullying, slandering, lying, stealing. immorality, and accidents. If a painful experience hasn't come to your mind in reading so far, try this little exercise. Pretend that your life is over, and by God's grace, you are enjoying your new life in eternal glory. Jesus comes to you and asks you to volunteer to go back to earth in your former body, family, economic status, and the same earthly circumstances as your life was before, with one exception. You are allowed to make one change. What would that change be? Whatever you wish could be changed about your life circumstances (e.g., height, weight, appearance, metabolism, birth order, gender, parents, relatives) likely reveals some disappointment, frustration, annoyance, discomfort, unrest, or dissatisfaction. These symptoms can create a tremendous amount of toxic stress (infection of the soul) and negatively impact your work, relationships, self-concept, and life's meaning and destiny.

To become completely free of the unwanted stresses, let us consider a few more basic principles of healing prayer. In order to discover the root cause of hurt, we must allow ourselves to "feel" the hurt long enough to identify specific feelings and emotions associated. These feelings and emotions are always driven by specific beliefs developed and reinforced by circumstances over time. Thinking patterns are accessed, perceptions are created, assumptions are made, conclusions are drawn, opinions are formed, and critical judgments develop to shape our view of how life works, and should work. The older we become the more our present core beliefs are so buried in our subconscious that we can't even remember how and where they came to be.

Another factor impacting our ability to remember is the intensity to which the hurt or wound was inflicted. Greater degrees of abuse, for example, tend to carry greater degrees of denial or dissociation. Denial is a useful self-protection coping strategy for a time, but becomes a huge burden as time goes on. So, naming our present feelings and naming our accompanying beliefs are big steps in the process. We will discuss "process" more later.

Beliefs are powerful. Every behavior and action we take has a belief behind it. If we believe we are competent and capable, we will step out in confidence and display self-assurance in our work, play, and relationships. If we believe the opposite about ourselves, we will be trapped by self-doubt, self-condemnation, and self-rejection. An example that demonstrates this principle involves the circus elephant. In former days, the training of an elephant began early in the elephant's life. The only environment the small elephant knew was a chain that kept him in the location the trainer chose for him. The elephant grew into adulthood believing he was limited by the confines of the chain. When the chain is removed for circus tricks he remains with the trainer because he knows nothing else. Freedom (escape) does not even occur to him. In general, animals are trained through repetition, and the natural inclinations of humans are the same. We gravitate to the familiar, even if the familiar is harmful or not in our best interest. A victimized person will subconsciously seek to be victimized because their beliefs confirm to them a lack of worth and value. Even depression and anxiety can be reinforced by believing life only offers despondent or scary circumstances.

Not only do some of our beliefs trap us, but they are guaranteed to be telling us lies. Our default tendency (from conception onward) is to perceive and interpret unpleasant surroundings in a negative way. This sets us up to believe things that are not true about God, ourselves, and other people. As children we are especially vulnerable to lies taking root in our thinking. For example, a five-year-old girl who overhears her daddy say to his friend about her, "We wish she had been a boy," can set her up for huge ramifications. I've heard numerous cases where seemingly harmless words or actions by a caretaker result in deep wounding. Generally speaking, children often tend to blame themselves for bad things that happen. The little girl's inner voice may hear her daddy's words as, "I should have been a boy," or "I'm really not loved because I'm not a boy, so I need to try to become a boy to be loved," or "I'm not lovable," or "I am a mistake," or all sorts of other lies. Parents' divorces usually result in their children blaming themselves for the breakup. Injury or illness to siblings can create false guilt and self-condemnation.

False beliefs tend to create more false beliefs so circumstances in adulthood are merely replays of childhood wounds. This negative bent in our personhood is part of the broken condition of humanity since sin and shame entered our world. Shame is at the root of all false beliefs. We will explore the topic of shame a bit more later.

The data stored in a computer's memory is only as good as the data put into the computer. Inaccurate data going in will cause errors in processing and errors coming back out. Good data is needed for accurate results.

Healing Through Truth

The solution for false beliefs (bad data) is true beliefs (good data). As noted above, our physical brain and mind is not the only part of us to be convinced of the truth. Our heart (inner being) must come to an understanding of truth that secures, preserves, and advances our whole being.

Jesus said of himself that HE is the way, the truth, and the life (see John 14:6). Jesus is the Healer and Transformer. We cannot know Father God except through Jesus his Son (see John 14:6-7). God as Father, Son, and Holy Spirit work together to provide healing for our innate broken condition. Healing prayer is an avenue by which we can allow the Holy Spirit to reveal hidden things in the broken parts of our subconscious, so they can be brought into light and take away the opportunity for shame to continue to condemn us. We exchange lies for truth. We exchange condemning judgments for empathy. We exchange despair for hope. Disappointment and dissatisfaction can turn to contentment and fulfillment.

Later, I discuss more on transformational healing prayer. Submitting to this process can be hard work. Not that prayer should be difficult, but being honest with ourselves and with God long enough to receive the truth God has for us is the "work" that makes for the sometimes difficult steps in our journey. Facing the pain in our experiences, confessing the error in our reactions, repenting, and surrendering to God's solution is viewed by many as too hard or scary to try. But I encourage all who read this to decide to be one of the few. I'm here to say the rewards are worth it. God is our Refuge and strength (Psalm 46). Holding on to old hurts and wounds becomes far more painful than seeking and receiving healing from Refuge. "Wait for the Lord; Be strong and let your heart take courage; Yes, wait for the Lord" (Psalm 27:14 NASB).

Chapter 3

Trade the Will for the Well

Perhaps the most common source of struggle and failure in a Christians life is a misunderstanding of the role of willpower in the transformation process. The belief that spiritual maturity is chiefly dependent on exercising greater willpower to change into a better (more godly) person, is exactly the opposite of the truth. If that statement is shocking to you, let me explain.

The reader may have heard the slogan "if it's gonna be, it's up to me." While there is an element of truth to the statement, it does not work spiritually speaking. Clarifying the difference between, and contrasting the physical realm and the spiritual realm, helps to bring understanding. The physical realm is identified by laws that govern how the natural world operates. For example, our bodies are subject to the law of gravity. Gravity keeps us from floating into outer space. Gravity is also demonstrated if we step out of a window on the tenth floor of a building. Our body will be injured in the fall, but this is to be expected. Even flapping our arms will not cause us to fly. Whether we believe in gravity or not, it is enforced on our physical body.

The spiritual realm is equally real, and similarly governed by laws (moral principles). God set in motion an orderly reality as revealed in the Bible. His commandments identify a standard of righteousness to protect us and provide passage for our experiences to go well for us. When we sin (disobey God's warnings), it can be painful because harmful consequences result when disrupting God's order for the way things work. As broken body parts show how misalignment with laws in the physical realm occur, brokenness in the spiritual realm separates us from God and misaligns us with his ways.

Weakness of Willpower

The intersection of the physical and spiritual realms is called the soul of man. This third realm of reality is called the psychological realm by author Ed Kurath in chapter two of his book *I Will Give You Rest* (see http://divinelydesigned.com). Kurath explains that it operates in accordance with our own powers and abilities. Habit patterns, our intellect, and our own willpower are aspects of the psychological realm. Our willpower has been given to us as a tool to manage this psychological realm, and it only has authority there. Kurath says, "But we have made a huge mistake, because we have believed that our willpower also has authority in the spiritual realm. However, our willpower only has authority in the psychological realm. We cannot overcome or defy the physical laws or spiritual laws with our willpower. Our willpower is impotent in defying the laws of the physical realm, and it was never given to us for this purpose. We cannot fly by flapping our arms. We cannot lift a 500-pound weight. We discover that no matter how much we want to lift it, we can't. We can will it, but we cannot perform it."

What is perhaps harder to understand is that our willpower is as impotent in the spiritual realm as it is in the physical realm. It was never given to us for the purpose of managing the spiritual realm. We discover this impotence when we try to do a spiritually impossible task, like obeying the laws of God. We discover that no matter how hard we want to do the good that we ought to, we cannot. We can "will" it, but we cannot perform it. As the Apostle Paul expressed, "So I discover this law: When I want to do what is good, evil is present with me. For in my inner selfhttps://www.biblegateway.com/passage/?search=rom+7&version=CSB - fen-CSB-28098f I delight in God's law, but I see a different law in the parts of my body, waging war against the law of my mind and taking me prisoner to the law of sin in the parts of my body. What a wretched man I am!" (Romans 7:21-24 CSB). Our failure to do the good that we want to do is not due to a lack of willpower, it is due to our misunderstanding about reality. We are under the illusion that we ought to be able to "will" it and thus do it.

Willpower can be used to our advantage for some things controlled by our intellect and reason. If we have a bad habit, for example, of eating snacks instead of healthy food, we may be able to change the foods we eat with practice and repeating the good behavior. But when a bad behavior or habit is rooted in a spiritually poor condition (in the spiritual realm), spiritual laws take over. Trying to stop (or even interrupt) the operation of God's spiritual laws is a bit like an ant in the middle of a highway telling a truck to stop as it is about to crush the ant.

Many problems people face in life (e.g., very destructive habits, addictions, generational curses, destructive relational conflict, chronic mood swings, chronic irrational fears, rejection of self, etc.) connect to some sort of spiritual roots that make them subject to spiritual laws. They are perpetuated by a delusion that willpower alone will gain the victory. Their failure is the result of "trying hard" to quit—making a decision with their intellect and relying on their willpower to bring it to pass. They are doomed to failure because God's laws are his, not ours, to uphold. This misunderstanding is a big problem, and it is widespread among Christ-followers.

The Bible makes very powerful statements regarding the illusion of our will. It is a universal flaw in mankind to think we can manage our own life in our own strength. It is so automatic, insidious, and covert that we don't even realize what we are doing. We will discuss some of these laws like the laws of judgment in the next section of the book. When the self-will is surrendered to God's will, transformation results. When the human will seeks God's will (the Well), well power takes over.

Well Power

There is a power to supersede willpower. That power is well power. Jesus is the well. Jesus is the provision for obeying God's commands. Well power calls us to *be* like Jesus and not just *act* like Jesus. Jesus invites us to drink from the well of living water. A story recorded by the Gospel of John about a woman drawing water at a village's water source (well), says this: "Jesus answered and said to her, 'Everyone who drinks of this water will thirst again; but whoever drinks of the water that I will give him shall never thirst; but the water that I will give him will become in him a well of water springing up to eternal life'" (John 4:13-14 NASB).

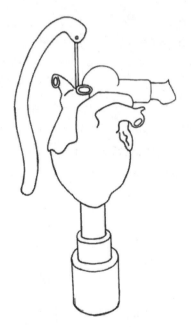

Well power calls us to *be* like Jesus and not just *act* like Jesus.

If someone is traveling in the desert, dying of thirst, and encounters a well, would they first try to dig another well beside the one that exists? The course of action would be to *recognize* the problem of needing water, *believe* in the ability of the well to pump the water, *decide* to work the pump, and act by working the pump. The spiritual realm works in a way similar to this physical world example. The deepest need for every soul is to reconnect with God through Jesus. The steps to meet the need are to first *recognize* the need, *believe* in Jesus as the provision for meeting the need, use willpower to *decide* to activate the provision, and *act* by praying and waiting on God for further direction and strength.

Jesus Is the Well

All through the book of John in the Bible, we are told how Jesus did everything according to the will of his Father in heaven. For all followers of Jesus this means that Jesus is the only way to eat spiritual bread and drink spiritual water. "For My flesh is true food, and My blood is true drink. He who eats My flesh and drinks My blood abides in Me, and I in him" (John 6:55-56 NASB). This statement from Jesus is part of an explanation after one of the first miracles he performed. Read it in John 6.

Jesus had thousands of people sit down on the grass and he took a boy's lunch box with five bread cakes and two fish, blessed and multiplied it, and fed the crowd to satisfaction. After their bellies were full, they acknowledged him as the great Prophet (John 6:14). Jesus was teaching them to put their complete faith in him, and not trust their own ways of thinking. By the end of this teaching people were ready to stone him to death (John 7:1), and very few disciples remained in the crowd (John 6:60-61,66-67).

So what made this such a difficult teaching to accept? Jesus performed a miracle which physically fed thousands of people to demonstrate a spiritual law (truth). God is the well. God is the provider of eternal life, and there is no way for people to work their way to God on their own willpower. They cannot even sustain their life on earth without his provision. Jesus was directly challenging their self-will and self-righteous behaviors when, "Jesus said to them, 'Truly, truly,

I say to you, unless you eat the flesh of the Son of Man and drink His blood, you have no life in yourselves. He who eats My flesh and drinks My blood has eternal life, and I will raise him up on the last day'" (John 6:53-54 NASB). Jesus is the only source of spiritual food and water that transforms our soul. No good deed performed by a person's will carries any significance in saving a soul—neither in conversion nor ongoing sanctification.

We do well to ask (as did Jesus' listeners in the story above), "What is our part in all this?" Jesus answered and said to them, "This is the work..., that you believe in Him whom He has sent" (John 6:29 NASB). In sum, our "work" is to surrender to the process of transformation. It can take much effort to change "beliefs" that are entrenched and harmful. These beliefs may include false assumptions gathered, erroneous conclusions drawn, condemning judgments cast, and bad subconscious decisions made. Our job is to exchange our beliefs for those of Christ Jesus.

Sometimes I find myself (even on a daily basis) in a similar dilemma as Jesus' followers in the story above. Do I really want to change (toward God's direction)? Do I want to let God be in control of the change? What beliefs (perceptions, assumptions, conclusions, judgments, choices) are in the way of God working his change in me? What ways of thinking need to change? Our work is to believe by surrendering to God's work of bringing things to our awareness, remitting the shortcomings we confess, forgiving the sins for which we repent, and giving us a future and hope for God's name to be famed through it all.

Leaders seem to have an especially hard time surrendering their will for the well. One reason is the overly high expectations of perfection on the part of followers. Those in the lead are expected to make things happens and implore others to make things happen (assuming willpower as the chief motivator). By definition leaders lead. Leaders are typically high energy, high achieving, highly will-driven catalysts who perceive dependence on outside motivational resources as a sign of weakness. Drinking from the well (with God as the source) can too easily become an afterthought. Whether parenting, pastoring, functioning as CEO, or just being a good friend to a neighbor in need, leadership requires first being good leaders of self. Like Jesus, good leaders must first be good followers of their Master.

Living a life that glorifies God is far less about willpower than most people have been conditioned to believe. Trading our will for the Well takes a lifetime of commitment to the process of transformation of our inner person. Trading the will for the Well is a must for pacing to peace.

Willfulness and Willingness

Understanding the difference between willfulness and willingness helps in understanding how it can be so difficult to drink from Christ's well instead of trying to create our own. Psychiatrist and author Gerald May, MD in chapter one of a book called *Will and Spirit: A Contemplative Psychology* writes,

> Willingness and willfulness cannot be explained in a few words, for they are very subtle qualities, often overlapping and very easily confused with each other. But we can begin by saying that willingness implies a surrendering of one's self-separateness, an entering-into, an immersion in the deepest processes of life itself. It is a realization that one already is a part of some ultimate cosmic process and it is a commitment to participation in that process. In contrast, willfulness is the setting of oneself apart from the fundamental essence of life in an attempt to master, direct, control, or otherwise manipulate existence. More simply, willingness is saying yes to the mystery of being alive in each moment. Willfulness is saying no, or perhaps more commonly, "Yes, but ..."

> It is obvious that we cannot say yes to everything we encounter; many specific things and situations in life are terribly destructive and must be resisted. But willingness and willfulness do not apply to specific things or situations. They reflect instead the underlying attitude one has toward the wonder of life itself.

Willingness notices this wonder and bows in some kind of reverence to it. Willfulness forgets it, ignores it, or at its worst, actively tries to destroy it. Thus, willingness can sometimes seem very active and assertive, even aggressive. And willfulness can appear in the guise of passivity.[2]

When we say "yes" to God (by believing in Jesus as our Savior), we take a first drink from the well of salvation. The sacrifice that Jesus made is enough. By spilling his blood on the cross, the provision for forgiveness of sin is completely taken care of. Our willingness to accept this provision is demonstrated by confessing, repenting, and accepting the free gift of forgiveness. Willingness to surrender delivers us from the slavery of willfulness.

We give up mastery for mystery. We begin a journey of self-surrender to relinquish self-will, self-determination, self-sufficiency, and any other part of "self" in opposition to the rule of God. Our journey is like traveling on a two-rail train track. We root out and let go of willfulness as it comes to light, and we cling to willingness to be transformed into the image of Jesus for more useful service and meaning in life.

Peeking further into the psychological realm discussed above, we find two parts that seem to battle at times. The psycho-somatic is the part of our soul most connected to our physical body. It manifests with physical sensations, thoughts, and feelings centered around the body. The psycho-spiritual is the part of our soul most connected with our personal spirit. It is far less sensory and more intuitive as it is centered around the spirit. When we believe in Jesus, and begin drinking from the well of "living water" as Jesus called it, the source of our life becomes more psycho-spiritual (spirit oriented) and less psycho-somatic (body oriented). The spirit part of our being becomes more and

---

2 Gerald G. May, MD, *Will and Spirit: A Contemplative Psychology* (New York: HarperCollins Publishers, 1982), 5-6.

more dominant. This is a key characteristic of the transformation of the inner person (see Romans 8:5-8).

The Holy Spirit is the well we are tapping into. The Holy Spirit becomes a greater and greater influencer of our whole being. As our willingness to surrender our soul to the Holy Spirit increases, our soul becomes more and more infused by the Holy Spirit. As our soul is filled more by the Holy Spirit, there is less space for the body-centered activity to operate. It's like clean water being continuously poured into a pitcher of contaminated water. Under a spigot (or fountain) of fresh clean water, the dirt (and dirty water) will eventually all spill out and be washed away as it is replaced by the clean. Willfulness is woefully inadequate to accomplish this transformation in our lives. We need the fresh fountain of the Holy Spirit rejuvenating our lives on a continual basis, pouring the cleanness into our being.

As disciples of Jesus, we are called to be disciple-makers. Staying connected to the well (fountain of Life) gives empowerment for pouring out to others. The Bible says, "Now on the last day, the great *day* of the feast, Jesus stood and cried out, saying, 'If anyone is thirsty, let him come to Me and drink. He who believes in Me, as the Scripture said, "From his innermost being will flow rivers of living water"'" (John 7:37-38 NASB). This is not only good news for our own soul, but every soul we come in contact with. God pours into us so we can pour into others. The truth is, we have nothing to give to others of redeeming value, that we have not first received from God. Our willful accomplishments have human limits, but willing surrender produces fruit beyond measure.

This is illustrated clearly by one of Christ's disciples, Peter. On the last night before his crucifixion, while in his earthly body, Jesus washed his disciples' feet. As John 13 records, Peter willfully resisted this physical and spiritual interaction with Jesus (see John 13:5-8). After Peter said, "Never shall you wash my feet!" Jesus answered, "If I do not wash you, you have no part with Me." Simon Peter said to Him, "Lord, *then wash* not only my feet, but also my hands and my head" (John 13:8-9

NASB). Peter's willfulness changed to willingness and demonstrated true discipleship. Jesus said to the disciples, "If I then, the Lord and the Teacher, washed your feet, you also ought to wash one another's feet. For I gave you an example that you also should do as I did to you" (John 13:14-15 NASB). Jesus was about to leave the earth, and for his message to be carried on, he needed his disciples to teach and do as he taught and did.

In these intimate moments at the "last supper" (as it is called), Jesus revealed to his closest twelve disciples that one among them was a betrayer. It soon became apparent that Judas was the one whose willfulness won out over willingness. Even one of Christ's closest disciples lost the battle within. Nevertheless, to the other eleven Jesus also used this opportunity to explain the foot-washing ceremony in more detail. He said, "A new commandment I give to you, that you love one another, even as I have loved you, that you also love one another. By this all men will know that you are My disciples, if you have love for one another" (John 13:34-35 NASB). As Jesus was surrendered to his Father's will, he is so commanding his disciples to do likewise. The way surrender is expressed is through love. Love demonstrates a willing heart. Love keeps the cycle of disciple-making going.

Spiritual Disciplines

One caution is not to equate or confuse our spiritual condition with so-called spiritual disciplines. Engaging in activity that attaches the word "discipline" to Bible reading, meditation, or prayer does not automatically (willfully) translate to transformation of the heart. I don't mean to minimize the importance of practicing self-discipline (especially in spiritual exercises), but the enormity of our need for divine intervention requires discipleship (following after Christ), not discipline (self-determined followership).

Relating to God as all three in One, Father, Son, and Holy Spirit, requires more than exercising the parts of our being over which we have direct control. It is impossible for a human in one lifetime to experience everything about God there is to experience. But what gives purpose and meaning in each day he gives us to live on this earth, is to experience as much of God's nature and character as we possibly can. The Bible further clarifies what it means to "drink from the well" of salvation when Jesus said, "true worshipers will worship the Father in spirit and truth; for such people the Father seeks to be His worshipers. God is spirit, and those who worship Him must worship in spirit and truth" (John 4:23-24 NASB). God is not a concept to be understood. God is a person to be known and be known by.

Forgiveness is one of the most practical examples of the need for practicing well power over willpower. Surrendering to God the ultimate rights of judgment requires a spiritual transaction that willpower cannot produce. Forgiveness is more than a willful decision. It is a decision to cooperate with God's means of justice and mercy. But the part of forgiving that requires surrender has to come through spiritual transformation and willingness to trust God to be the rightful Judge in any and every situation. Deciding to forgive is incomplete without following through to receive and carry out God's direction on how to show his love to the offender. I can speak from hard-learned lessons that showing love to an offender takes great well power.

We may think willpower is enough for a season, but sooner or later an offense becomes so big that we discover our need for a deeper well than we can ever will to dig on our own.

Much of the brokenness in our world today revolves around broken relationships with people. I find it interesting that the woman Jesus chose to interact with (at the well in the story of John 4), was a person who had many broken relationships in her background. She had numerous husbands. Unforgiveness is often at the heart of most marital struggles, for example. When divorce is considered as an option, most times issues left unresolved are the same issues that will pop up again in another relationship. We cannot depend on someone else's well to supply our need for the "living water." Each of us taking personal responsibility for our own inside-out change is a needed "discipline."

Make or Break

As noted earlier (see story in John 6), most of the people following Jesus liked his "free food" and teaching on a better way to live, but when "push came to shove" they were not willing to commit to discipleship. It was a make-or-break moment to decide to allow Jesus to radically change their life patterns and direction. Will it be similar for us? Is change too scary? Do we see inside-out change as too costly or bringing up too many uncertainties? Do we see ourselves as too broken to be able to be put back together?

God is only looking for a willing heart, not a willful heart. The Psalmist reminds us, "A broken and a contrite heart, O God, You will not despise" (Psalm 51:17 NASB). We only need to earnestly desire to change, not perform the change by our own will. The next part of this book will help the reader see that accepting our heart's broken condition is a crucial step in the journey.

Part 2

Accept Our Broken Heart Condition

Pursue peace with all men, and the sanctification without which no one will see the Lord. See to it that no one comes short of the grace of God; that no root of bitterness springing up causes trouble.
Hebrews 12:14-15 (NASB)

God is our Creator. We are his creatures. His ways are far above our ways. Ignoring, redefining, or flat-out rebelling against his ways has serious negative consequences. Man's bad choices to sin bring brokenness into the world. Every baby born since Adam and Eve enters the world with a broken heart. Through much travail the heart can be made whole again when we choose to honor God's ways and yield to his process of transformation.

Chapter 4

Spiritual Laws that Govern Life

The Bible is filled with descriptions of the way God works. Remember the three realms of reality discussed earlier (physical, spiritual, and psychological). The spiritual realm is just as relevant as the physical realm in placing boundaries on how life works. Spiritual laws govern the way the spiritual realm operates, affecting all of our lives, all of the time, and in all places.

Four Principles

If the word law is a bit too "legal" sounding, think of them as principles, guidelines, or commands to follow. Proverbs is full of wise words describing good conduct. As noted earlier, Jesus often explained how heart attitudes and motives are expressed in our behavior. For transformational living, four key laws are explained in a book called *Transformation of the Inner Man* by John and Paula Sandford. These are:

1. Honor your father and mother (Deuteronomy 5:16)

2. Judge not that you be not judged (Matthew 7:1-2)

3. You reap what you sow (Galatians 6:7-8)

4. For in that you judge another, you condemn yourself (Romans 2:1)

Almost all difficulties we face in life can be traced back to violating one or more of these basic laws. Bad roots are caused by violating these laws, which create the difficulties and bad consequences.

One of the Ten Commandments is to show respect for our parents. It is the only one of the ten with a promise. "Honor your father and your mother, as the LORD your God has commanded you, that your days may be prolonged and that it may go well with you on the land which the Lord your God gives you" (Deuteronomy 5:16 NASB). Our parents, or our primary caretakers in our earliest years, shape our entire life. Our deepest and most impactful roots lie in how our parents treated us in those years and our responses to them as people. Although there are no perfect parents in the world, they deserve our honor merely for the authority they represent in God's order of things.

Much more will be said about these laws later, but for simplicity I'll combine the second and fourth on judging, into one. The key idea here is condemnation. Whenever condemnation of a person is involved, it creates bad roots. Condemnation of behavior is permitted (and sometimes necessary), but condemnation of a person (including oneself) creates bad roots (sin) which create bad fruits (bad results).

Reaping what is sown has to do with facing the consequences of thoughts and actions. For every action there is an equal and opposite reaction. For every conscious thought, there is a moment of decision to allow its influence as a good thought or resist its influence as a bad thought. Thoughts build and turn to ideas which eventually turn into actions. Feelings and emotions are added to the mix and give the actions intensity.

Another helpful thing to realize is how our identity is affected by what we allow ourselves to focus on. We become (as a person) what we give the most attention to. Sowing thoughts and actions develop patterns and habits. We reap a lifestyle of sown ideas and accompanying choices.

A related law of blessing and cursing operates in the spiritual realm. It is determined by how well we align ourselves with God's ways. Generally speaking, when we live in obedience, we experience good things (blessings). When we disobey, we bring on ourselves the bad things (curses). All the way back to Adam and Eve in the garden and in our lives today, we can see how whether or not we make God the rightful center of our lives opens heaven's doors for good or bad things to happen.

A practical example of how this law may flesh out is the practice of generosity. When we understand that God is the real owner of all the resources, we can freely give whatever he tells us to give. Whether it be time, money, or talents, it is all the Lord's to begin with. He freely gives to us so we can freely give. On the other hand, if we are stingy, or overly demanding in our conditions of giving, we fail to show our trust in God to meet our needs. We may end up as victor on the side of blessing, or victim on the side of cursing.

Gratitude works with similar results. Being thankful and grateful opens our heart to receive more. Nursing bitterness and complaining closes the opportunity to receive more of the goodness God desires to bless us with. Of course, there are limits to this, and I am not advocating a so-called "name it and claim it" persuasion. But when we aim to please God, we set in motion God's laws to reap blessing. When we sin, we set God's laws against us and reap cursing.

Understanding how spiritual laws work helps us identify and address areas of our lives ripe for transformation. The dark areas of our heart created by breaking spiritual laws are at the root of the undesirable results we see on the outside.

Bad Roots

In comparing our heart (inner person) to the new ownership and reconstruction of a house, we see there is much cleanup work to be done for the house to become a more welcoming place for God to live. There is a profound misunderstanding that keeps many from pursuing transformation. Many believe giving their life to Jesus makes their whole house immediately perfect and all the work is done. They believe all their sins are forgiven and they are pure inside. Now that they are pure on the inside, they should be able to act pure on the outside.

In reality, that is not the way it works. It hasn't worked that way for me or for anyone I know. Nor is sinlessness attainable for people spoken of in the Bible. In fact Paul speaks of the tension between knowing what is right and wanting to do it, but not being able to. "Wretched man that I am! Who will set me free from the body of this death? Thanks be to God through Jesus Christ our Lord! So then, on the one hand I myself with my mind am serving the law of God, but on the other, with my flesh the law of sin" (Romans 7:24-25 NASB. The work of Jesus is done, but working himself inside of us is never done.

Some of the compartments of our heart (corners, closets, rooms of a house) remain in darkness and need to be brought into the light. These bad roots (dark attitudes and desires) still produce bad fruit (bad behaviors). We need to allow Jesus into each compartment that has darkness in it. This revitalization (transformation) is a process. As more and more compartments are cleaned up, we become more like Jesus (2 Corinthians 3:18). This salvation work continues to other compartments as described in Philippians, "So then, my beloved, just as you have always obeyed, not as in my presence only, but now much more in my absence, work out your salvation with fear and trembling; for it is God who is at work in you, both to will and to work for His good pleasure" (Philippians 2:12-13 NASB).

Consider how plant life grows. In every forest, on every farm, in every orchard on earth, it's what's under the ground that creates what's above the ground. The invisible underworld creates the visible results. Past successes in previous seasons of life don't necessarily guarantee good fruit today. That's why placing your attention on the fruits that you have already grown is futile. You cannot change the fruits that are already hanging on the tree (bad or good). You can, however, change tomorrow's fruits.

Life of a Tree

Visible

Appearance

Fruit
(External Behaviors)

To

Invisible

Reality

Root
(Inner Workings)

Conquering an addiction to alcohol or pornography, for example, does not make a person immune to yielding to temptations that may cause a recurrence of problems. The tiniest seeds of lying, cheating, or stealing can develop (or redevelop) into roots (attitudes and desires) that form fruit-bearing plants (speech and actions) which cause mistrust and discord in relationships. A "white lie," fudging a date or signature on a document, or deciding money you found on someone else's property belongs to you as "finders keepers," tend to lead to bigger deceptions, forgeries, and thefts. Integrity can disappear before one realizes it's gone, but the damage is done. Cleaning up, even the smallest spots of darkness, keeps us healthy and fit as image-bearers of God.

Even good roots that produce good fruits can become compromised and turn into a damaged root. Jesus tells a story about a farmer sowing seed which falls on four different types of soil. Three types were bad and only one was good soil producing a crop (see Mark 4).

Good fruit is produced by good soil and proper growing conditions. Transformational living keeps the soil in good condition. When we fail to stay connected to the Master Root (Jesus as described in John 15), we are vulnerable to the dangers that the enemy of our soul has in line to kill, steal, and destroy (John 10:10).

Judging

One more very important spiritual law must be explored. It is so important that I devote the whole next chapter to it. The author of the book of Hebrews writes, "See to it that no one comes short of the grace of God; that no root of bitterness springing up causes trouble, and by it many be defiled" (Hebrews 12:15 NASB). Bitter root judgments defile. Condemning judgments destroy lives. Critical judgments made in the heart become visible in condescending speech and prideful actions. A critical spirit is sinful and can never be rooted out too soon. In my own personal transformation journey, and in observations in others, this is one of the most challenging of the dark corners of the house for us to expose. Condemning judgments often present themselves as "normal," intelligent, justifiable, and automatic responses that keep them disguised as light (instead of the truly dark evil they represent).

Earlier we discussed the idea of ANTS (automatic negative thoughts), and how common they are. More examples of judging will be discussed later, but critical judgment is so common in our relationships that we don't recognize it as such. For example, here are three typical examples of how easy it is to think less of someone with condemning thoughts: As a wife, my husband did not recognize a new outfit I am wearing for the first time. Or, a person walks into a room and says "hi" to others but not to me. Or, as a husband, my wife failed to thank me for fixing something that had been annoying her for a long time. In these cases we may feel insignificant, ignored, or unappreciated. We may even take it more personally and feel worthless, devalued, dishonored, disrespected, or unworthy of love. When we allow our undesirable feelings to negatively influence our thoughts toward a person's core individuality, we are condemningly judging that person. Our erroneous beliefs about a person's identity causes us to perceive them as a "bad" person. These bad perceptions turn into bad assumptions like the person "doesn't love me," "doesn't care," "doesn't understand," "isn't willing to listen," "isn't going to change," etc. With that untrue assumption about the person, negative opinions are formed like, "this marriage is terrible," "I can't continue working with this person," "this situation will never change," "I can't let them get away with this," "they are going to have to pay," etc. From the initial lie-based, bitter thoughts, the bitter root develops into blaming others, justifying self, hatred, resentment, and perhaps even retaliation. Bad decisions are then made like, "telling them off," "cutting them off," "getting back at them," "they did bad to me, so I'll do something bad to them," etc.

The driving force in the escalation from offended feelings, to believing lies about a person's identity, to wrongful assumptions, to forming damaged opinions, to choosing bad behaviors, is the sin of judging. Entertaining bitter thoughts toward a person (or institution or situation) creates a bitter root. If not detected and dealt with, over time a narrative or pattern of bitterness develops into hurtful actions. These are examples of how the verse quoted above in Hebrews 12:15 shows how the "root of bitterness springing up causes trouble, and by it many be defiled."

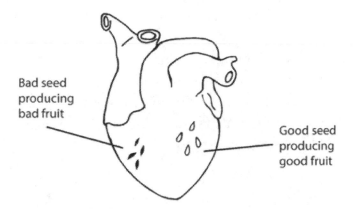

Bad seed producing bad fruit

Good seed producing good fruit

Jesus commands a wonderful cure (law) for judging. He reminds us that the standards we use to determine the rightness or wrongness of other people's behavior should first be applied to ourselves. "Do not judge, so that you won't be judged. For with the judgment you use, you will be judged, and with the measure you use, it will be measured to you. Why do you look at the speck in your brother's eye but don't notice the log in your own eye? Or how can you say to your brother, 'Let me take the speck out of your eye,' and look, there's a log in your eye? Hypocrite! First take the log out of your eye, and then you will see clearly to take the speck out of your brother's eye" (Matthew 7:1-5). Applying this solution to whatever bitterness we feel toward another person quickly puts things in perspective.

Good News

Fortunately, although we are bound to the natural laws which govern life, we also have access to a supernatural realm with God providing an oasis of love and faithfulness unmatched in the universe. We are reminded of some verses in the book of Romans that give us great hope, "You, however, are controlled not by the sinful nature but by the Spirit, if the Spirit of God lives in you. And if anyone does not have the Spirit of Christ, he does not belong to Christ. But if Christ is in you, your body is dead because of sin, yet your spirit is alive because of righteousness. And if the Spirit of him who raised Jesus from the dead is living in you, he who raised Christ from the dead will also give life to your mortal bodies through his Spirit, who lives in you" (Romans 8:9-11).

The spirit part of our being can influence the results of what we experience in the other planes of our existence. When we allow God to take his rightful place as creator and ruler of our heart, the conditions are in place to get planted in the right kind of soil to continue growing into a healthy tree for bearing good fruit.

Chapter 5

Bitter Root Judgments

In the year 2011, I authored a book called *Escaping the Pain of Offense: Empowered to Forgive from the Heart*. The content of the book is largely a culmination of a three-year research project I completed for my seminary degree dissertation. Digging deeply into the topic of forgiveness radically changed my life for the good in so many ways. We will look at the topic of forgiveness in more detail in the next section of this book.

What I discovered in writing and promoting the book is a widespread indifference to the topic of forgiveness. Besides those who think forgiveness is all taken care of at conversion, many do not realize the great degree of unforgiveness burden they are currently carrying in their lives. Many physical symptoms and unpleasant emotions are rooted in bitterness that can go undetected for years or even a lifetime.

Disappointments and offenses can contaminate the soil and cause bad fruit even sometimes without us being aware of what is going on. In my opinion, one of the greatest needs in the life of most people is a reprogramming of their understanding and practice of forgiveness. Common effects (bad fruits) of unforgiveness include pervasive stress and anxiety, self-inflicted condemnation, lack of trust and love, anger and bitterness, perpetual conflict, building of harmful emotional walls, depression and hopelessness, chronic illness, and sleeplessness or appetite loss. If any of these are consistently bad fruits in our lives, the transformation journey likely includes a deeper look at the invisible roots that almost always include a root of bitterness somewhere. Soil cleansing and rooting out frustrations, disappointments, and offenses in these areas will increase the quality of fruit produced in our lives. We must beware not to become too comfortable with unpleasant emotions so as to treat them as a normal mode of operating.

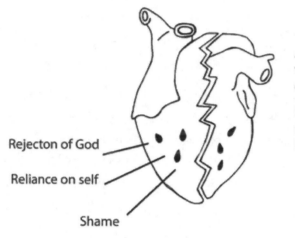

A broken world breaks our heart

Bad seeds/bad roots producing bad fruits

Rejecton of God

Reliance on self

Shame

Bad judging causes bad roots. Bad (sinful) judging begins in the heart and produces bad (sinful) actions. We all sin frequently in this way. Bad roots develop by misinterpreting information, creating wrong perceptions, making false assumptions, thus forming inaccurate opinions, drawing mistaken conclusions, thus making bad decisions, which turn into condemning judgments. Like a computer, bad data in, processed by bad programming, yields bad data out. In our repossessed house illustration earlier, bitter root judgments are what create and maintain the "dark" places of our house. These bad judgments create what the Bible calls a root of bitterness.

"Watch over each other to make sure that no one misses the revelation of God's grace. And make sure no one lives with a root of bitterness sprouting within them which will only cause trouble and poison the hearts of many" (Hebrews 12:15 TPT).

What Judging Means

The English word judge can mean many things across a spectrum of "good" judging and "bad" judging. Good judging may include rightly perceiving, discerning, and wisely discriminating. "Bad" judging is unfounded criticizing, pre-judging, misjudging, demeaning, and condemning. Bad judging usually involves an assumption of unfair or unjust treatment (real or perceived). Communication via language can be very difficult, but with this word judge, it can be especially difficult to determine meaning. For example, the word *discrimination*. Discrimination is a word of "good" judgment, hijacked in recent years to be widely associated with unfairness.

In languages other than English, the problem is similar. The Greek text of the Bible uses the same word for four different meanings. The context defines its meaning. Three are the good kind of judging. These are the judicial authority practiced by Church leaders, the judging Jesus himself does, and the discernment practiced to determine wise and moral behavior. The fourth, and sinful type, happens when we make ourselves the sole judge, jury, and hangman. Bad judging condemns a person and not just the behavior.

Thirst for Justice

Desire for justice is an innate part of our being. Unfortunately, since the moment sin entered the human race through Adam and Eve, our default mode of judging is "bad" judging. When man chose to give up existing solely on the "tree of life," he chose "the tree of the knowledge of good and evil." Judging (in the sense of knowing good from evil) was not originally meant for human practice. Only God is the ultimate Judge. God's laws (ways of operating) are supreme. Therefore, any judgment a person makes, (even a "good" judgment), is subject to reinterpretation by a higher power. Only God can satisfy our ultimate desire for justice. God is a God of perfect justice and perfect mercy.

So, although God did not design and desire man to carry the burden of judgment, the problem is that man wills (and demands) to be his own judge. Our human nature does not want to accept God as Judge. However, God is Judge, Jury, and Executioner. He makes judgments, is not subject to anyone else's interpretation, and acts as he wills on his judgments. Our rebellion against this authority is sin. We are doing the bad judging because we do not trust God to take care of us and to hold others accountable when they sin against us (and therefore hurt us). We think we must take the law into our own hands, because if we don't, we falsely believe (assume, imagine, conclude, and decide) that nobody will.

How to Know the Difference

How do we know when we've crossed the line from good to bad judging? Understanding our problems of "bad" judging requires much more than intellect and reason. It must include searching the inner heart of our own being.

When judgment transfers from a person's behavior to the person themselves, we've crossed the line. It's okay to expect behaviors appropriate to the situation, but when an offense (real or perceived) causes negative feelings and emotions toward an offender, the bitter roots begin forming. Think of the word jerk. When thinking of someone as a jerk, that is bad judging. It's okay to judge a person's actions as bad, but not the personhood (their value as a human being).

Let's look at an example. You are driving 70 mph on an eight-lane expressway. A driver in a car in the lane to your left is traveling faster than you, slightly ahead of you, and suddenly decides to slip over into your lane, barely missing your left front fender. You react slightly, almost swerving to the right to avoid a collision. What are you feeling at this point toward that driver? Then you see him cut off another driver in front of you twenty seconds later. Do you think now that you are justified in calling the driver a jerk? It's okay for you to expect the driver's behavior (driving habits) to be safer, but not to condemn the driver's personhood as unworthy of the grace of God.

Sometimes frustration and anger can turn to rage. So-called "road rage" has a bitter root at its core. A person angered to the extreme of rage is forgetting there are two sides to every offense. When we are on the offended side, it's easy to identify the offender's actions as wrong. When we're on the offending side, we so easily identify with our own intentions that we may forget what our actions look like to others. In the highway reckless driving example, what if we are the person driving erratically? What if we are caretaking for a family member and couldn't leave the house any earlier? Furthermore, we were late for work already twice and the boss said the third time we would be fired. There is still a chance to get to work on time, but it means taking some chances while driving that we know are a little reckless, but as long as we don't put anyone else at great risk, God might overlook our breaking a driving rule, for this time at least. In this case we want mercy.

Why is it so hard to grant mercy when the roles are flipped? It is because our default nature is bent in the direction of bad judging. For an example in the Bible, see the story Jesus told in Matthew 18 about the debtor's unforgiveness of a lesser debt. When we realize we have done the bad judging and are honest with ourselves enough to own it, we can be free to humble ourselves and forgive. Forgiveness, as the way to get free of the bad feelings caused by the bitter roots embedded (that result in calling someone a jerk), is what drives our pace to peace.

Judging Self

We will talk more about shame later, but shame and judgment work together to condemn our personhood. Shame tells us we are not worthy to be the sons and daughters God created us to be (which is a lie). We confuse shame (who I am) with guilt (what I do) to condemningly judge ourselves unworthy.

This rebellion and shame is so rooted in our nature we accept it as a fact of life. It shows up in the earliest days of childhood. Babies have legitimate needs and cry when they are hungry or uncomfortable. But they sometimes scream in anger for no apparent reason. Toddlers sometimes throw tantrums simply to demand their way. Children do not have to be taught how to disobey, steal, manipulate, and the like. The broken world in which we live imposes hurtful experiences causing perceived wounds and reactions ("bad" roots) of bitterness, resentment, blaming, and justifying. Reactions turn into learned patterns of behavior, forming who we are on the inside. It is important to recognize that what goes wrong in our life is not because of the bad things others have done to us, but because of our bitter reactions to them.

We also do not have ability to recognize this poor condition. Each person is blind (for the most part) to his or her own bitter reactions, wounding, and critically judging. Our heart could be compared to a vegetable garden with good plants and weeds growing together. The soil feeds the roots of both good plants and bad. The good plants try to bring forth fruit in keeping with what they were designed to produce, unaware of the weeds stealing nourishment and limiting their ability to produce. God as the Gardener of our heart is the only one who can solve the problem by providing a means for taking care of the weed problem.

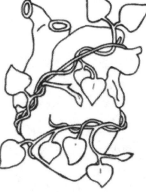

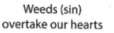
Weeds (sin) overtake our hearts

No garden will ever be completely free of weeds. Even after a good weed-pulling session, seeds are in the soil that will eventually produce more weeds. The seeds of sin are with us as long as we live. It's an unending problem and just part of natural laws. So too our hearts produce weeds as part of our natural existence. The nicest, most good-hearted, loving person carries the same seed as the most inconsiderate, unloving, or abusive person. Even unrecognized or unacknowledged bad behaviors (rooted in bad judging) will grow into unmanageable weeds. Only the Gardener (God) can take care of the weeds with finality. Jesus is the Gift God provided to make things right in our heart. The miracle cannot be finished with one weed-pulling session. It takes a lifetime of pulling weeds. This is called transformation and sanctification.

Common Problem

The greatest enemy in the garden of the heart is the will to critically judge. Our deep desire for justice becomes an excuse for condemning ourselves and other people for who they are instead of merely for their actions. We explain away many condemning judgments on a daily basis. For example, when you think or verbalize the following with a person or persons closest to you in relationship: "I told you a million times not to do ____ (whatever annoys you)_____ , but you keep being a jerk about it." Or, "You really don't love me when you _____." Or, "I cannot love you if you keep doing _____ ." Or, "Drivers on the highway are jerks when they _____ ." We accuse and confuse the guilt of "wrongdoing" with the shame of "wrong being." In God's eyes (God's judgment) there is no such thing as "wrong being." God does not think of any person as a jerk. So, if we believe in justice, we cannot think and act that way either.

An example recently occurred when a holiday greeting card and letter showed up in our mail as "undeliverable." We had sent the card to a close family member about two months prior. For some time, this family member was judging my wife and I unfairly, and not answering our calls and messages to reach out and try to make things right between us. When the card sent to this person came back, I immediately assumed they were unwilling to receive mail from us. I began thinking thoughts like, "That's just like them," and saying to my wife, "I can't believe they would be so disrespectful." I thought other unkind and critical things about them as a person, and also believed their actions condemned them as guilty.

The stickers the United States Postal Service placed on the envelope that was returned in our mail had some unclear remarks about how the letter was handled. My wife took the letter to our local post office to get clarification. The postal worker explained that, in recent months, they had already received many complaints about this type of letter being misdelivered. In fact, her description of the problem meant that the recipient likely never received the letter in their mailbox. What seemed so reasonable in assessing the situation turned out to be feeding false assumptions, perceptions, and beliefs. These led to condemning judgments of the person. I had to confess and repent for the bitterness that had gripped my heart. Otherwise, the bad root would have kept on growing.

The more bad roots we have, the more bad fruit we have. This is why bad judging is so damaging to us. To make matters worse, the longer a bad root grows inside us, the bigger it gets, the more entrenched it is, and the more difficult it is to eradicate. The bigger the root, the more pervasive is the bad fruit.

Again, there is no one exempt from this condition of humanity. As we discussed earlier, no amount of willpower can correct it. Instead of the "tree of judging," God wants us to enjoy the "tree of life." Eating fruit from the tree of life means that our thirst for justice is satisfied by the Judge of all judges, not by our own self-determination. God judged sin and shame to be taken care of through the justice and mercy provided by his own Son, Jesus Christ.

Inner Vows

An Inner Vow is a mechanism that is always linked to a bitter root judgment. Working together, they cause us to do the things we don't want to do. When an Inner Vow is operating, it produces rigid and inflexible behavior, and our willpower is unable to overcome it. All toxic Inner Vows, even "good" ones, need to be removed. Otherwise, they will hold us in bondage, and they will obstruct our ability to obey Jesus.

A classic example is a person who declares they will not be like one of their parents they were offended by. John, a ten-year-old boy, has a father who is a very angry man. His father's inner anger is taken out on John, his mother, and his siblings. John comes to hate his father, and he judges him. So, the consequences of the first sin of judging takes effect and will cause him trouble later in life. But at some point John also says to himself, "I am never going to be like my father." John has just made an Inner Vow (binding promise which includes condemnation), and this condemning vow compounds and expands his future problems.

The contemptable judgment against his father is sin, and it plants a bitter root that will grow inside him and produce bad fruit in his life as a result of the operation of God's law. It is simply the way the spiritual universe works. But he has compounded his problem by taking his life into his own hands. John decides that he will never be like his father, whom he despises. He has just entered into bondage. What will likely happen in John's adult life is that usually he will not get angry, because the Inner Vow represses his anger. But now and then he will explode in a fit of rage, and those around him will be wounded. Afterwards he will be angry with himself because he has just acted exactly the way his father did!

During those times when he is successfully repressing his anger, other people may sense the anger seething below the surface, but John will be unaware of it. After all, he has decided that being angry is bad, and he doesn't want to admit to himself that he has anger inside.

The problem for John is that he is locked into this pattern of behavior. He hates it, but he is powerless to change it. He is again reaping from the operation of God's law, and needs the transformational power of Jesus to change it. We will see in the next chapter how emotions like anger are friendly message carriers to help get to the root of things.

The difference between resolutions (nonjudgment-based vow) like a New Year's resolution and an Inner Vow is that the resolution was made with our head, whereas the Inner Vow was made with our heart. The way the Inner Vow got into our heart was that at the time we made it we were very much influenced by wrongful perceptions created in our heart. We were in a state of bitterness, and our emotions were greatly stirred. When we made an Inner Vow we were judging, and it is the strength of the sin of judging that gives the Inner Vow its power.

An Inner Vow is a heart-based decision we make and usually contains the words "always" or "never." Many Inner Vows are not consciously spoken or even thought. This is especially true with small children. Even though they may not yet know how to talk, they can still make Inner Vows.

There was another powerful dynamic going on when we made the Inner Vow. At that moment we were taking our life into our own hands. We decided that nobody else was going to rescue us from this awful situation, and so we were going to have to take control of our own life. Thus, we judged God and we were presumptuous. In our opinion God was not fixing the situation, so we needed to do it. We presumed that we had the ability to protect ourselves with our own power. This sin goes all the way back to the beginning of mankind.

Recall that when we condemningly judge another person we are usurping God's role, because we don't trust him to be the just judge. In the case of an Inner Vow, when we decide to do it ourselves, we are again usurping God's role. We do this because we don't trust him to take care of us. From the Garden of Eden onward, there has been a tendency for man to demand, "I'll Be My Own Judge" (IBM-OJ).

The Inner Vow itself is not sin, because we have a right to make decisions. But at the time that we make an Inner Vow, we have bitterness in our heart. In that moment we don't trust God to be our protector, and we decide to take control. We decide to take God's place and to be our own protector.

When we do that, we are in sin. When we sin in this way, our willpower no longer has authority over the decision that we made in our moment of bitterness. In that moment of bitterness, a bitter root was planted in our heart. A spiritual event occurred, writing the decision in our heart. Now that decision is no longer under the authority of our own power. God's laws are now impelling it to operate as we had decided. After this point it becomes embedded in our below-conscious memory beyond our awareness. We cannot decide to renounce it and make it stop operating. From then on it will direct our life, perhaps making us do things we no longer want to do.

What about making "good" Inner Vows? When John said, "I will never be like my father," he might also have said, "I will always be nice." What is wrong with this vow? Isn't it a good thing to always be nice? Sometimes we are reluctant to see that a "good" Inner Vow is a problem, but Inner vows always create difficulties for us. To further illustrate, John has his car repaired and the mechanic overcharges him by $50. If John has made an Inner Vow to always be nice, it will be impossible for him to confront the mechanic, because that wouldn't be "nice." So he may rationalize his behavior: "Oh, well. It's only $50, and I know he has a family to support, so I won't say anything." It would be appropriate to ask the mechanic politely about the overcharge, but the rigidity of the Inner Vow interferes with John's ability to do this.

John may also rationalize that it is good to be "nice," and so a "good" Inner Vow is okay. However, Jesus never told us to be "nice." Was He "nice" when he called the scribes and Pharisees *"a brood of vipers"* (Matthew 3:7), or called them *"whitewashed tombs"* (Matthew 23:27)? Was he "nice" to the moneychangers when he overturned their tables in the temple? He didn't tell us to be "nice," but to be "loving," and there is a big difference between the two. It was because of his love for his Father that he cleansed the temple and love for people that motivated his confrontation of their leaders. I remember a former pastor of mine saying, "There will be a lot of nice people in hell."

The so-called "good" Inner Vow that John made was based upon sin, and therefore it is not "good" whatsoever. We need to be free of anything that is based upon sin and bondage. Therefore, we need to be free of all Inner Vows (binding condemning judgments), including "good" ones. "Good" inner vows compel us to establish our own righteousness, whereas Jesus came to express his righteousness through us. We need to be free to let him do this, rather than to be locked into our own decision which may be different than what the Lord wants.

In the next section we will discuss more about how to renounce and become free of bitter root judgments and inner vows. Sometimes people are afraid to renounce their Inner Vows. Because John wants so desperately to not be like his father, he may find it difficult to renounce his Inner Vow. He is afraid that if he does so, he will become like his father. That would be intolerable (even though he currently acts like him anyway). But what actually happens when he is set free of the bondage of the Inner Vow is that he is free to feel the anger when it is present. After all, the anger was always present, but previously he wasn't free to feel it. He needs to feel it so that he can recognize that he has condemningly judged the person who currently transgressed and offended him, and then he can process it by forgiving and being forgiven.

Two Parts

I offer a word of caution here. In recognizing "bad roots" in our hearts, we must never forget the "good roots" God has planted in each of us. God has created each human being with good traits and characteristics unique to him or her as an individual. Lest we become overwhelmed by the bad (because of the brokenness inherent in the world), we must remember the God of the good. The bad and good simultaneously dwell in the same heart. The bad is only a part of us, and as we yield to God in transformational living, the bad has less and less influence, while the good produces more and more good fruit.

So, the bad roots do not cancel out the good, but the two coexist. Just as good plants in a garden grow in the same soil as the weeds, our heart contains portions of light that flourish, and portions of darkness that create problems. Jesus taught a parable in Matthew 13, where he explained that while we are in this world, "wheat and tares" (good and bad) exist together. The enemy who tries to spoil the wheat (good) by sowing tares (bad) will be dealt with at the end of time.

Let us therefore not allow bad roots to define us, but see ourselves as a work in progress. Our worthiness comes from the Lord, and no amount of damage or brokenness can keep us broken forever.

Understanding our inner person as a makeup of two parts is especially helpful for those of us who lean toward being our own harshest critic (perfectionist). But it also helps us not jump to judgment on others we observe to be judgmental people. Let me explain.

Although the truth in this chapter is absolutely essential in healing from the inside out, it is so rarely taught in pulpits. I often hear people who have been Christians for years ask the question, "Why haven't I been told this before?" An awareness is awakened inside that can create heightened sensitivity to things that were always there, but not noticed before. When people start realizing how commonly condemning judgments are made, they likely start seeing it in everyone around them. They observe their friends' and families' condemning judgments quicker than they see their own judgmentalism. Some people tend toward judgmentalism more than others.

In my personal experience, I didn't realize how "quick to judge" was so much a part of my interactions with people. I began to become more aware of how my thoughts, feelings, assumptions, and conclusions so easily formed condemning judgments. I also started becoming more keenly aware of other people's judgments against me. It became very tempting for me to want to point out the judgments in my wife, for example, especially when I was the one who felt judged by her. Obviously, insisting on pointing out her judgmentalism did not go over well with her. Her judgmental reaction could not be an excuse for me to avoid taking responsibility for my own error in the issue at hand. My enthusiasm for practicing this new truth in identifying and releasing critical judgments to the Lord was meant for me personally, and could not be forced on other people. I had to realize it's much easier to see others' errors than to see my own. Also, I cannot let the tendency for bad judging I see in a person overshadow the value and good in that person.

Recognizing human nature's propensity toward bad judging, combined with recognizing the nature and power of emotions, are at the core of inner person change. Next, we look at emotions.

Chapter 6

Emotional Trunk

Emotions are not easily understood. Volumes have been written on emotional theory and attempts to try to figure out how they work. Emotions are powerful, they are a very real part of our being, and they carry messages that reveal what is going on in our inner world.

Like the trunk of a tree that carries life from the roots to its branches and fruit, emotions carry life (inspiration, motivation, vitality, "umph") through a person. Like the electrical system of a house, emotion powers the activities of a person.

I believe it is helpful to distinguish feelings from emotions. Naming the feelings that make up emotional responses helps us interpret the message contained in the emotions. Feelings and emotions are experienced more below our level of consciousness, but they can be compared to thoughts and ideas in our consciousness. Ideas are made of thoughts. Some thoughts are good and some are bad. Not all thoughts help in making good ideas. You may have heard it said, "Ideas have consequences; bad ideas have victims." Feelings have similar value to emotions as thoughts have to ideas. Feelings just are. Some feelings contribute more value to the message of the emotion.

Emotions can be pleasant or unpleasant. We all have needs and desires that get met, or not met, producing thoughts and feelings processed at the conscious and below conscious levels. The responses generated cause pleasure or pain. The areas of pain usually get the most attention.

This dynamic is often compared to an alarm system. Like the smoke alarm in a house, the sounding of the alarm is meant to draw attention to a danger. Ignoring the alarm, or prematurely cutting it off without finding the reason for its sounding, can lead to disaster. If an electrical fire is about to burn down the house, action must be taken to put out the fire. So too, our inner (below conscious) being is like an alarm system to give a message of warning (pain) when something is wrong.

How do we know what the warning message is telling us? Answer— we identify specific feelings and emotions to track to the source of the problem. Unpacking unpleasant emotions can be hard work. Many people would rather try to ignore the warnings (denial), or try to escape the reality of the danger (numbing the pain).

Loss and Pain

The loss and pain (everything from failures and disappointments to injustice and serious abuse) are experienced as a result of the broken world we live in. Loss and pain are to be expected, and are common to all. Losses create needs. We must be aware of our needs and recognize the pain of unmet needs and expectations. If we wish to recover from loss and pain, we must stop trying to hide it, and allow it to be found by Jesus. Breaking through denial and positioning our hearts for healing involves the following three considerations.

First, consider the purpose of pain. Physical pain in the body is meant to signal a warning of disrupted functionality. If a carpenter accidentally hits his thumb with a hammer, the physical pain he feels tells him something bad is happening to his body. A physical injury to a body may demand treatment and healing for functionality to be restored. Mental, emotional, and spiritual hurts need to run a healing course as well.

Second, consider what governs our actions. Reaction of the physical or tangible (outer man) is determined by the nonphysical or intangible (inner man). Jesus taught us that the sinful actions we take part in have their source in our heart (see Mark 7:20-23). If the heart is at rest, a person's behavior will reflect peace and calm. If the heart is unrestful, the person's behavior will reflect frustration, dissatisfaction, and all sorts of emotional pain, and all sorts of unpleasant, undesirable, or harmful behavior.

Third, consider what lies at the root of painful feelings. From our conception in the womb, our own brokenness, and the brokenness of people around us, creates critical judgments, bitterness, injustices, and wounds of soul and spirit.

So, if 1) our bad behavior is undesirable or destructive (sinful), which is, 2) caused by a heart full of pain, which is 3) caused by unresolved bitterness and woundedness, then doesn't it make sense to go after the "bitter root" to bring healing to the problem? This is actually commanded in Hebrews 12:15, "See to it that ... no bitter root grows up to cause trouble and defile." (NIV) Why is this so difficult? It is hard because it cannot be done with mere knowledge or sheer will power. It requires surrendering to the power of God for transformational healing.

Only Jesus can truly redeem the broken condition of the human heart. He has given us the gift and power of the Holy Spirit to accomplish this in our heart.

Let me encourage you to take inventory of your heart. What might be a remaining loss (and waiting to be found by Jesus) in your life? Is there a behavior, habit, or pattern of reaction that may indicate some degree of unrest in your soul? Is there a root of bitterness and unforgiveness you already know about but haven't surrendered to God for him to be the Judge? If you think there's nothing, let go of your denial and start feeling. Let the pain surface. It wants to be your friend. Let the ashes of loss, failures, discomfort, uneasiness, restlessness, confusion, doubt, and worry be turned into beauty of pain-free circumstances (see Isaiah 61:1-3).

Ridding Painful Judgments

Unpleasant feelings and emotions can be seen as our "friend" since they reveal to us the bitter root judgments that cause destruction. God has provided Jesus to forgive our sins of condemning judgment. When we forgive and are forgiven, our sin is washed away and healing comes into that place in our heart. The pain is driven out. Jesus is our Healer. Jesus is our Pain Bearer (see Isaiah 53:1-6).

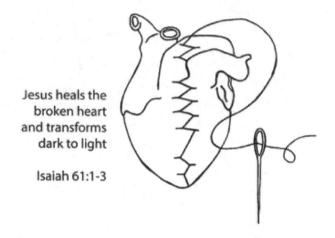

Jesus heals the
broken heart
and transforms
dark to light

Isaiah 61:1-3

How does this work practically? Consider the example in the last chapter when a careless driver is encountered on the highway. When Driver A gets angry with Driver B for cutting too closely in front of him, he judges Driver B condemningly by calling him a "jerk" (whether in his heart or with his mouth as well). Driver A needs to take care of this as soon as he can, immediately if possible. That way the initial warning is heeded, and the root can go no deeper to take hold. But if after praying and releasing it to God, the agitation persists and more unpleasant emotions surface over the incident the rest of the day, a deeper buried root of bitterness (sin) must be considered. Perhaps Driver A had judged his parents for not considering his opinion when key decisions were made in the family-of-origin household, or for not considering his needs, or for cutting him off in some other way. Perhaps even worse, Driver A may have judged himself as being unworthy to have his needs met by others; and therefore, it is left up to him to take care of himself. Yes, it is true that the other driver was not sensitive to his needs, and it was the behavior of the careless driver that touched that wound deep inside him. But it wasn't what Driver B did that is the problem. What planted the bitter root was Driver A's reaction to what was done to him. Allowing himself to feel the unpleasant emotion gives him an opportunity to know what happened, and thus he can pray and be set free from the consequences of the bitter root.

Surfacing Feelings

Though turning to Jesus and praying is simple, appropriately working through emotions of a hurt can be complex. It becomes complicated because many of the old roots of bitterness are deeply buried and forgotten about. Although they may be forgotten by us, they did not escape the notice of God. Although it seems complicated to us, nothing is too complicated for God. Jesus can lead us through the process of finding the bitter root(s) and being healed. Sometimes another person walking alongside us (such as a trusted friend or counselor) is helpful or necessary in the process.

Some people claim that "bad" feelings are sinful. For example, some think it is a sin to feel angry or jealous. It is not a sin to feel. There is no sin to repent of when you feel angry. There may be a sin present, but it is deeper than the feeling of anger. The emotion of anger is carrying a message. The message is trying to tell us about a root of bitterness inside us (planted by a sinful reaction of judging), and we need to know about the presence of this bitter root.

There may be a sin present, but the sin is not the emotion. The sin is the condemning judgment. The feeling and emotion of anger is not sin. If we fail to take the message of anger to Jesus, the bitterness may turn into rage which may eventually turn into another type of sinful behavior (like physical aggression to harm an offender). So we see that there is a difference between the emotion and the root. The root needs the healing, not the emotion. When a bitter root exists, the emotion is just a signal telling us about the root. The signal is sounding an alarm as a faithful friend to avoid disaster.

Repressing or trying to squash our emotions produces negative consequences in our lives. We are the ones who suffer. When we repress the unpleasant emotions to keep from feeling the pain, we miss out on the awareness that something inside needs attention. That is what the negative feelings and unpleasant emotions are telling us. If we continue to ignore them, there will be unfortunate consequences. Whatever is wrong inside will eventually come to the surface in some way, because the problem inside will become too large to ignore. Ulcers, insomnia, eating irregularities, and uncontrolled outbursts of anger are common examples of this. When we do not allow emotions to come "straight out" (intentionally listen to them and resolve them) as God intended, they eventually come out "sideways" (unintentionally) and produce problems in our life.

Emotional Capacity

The term emotional intelligence (EI) has become a buzzword to address the role of emotion in relationships, work, organization, and family environments. But most of what we hear about EI, in my opinion, has very little to do with emotions. EI seems to have more to do with cognitive awareness and attempts to *avoid* or subdue emotions.

I think Emotional Capacity (EC) is a better way to consider the emotional aspects of a person. Intellect draws on the memory bank of the mind, but the capacity of emotional experience goes deeper to the heart of our being. Unwanted feelings may produce unpleasant emotions, but the capacity to change these to pleasant emotions requires more than a mere decision to change. Deeper qualities of love, joy, peace, temperance, gratitude, contentment, kindness, and faithfulness must go beyond the imagination of the mind to provide meaning for ourselves and others around us.

EI focuses on controlling behaviors. EC focuses on positively influencing behaviors by expanding core belief systems to engage, enrich, and transform a person. Mere cognitive awareness of emotion does not produce transformation. Inside-out change is much more rewarding, productive, and longer lasting.

Since emotions carry messages, the messages they report are gathered from thoughts and feelings about the environment. Who we are as a person is based on our constant evaluation of our value and worth in our environment. Therefore, our identity directly relates to our EC.

EC can be defined as the ability to interpret and express inner emotional messages with unshaken assurance of personal worth and identity. I discovered valuable insights on EC by reading work by Dr. Richard Ecker. We learn how to navigate our environment by developing coping skills. Ecker points to Webster's definition of coping as "successful striving." In the *Emotional Survival Training Manual*, Ecker writes that coping, "is the ability to stand and endure in the face of difficult circumstances— or maneuver to avoid them. But we do not cope when we merely stand and endure or run and hide. We cope when we strive actively against the realities we face— and succeed."[3]

Ecker also says, "Typically, coping success is believed to be tied to the ultimate outcome of the situation that has made the coping necessary. If the outcome is good from the standpoint of the individual who is trying to cope, then that person is generally considered to have coped successfully. If the outcome is undesirable, then most people

---

3 Richard E. Ecker, PhD, *Emotional Survival Training Manual* (Bradenton, FL: Booklocker.com Inc., 2013), #.

tend to feel that they coped badly. The fact is, outcomes have nothing at all to do with whether or not an individual coped successfully with the situation. The only real measure of coping success is whether or not that person emerged from the encounter with a positive feeling of personal value— that is, has successfully striven."[4]

What I believe this means is that, judging whether we are better off as a person by going through difficult circumstances, is not measured by the circumstances, but by our inner condition as a result. When adversity causes us to surrender more of our heart to God, it has done us good on the inside, regardless of what the externals may look like. Our identity is at the core of our belief system. The more we are surrendered to God, the closer we become to seeing ourselves the way God intends for us to be. The more we accept ourselves for who God made us to be, the greater the capacity to accept whatever circumstances may come our way.

The ability to cope is based on increasing a sense of God-given personal value and worth. Let me distinguish between self-worth and self-esteem. Value and worth is an attribute given by God inherent in the existence of every human life. Nothing a person does (or doesn't do) can add or detract from the image of God in personhood. Esteeming self by exalting one's human ability to create or maintain superior value is not the kind of striving Ecker means in the quote above. Selfish satisfaction of personal desire works against the created order of God. Self-worth comes from selflessly accepting and loving the person who God made you to be.

Ecker also says, "if you learn how to confront the realities of life in such a way that you can emerge from each experience with a positive sense of personal worth, then you can gain from each experience valuable equipment that will make you even more successful in succeeding

---

4 Ecker, #..

confrontations."[5] Increasing emotional capacity is the goal. Accepting your unconditional personal worth is the means to that goal.

Managing vs. Engaging

In order to obtain the full message from emotion, one must be able to identify specific thoughts and feelings and determine the reality of their impact. EC allows a person to feel. Fear of feeling shuts a person down so that the true messages being sent by emotions are not received. If a person denies or minimizes the feeling of sad, they will also not be able to feel glad. Pushing away the feeling of alone will also prohibit a feeling of belonging. Refusing to feel wherein one's discontent lies will also limit the capacity to feel true contentment. Whatever negative feeling is avoided will inevitably cut off the ability to feel the positive counterpart.

Anger "management," for example, without anger engagement, may actually diminish one's EC. Anger is a surface emotion in that a deeper message is always behind the anger. If feelings like rejection, guilt, or shame are the source of the anger, a cause or solution has no chance of being discovered if the anger is merely "controlled" and not also engaged at a deeper level. EI may offer a solution to anger that would include withdrawing from situations that make you angry. EC would build the ability to cope with the inner source of anger so that tougher and tougher situations can be endured without triggering the anger.

At one time or another, we all face overwhelming emotional circumstances in life. Our coping skills have limitations based on our perceptions of our personal worth. Our capacity to overcome (or lack thereof), is most significantly influenced by our parents and the people in our background who shaped core beliefs about ourselves and the world around us.

---

5 Ecker, #..

Another thing to realize is that negative feelings are the default mode of our human condition. From birth we feel things like the following without having to take lessons: rejected, deserted, left out, ashamed, trashy, unfit, unworthy, anxious, desperate, fearful, powerless, helpless, oppressed, weak, damaged, flawed, inferior, insignificant, unappreciated, unloved, defeated, hopeless, disoriented, and depressed. From a very young age we assimilate these into our concept of self-worth and unconsciously create conditions for accepting love and affirmation from other people. We form habits of interpreting and expressing inner emotional messages that condemn rather than build up. When this negativity is reinforced or aggravated by those around us, developing a positive sense of self-worth is all the more difficult.

It takes some effort to increase the capacity of the emotional part of our being, but it is worth every bit of effort. Building resilience is like filling a reservoir with clean water in preparation for an unknown drought season. We may not know when the next conflict or crisis tests our stamina or stability, but we know our personal worth is not based on how the situation turns out. We fill our soul with "clean water" by uncovering and healing the source of damaged self-concept, learning and developing new coping skills, and replacing bad habits with good habits.

The toxic stress of holding an offense causes a block to EC. The bitterness often turns into a grudge, resentment, or rage that can cause great damage (Hebrews 12:15). Taking the bait of offense means we've allowed our self-worth to be challenged. This shows up in one of two forms: blaming or justifying. Blaming is putting others DOWN to make oneself look good. Justifying is putting oneself UP to make others look less worthy (because one's own concept of self isn't able to stand on its own). We are very prone to self-deception and hiding our tendency to wrongful blaming and over justifying.

Increasing EC improves the ability to empathize with others. One cannot feel how others feel if one does not allow oneself to first feel similar kinds of feeling within. Empathy goes a long way toward curing toxic self-focus and seeing other people more as God created them to be.

In the next section of this book the reader will discover more key ways for increasing emotional capacity. But first, there is one more major factor in the human condition we must explore—shame.

Chapter 7

Identity and Shame

Shame is the most powerful of human emotions. But the role of shame in the human condition makes it much more than an emotional response. The original sin of mankind made shame a part of our identity. Our identity reflects the degree of shame we tolerate in our being. Our perception of reality is governed by the ongoing transformational power of Jesus turning shame into the joy of his salvation and turning victimhood into victory.

> Fixing our eyes on Jesus, the author and perfecter of faith, who for the joy set before Him endured the cross, despising the shame, and has sat down at the right hand of the throne of God. (Hebrews 12:2 NASB)

Shame is the greatest obstacle to receiving our true identity in Jesus. Jesus conquered shame once and for all. He did it *for* us (see Isaiah 53:1-6). He didn't leave shame for us to conquer. A huge part of our broken human condition is rooted in the problem of shame. Therefore, a huge part of our transformation journey involves identifying and eradicating shame.

Sometimes shame is confused with guilt. In the Bible there are some instances of the word shame being used as a means of inducing feelings of guilt for the conviction of sinful behavior. Condemning bad behavior with the goal of redemption for the person is different from condemning a person himself as irredeemable and without value to God. Shame in the deeper sense of condemning personhood steals our true God-given identity.

> **Shame is the greatest obstacle to receiving our true identity in Jesus.**

We get rid of our shame, and find our real identity, by surrendering it to Jesus. Recent research has revealed some workings of shame we will consider later in this chapter. First, we need to explore some general aspects of identity.

Identity Parts

Man is different from the animal kingdom because he has a personal spirit. The spirit part of our being is what allows us to connect to our Creator. Besides our personal spirit, in broadest of terms, who we are can be considered in two major parts. The parts are conscious and below conscious or mind and heart. The head (or mind) and the heart are divided along the lines of, 1) cognitive function (intellect, willpower, consciousness), and 2) all the rest of our core self (feelings, emotions, intuition, creativity, curiosity, gifts, talents, masculinity or femininity, imagination, spontaneity). God created us in such a way that the head and heart have to work together to make the whole person.

The working of Mind and Heart is not a "clean" division of functions. Many aspects of the "mind" (besides brain power) are present in the "heart" (core inner being). And many aspects of the "heart" are present in the mind. For purposes of our discussion here, it helps to think of them separately. Mind and Heart is also one of the ways the Bible speaks of the way people are organized inside. I discuss more detail about "living from the mind and heart" in Chapter Four of my book *Escaping the Pain of Offense*.

As creatures of habit, our subconscious mind develops patterns (grooves) of operation so that routine thoughts and behaviors can be processed without consciously thinking about the detail each time an action is called for. Our parents are the primary environmental influence in the early years when the inner parts develop lifelong patterns. Our childhood experiences are what form the relationship between the two parts and how well (or not) they work together.

Our conscious mind is constantly comparing the messages coming from our inner world (inner voice) with the messages we get from our environment (outer world). Because our world is a broken place, our mind (conscious self) tries to protect our inner treasure from real and perceived dangers. The inner treasure is longing for basic needs of love, safety, and belonging. When these are threatened, a wall starts to build for protection.

Often a more significant factor in building a wall for perceived protection of our inner treasure, is a second part of our heart that is also broken from its original created design. Along with our inner treasure, our heart has an inner dark part to it as well. This dark part functions as inner treason. It is hidden in darkness because it has been passed down through every generation since it entered Adam and Eve with the first sin. It works from the inside out to self-protect. Being dark, with no light to see, it has the result of distorting the true, light, good part of us. Hence, self-deception is often a big part of this wall-building as well.

Broken Coping

This wall building on our inside is a "broken" way of trying to deal with brokenness. The more brokenness in our background, the higher and thicker the walls may become. God created us with our inner treasure to give voice to who we are as a person. With a wall in place, the person we were created to be cannot be fully expressed. That is, all of our parts cannot work together as a whole (whole self).

Little children have countless interactions with their world as they grow up. If the messages coming up from their inner treasure are validated, they grow in their ability to trust and value their inner treasure. If they are not affirmed and validated, they can form patterns of repression, or even despising the messages (coming from within) to avoid painful feelings and emotions created.

An example would be the nurture received from their mother as a baby. A mother who expresses love in feeding and diaper changing to provide nourishment and comfort for the baby is affirming the child's value. Nursing and lovingly gazing into the eyes provides a sense of connectedness and belonging in the world. On the other hand, a mother who does not provide these validating experiences for the child causes a conflicted message within the child. The needs and desires to be loved, safe, and belong for all children are the same. If a mother drinks alcohol too much, hangs out with men who think children get in the way of a good time, swats the child for crying, or otherwise treats the child as an annoyance, the child reacts in pain. The child's inner treasure tries to defend itself against the pain. Worst of all, they may doubt and distrust their inner treasure. This disconnects them from who they were meant to be as a person.

The Unwholesome Wall

God created us in wholeness and to be his image bearers. We need all of the attributes that are in both our mind (head) and heart (inner treasure). Neither part is bad, and neither part is redundant. Sometimes we need to analyze a situation with our intellect and then simply go and do it. Sometimes we need to stop and listen to the messages from our inner treasure and act on what they tell us. However, the wall we have built interferes with our ability to hear these internal messages and allow them to interact. The wall wasn't supposed to be there, and is very damaging to our personhood. With a wall present, we have to try to live all aspects of our life from our Head, and we may not even be aware that the inner treasure exists. Without access to those attributes inside, we fail in some key aspects of our life.

For instance, a wife may be complaining that her husband can't communicate with her. She expects him to know what is going on inside her, yet she does not communicate her needs directly. Her husband is very frustrated because he is not a "mind reader." He asks himself, "How in the world am I supposed to know what she is feeling when she does not seem to know herself?"

The problem comes about because the husband is cut off from his Inner Treasure. Inside he feels her pain and does know what is going on inside her. There is ongoing communication between her Inner Treasure and his Inner Treasure. However, the awareness of that information never makes it through his Wall to his conscious mind (his Head). He becomes frustrated, and his wife does not feel heard. Because of the presence of the Wall in him, the marriage is much less intimate and rewarding than God meant it to be.

It is also quite likely that the wife also has a Wall, and therefore she too may not have a clear awareness of what her own needs are. Oftentimes marriage problems are best solved by each spouse first making progress on tearing down inner walls individually. A marriage (or any other relationship) cannot be whole if the two parties are not "wholly present" in the relationship.

Separated from God

Our relationship with God is similarly affected by an inner Wall. The living Lord communes with our personal spirit. We are designed to have a personal relationship with him through this part of our Inner Treasure. When we can hear God's voice, we will be reliably guided by him and prevented from sinning. We will be able to discern our chief enemy's traps and accurately identify the deceptions of the World. The devil loses, and we win.

However, when we have shut ourselves off from our Inner Treasure, we become unaware of God's presence. We are separated from him by the Wall, and our ability to hear him is impaired (sometimes totally)! This is the greatest tragedy that results from the building of the Wall. The building of the Wall is our enemy's grandest scheme because he loves to see us cut off from God. When we are cut off from God, we have to rely on our intellect, which is ill-equipped to discern good and evil, right and wrong. Our enemy can then lead us into all types of error. The devil wins, and we lose.

Separated from Other People

In addition to cutting off God, the Wall also affects our ability to have relationships with other people. Our inner treasure is the part of us that is sensitive to have compassion, for example. It is the part of us which has relationship with another person. Real relationship is heart-to-heart (Inner Treasure to Inner Treasure), not Head-to-Head. There is actual communication that occurs at the heart level. Jesus could tell what was going on in people's hearts, and so can we (at least to a degree). When we have access to this part of us, we can then feel what the other person is feeling. This sensing is called "empathy." Our personal spirit was given to us so that we can communicate heart-to-heart in this way. However, if there is a Wall inside, our ability to consciously hear what our personal spirit is saying is impaired, or perhaps completely blocked. If completely blocked, we are forced to try to figure out what is going on in the relationship with only our head.

Consequently, our relationships are shallow. We cannot feel what others feel or sense what is going on behind the personality they present to the world. It is not possible for us to have intimacy in our relationships because intimacy is only made possible by the heart-to-heart connection. With our Wall in place, other people who are sensitive to their own Inner Treasure will be able to sense that they are not connecting with us. We have them locked out. Our relationships are hollow and not very rewarding to either the other people or to us.

Separated from Self

Great tragedy results from the Wall that separates our conscious self (head) from our below-conscious self (heart). Most of our daily activities proceed out of habits stored below consciousness. Our "true self" mostly resides in our Inner Treasure and thus is very important to our being.

The most obvious loss of separation from below-conscious self is that we are shut off from the benefit of all those attributes contained in the Inner Treasure. In fact, most of our personhood, most of who we are, is in our Inner Treasure.

But there is a more debilitating result than not being all we are meant to be. Being cut off from ourselves causes incredible internal pain. Our Inner Treasure is meant to be the best friend of our Head, and suffers greatly when cut off from this relationship. The pain comes about because we have decided that who we are in the Inner Treasure is not acceptable. In fact, we conclude that this part of us inside is bad! In his book *I Will Give You Rest*, Ed Kurath calls this internal pain the "Big Hurt," because it is the most excruciating emotional pain we experience. The "Big Hurt" is our rejection of self. Self-rejection and shame interact in very crippling ways. More about shame is soon to come.

Contents of the Wall

So, the Wall is made up of condemning (bitter root) judgments and inner vows. The judgments are against yourself (your Inner Treasure), and the inner vows are decisions to not listen to the messages that come up from the Inner Treasure. For example, the little boy who skins his knee feels pain coming from the Inner Treasure. That Inner Treasure is compelling him to do something that Dad disapproves of (to cry), and it thus threatens to cause him the loss of Dad's approval. Therefore, the little boy judges that place, the Inner Treasure, as being trouble. He decides, "I'm not going to be a wimp. I'm going to be brave. I'm not going to listen to the pain anymore." This is an inner vow.

I will discuss more in the next section about how to be cleansed of bitter root judgments and how to renounce inner vows. The judgments against your "self" and the associated inner vows are dealt with in exactly the same way as dealing with them in relationship with other people. First you need to forgive and be forgiven in order to cooperate with the operation of God's laws. This takes away the power that drives the inner vow.

Then you need to renounce the inner vow. For example, "In the name of Jesus, I renounce the decision that I made to never pay attention to my emotions."

Finally, you need to restore the relationship, in this case your relationship with your "self" (your Inner Treasure). Your Treasure Inside is fully human and is wounded by your rejection, and yet your Inner Treasure is a part of you.

You need to restore this relationship (with yourself) in the same way as you would restore a relationship with any other person. You need to be proactive and pursue the restoration. You need to persevere, and to correct immediately any future critical judgments you make against yourself. And you need to spend time in relationship with your Inner Treasure (listening, valuing, attending to, protecting, nurturing, blessing). Relationships require time spent together and interaction.

This may sound strange, but keep in mind that your relationship with yourself is the most important human relationship you have. Being able to have access to those attributes in the Inner Treasure depends upon you having a loving relationship with yourself. Having a Wall inside interferes with your ability to hear God, to love him, and to love other people. Therefore, if you are at war within yourself, you cannot possibly fully and freely love others.

"Love the Lord your God with all your heart and with all your soul and with all your mind. This is the first and greatest commandment. And the second is like it: 'Love your neighbor as yourself'" (Matthew 22:37-39 NIV).

Love Yourself

Jesus summarized the Ten Commandments into two as stated above. In order to genuinely love your neighbor, you have to truly love yourself. That means being comfortable with the unique traits, abilities, disabilities, talents, characteristics, etc. you were meant to personify. Your identity and purpose in life hinges on what you value and perceive as meaningful. Loving others is a choice, impossible to make if you haven't first chosen to love yourself as God made you and loves you.

I would like to draw on the wisdom of one of my favorite thinkers named Viktor Frankl, MD. In his best-selling book *Man's Search for Meaning* he writes, "Ultimately, man should not ask what the meaning of his life is, but rather must recognize that it is *he* who is asked. In a word, each man is questioned by life; and he can only answer to life by *answering for* his own life; to life he can only respond by being responsible."[6] The Austrian psychiatrist Frankl won the battle in his mind to find life's meaning. Frankl did not allow his imprisonment in four Nazi concentration labor camps to demean his existence. He survived because of his desire for meaning. His logotherapy teaches us to inquire of life for meaning rather than to inquire of meaning for life. Finding meaning is believing in yourself enough to know you're here for a purpose, and you are committed to your responsibility to find the fullness of that purpose.

Loving the person God made us to be helps to remove the Wall and keeps us from rebuilding it so that we can connect with the Inner Treasure. This is not selfishness or narcissism. We were made for love. True love is expressed from the inside (Inner Treasure) in order to manifest on the outside. God is love, and as we are changed into his image, love must permeate our being. Loving ourselves does not lead

---

6 Viktor E. Frankel, *Man's Search for Meaning* (Boston: Beacon Press, 1959, 2006), 99.

to selfishness. We become selfish when we are empty of God's love and needy inside. When we are needy, that need compels us to strive for more of what we are missing. That is the nature of any need. If the need is severe enough, we are compulsively driven to fill that empty place, even in unhealthy ways. That is when we become self-focused.

Often what happens when we lack love for our Inner Treasure, we try to draw love inappropriately out of life and other people to fulfill the "need." We become "selfish" because the demand to fill the need screams so loudly, we cannot hear or sense others' needs. We have no love reserves from God to give them.

Transformational living involves growing in the practice of loving yourself. As you daily, and moment by moment, dismantle the Wall by loving God and discovering the person he made you to be, you will find it easier and easier to connect with your Inner Treasure and love people around you. You are loving them because you have a surplus of love in your Inner Treasure. The overflow of love is good fruit from a good root. Your identity is re-rooted in the original design of creation.

Self-Rejection

The opposite of loving oneself is rejecting oneself. Severe emotional pain results from the separation from the Inner Treasure. The deepest hurt that humans experience is rooted in rejection of self. Self-doubt, self-blame, self-criticism, self-indignation, self-condemnation, self-judgment, self-bitterness, self-contempt, and self-hatred all tie in to rejection of self.

Rejecting self compels people into all sorts of undesirable behaviors in trying to avoid painful feelings of rejection and abandonment. Most addictions, codependence, and compulsive actions are attempts to dull feelings of separation from self. Excessive use of alcohol, drugs, pornography, technology, and other addictions result from trial and error with things to numb or lessen the intensity of the pain. These things only temporarily cover the pain, instead of fixing the source of the pain (which is condemning judgment of self). Addictions require greater and greater use of the substance or behavior, with less and less relief, dominating more and more of life. Fear of being rejected by others (because of the undesirable behavior) makes the pain even greater, increasing the desire to use, creating a cycle of more and more destruction. Self-rejection in its worst form can truly be disabling.

Shame

The chief forces driving rejection of God, self, and others, are rooted in shame. Shame hijacks our sensing, imaging, feeling, thinking, and behaving to separate us from knowing God and being known by him. Shame's foremost aim is to SIFT our true destiny and purpose for being (using our S-ensing, I-maging, F-eeling, T-hinking). There is a whole lot more to shame than just an unpleasant feeling. In fact, most shame experiences of humans go completely unnoticed.

Shame is hard to define and not a topic most of us want to think about (very often or for very long, at least). I admit that I have a lot more to learn and practice regarding shame. What a shame. Actually, it's not a shame because the first step in pacing our way toward peace is awareness of our need. Finding out when and how shame presents within ourselves, between us and other people, and between us and God is our first challenge on the transformation journey. Some of my most helpful insights on shame have come from psychiatrist Curt Thompson who authored a book called *The Soul of Shame: Retelling the Stories We Believe About Ourselves*.

Dr. Thompson writes, "Shame is not just a felt emotion that eventually morphs into words such as 'I'm bad.' As I will suggest this phenomenon is the primary tool that evil leverages, out of which emerges everything that we would call sin. And as such is actively and intentionally at work both within and between individuals. Its goal is to disintegrate any and every system it targets. ... Its power lies in its subtly and silence and it will not be satisfied until all hell breaks loose, literally."[7] In his book on shame, Dr. Thompson explains many of the topics above in more technical terms of interpersonal neurobiology.

He states his premise in the Introduction of the book:

> From the beginning it has been God's purpose for this world to be one of emerging goodness, beauty and joy. Evil has wielded shame as a primary weapon to see to it that would never happen. ... The premise of this book, then, is that shame is not just a consequence of something our first parents did in the Garden of Eden. It is the emotional weapon that evil uses to (1) corrupt our relationships with God and each other, and (2) disintegrate any and all gifts of vocational vision and creativity. These gifts include any area of endeavor that promotes goodness, beauty and joy in and for the lives of others, whether that be teaching our first graders, loving our spouse well, managing forests, conducting healing prayer services, creating a new medical technology, offering psychotherapy or composing symphonies. Shame is a primary means to prevent us from using the gifts we have been given. And those gifts enable us to flourish as a light-bearing community of Jesus followers who work to create space for others who wish to join it to do so. Shame, therefore, is not simply an unfortunate, random, emotional event that came with us out of the primordial evolutionary soup. It is both a source and result of evils active assault on God's creation, and a way for evil to try to hold out until the new heaven and earth appear at the consummation of history.[8]

Every minute of every day we choose between shame and love. I encourage the reader to read Dr. Thompson's book for a more comprehensive look at the topic of shame. What we will discuss in the remaining two sections of this book are some ways to win over shame.

---

7 Curt Thompson, *The Soul of Shame: Retelling the Stories We Believe About Ourselves* (Downers Grove, IL: IVP Press, 2015), 22.
8 Thompson, 13.

Here are some bullet thoughts about shame:

- Shame is humanity's greatest enemy.

- Shame is the craftiest thief of inner rest and disrupter of our PACE to peace.

- Shame and condemnation hang out together, are always linked together, work together, and are packaged together like a bomb and its fuse.

- Shame is the darkest of darkness.

- Shame is most destructive of destructions of fruit of the Spirit (in Galatians 5).

- Shame is the Master of bitter root judgments.

- Shame is the most condemning of the thoughts, feelings, sensations, images, and behaviors humans experience.

- Shame is the deepest, thickest, strongest, and most poisonous of bitter roots.

- Shame is the most binding of Inner Vows.

- Shame condemns our Inner Treasure, builds a shame wall to filter messages in and out, and then uses our Inner Treasure as a tool to destroy everything outside the shame wall.

- Shame is the most damaging expression of evil ever to enter the world.

- Shame disrupts God's creativity, man's creativity, and the joy that is felt by the two working together to fulfill God's purposes.

- Shame is at the root of all sin.

- Shame cannot be overcome with sheer willpower or good deeds.

- Shame can only be truly overcome through the suffering and blood of Jesus Christ. Jesus is the only way to deactivate the work of shame in our lives.

- Shame is remedied through vulnerability, the ultimate expression of which is admitting the need for a Savior, and surrendering to the transforming power of Jesus Christ.

God's redeeming grace, through the work of his Son Jesus, frees his Holy Spirit to work in our hearts to dismantle our shame wall. God replaces our self-erected shame wall with the shame shield of his presence. The more we surrender to God, the more this good work is completed. The more we seek God's presence, the more we know who God is in reality, and the more we are known by him. This completes our chief purpose for being as stated by the often-quoted Westminster Shorter Catechism, "The chief end of man is to glorify God, and to enjoy him forever."

One of the ways shame manifests in our culture today, is in victimhood. R. Loren Sandford, the late pastor of New Song Church and Ministries in Colorado had recently posted this on social media:

> I've concluded that some people have a sick NEED to hate. It might be hate for a Christian leader. It might be directed at a political figure. It might be directed at the opposite sex. It can be racial. It can be religious. In any case the need will be there and it will manifest in damage done to relationships of all kinds.
>
> Why is it there? Because it promises power and significance while turning the hater ultimately into a victim. For at least a generation now we've been conditioned as a culture to think of ourselves as victims instead of sinners who are saved and victorious in Jesus. Victims of sexism. Victims of race. Victims of abuse. Victims of injustice. Victims of circumstance. Victims of politics. Victims of the big corporations. Victims of unfair treatment. On and on it goes.
>
> And now hatred consumes the land. I think we need to remember that we are called to be conformed to the image of the Son of God. He was not the victim of the cross. He accomplished the cross. And then rose again.

I like this quote because prophetic pastor Sandford doesn't just state a problem, but also states the solution. This solution requires a radical, daily commitment. Sometimes moment-to-moment intentionality is necessary, especially when we seem surrounded by "haters," or you feel that "hatred" is trying to make yourself out to be a victim, a hallmark characteristic of shame. To help combat these sorts of challenges, increasing our emotional capacity becomes necessary.

EC and Shame

Earlier I contrasted EI with EC. It takes much more than intelligence to deal with the realities of life. We defined Emotional Capacity (EC) as follows, "the ability to interpret and express inner emotional messages with unshaken assurance of personal worth and identity."

Challenging circumstances create inner emotional messages perceived as threats (real or imagined) upsetting a secure image of self (named the Wall above). The capacity to regulate what role emotions play in making things better or worse is EC. A person's quality of life is largely determined by EC.

When facing a challenge, EC is not dependent on whether or not the circumstances improve, but whether the reservoir of positive self-worth is improved. A person is not always in control of external events in life, but our EC can control our response to those events. We may ask, "I know increasing EC dramatically improves my health and relationships, but how is it possible to cleanse (or maintain a clean) emotional reservoir?" Below are three points of direction.

First, and most important in emotional health, is knowing the God who designed and authored the human being (including the emotions). I believe the basis for understanding identity and worth for each person is understanding the divinity and worthiness of the One who knows us better than we will ever know ourselves. The attributes of God, his relatability as a personal God, and how much he loves each person, sets him apart as supreme authority. All humans are created in his image with a unique stamp of his likeness. Also understanding some things about his emotional qualities can help give us a glimpse of ours. Knowing God as Father (similar to how a child depends on an earthly father) provides identity and security (including assurance of value and worth) like nothing else can. This inexhaustible topic is obviously too much to give adequate attention to in this book. I discuss it a little more in a later chapter. The point here is that God is the source for living from the heart, eradicating shame, and restoring emotional capacity of the human being.

Ironically, esteeming self above God and other people ruins our sense of worth and value. Removing self-focus from our identity is essential for emotional health. Ego-centric living destroys our true identity. For some modern-day examples of how this works I recommend Ryan Holiday's book called *Ego Is the Enemy*. We must give up our "me centered" worldview and take on a view of the world that puts God at the center of our universe and our soul. God is not only a *great* God in charge, but also a *grand* God in love with all he created. As the ancient psalmist says, "Great is the Lord, and most worthy of praise. … the Lord's unfailing love surrounds the one who trusts in him" (Psalm 48:1; 32:10 NIV).

A second way to increase our emotional capacity is to allow our hurts and wounds to heal properly. A broken arm needs to be set in correct position, placed in a cast, and perhaps a sling for recovery. Similar to our bodies' vulnerability to physical injuries, our hearts are subject to brokenness and disrepair. From the beginning of life, we prejudge, misjudge, and critically judge as a default tendency. Even when our felt self-worth is secure in who God created us to be, our "sinful nature" severely handicaps our ability to accept this without self-imposed conditions. Unmet expectations create disappointments and all sorts of negative reaction. Hurts and wounds fester and pollute our core beliefs (even without our awareness). Although our minds try to settle into adulthood, our hearts remain in the limited capacity of broken conditions of childhood. Some people turn to God and receive spiritual healing. Even as a God-follower, the process of healing the soul must continue throughout our remaining days on earth.

The greatest loss in human history was Adam and Eve's decision to reject God's supreme authority. This error released shame into the world. Shame is the *root of all roots* of brokenness and emotional pain. Shame and vulnerability researcher Brene Brown defines shame as the fear of disconnection. Brown's findings reveal that self-worth is rooted in a sense of connection. Shame (based in our hurts and wounds) keeps us from the truth and wholehearted (capacity-filled) living. Dr. Brene Brown has authored a number of books including one that helped me greatly called *The Gifts of Imperfection*. She has found vulnerability as the only way to attempt to resolve shame.

Shame keeps a person from believing they are worthy of love and belonging. As a God-follower, I believe I am worthy, not because of anything I have done (or not done), but because of what God has said and done for me. As a Christian I believe Jesus is the complete connection to resolve our fears of disconnection. You may not believe in God the same way I do, but reading on will help you grow in emotional capacity. Or, you may already believe in Jesus, but to grow in your relationship with God, you must embrace vulnerability and the reality of a shame-infected soul.

To be vulnerable is to be authentic, transparent, and completely honest with oneself. Vulnerability is not weakness, but builds strength and capacity. Here are some qualities Brene Brown mentions. Vulnerability means you must allow yourself to be real and seen, deeply seen. It means you must love with your whole heart, even when there is no guarantee. It means you must practice gratitude and joy, even in the face of fear. It means you must believe you are enough, even when you feel "not enough," not good enough, not smart enough, not beautiful enough, not capable enough, and so on. And vulnerability "walks into" awkwardness, uncertainty, and imperfection.

But under the cloud of shame we resist vulnerability. What does that look like? We try to be perfect (perfectionism). We expect "perfect" from others. We try to "make certain" (control). We blame (as a way to discharge our pain and discomfort). We justify ourselves (and pretend that what we do does not have an impact on other people). These are all signs of trying to numb vulnerability.

Numbing feelings may filter the bad, but it also prevents the good feelings. As Brene Brown says, "You can't selectively numb emotion." If you try to numb disappointment, failure, and sadness you will also be numbing happiness, gratitude, and joy. Americans are the most "numbed" society on earth as evidenced by overindulgence and addiction: food (obesity), alcohol (alcoholism), drugs (medications and illegal use), work (workaholism), shopping ("retail therapy"), busyness (filling schedule with things to do), technology, and all sorts of distractions. So, we set ourselves up for dissatisfaction and emptiness (lack of emotional capacity).

Here are some examples of things that may trigger feelings of vulnerability: asking someone for help when you're sick or injured, initiating sex with your spouse, being "turned down" (for promotion, election, team participant), waiting for the doctor to call back, getting laid off a job or having to lay off people, and practicing servant leadership. Many common, ordinary experiences reveal our capacity to meet the challenges of uncertainty, making us vulnerable to shame. Other indicators may include things like whether or not we can easily admit offense when offended, accept differences (cultural, ethnic, or gender), own bad habits or addictions, take responsibility for actions that put others in peril, listen to others giving us criticism, receive advice, and stop making excuses for too much eating, drinking, working, spending, sensualizing, sexualizing, hoarding, or technologizing (too much time on electronic devices).

We discussed the God factor and the shame factor. Now let's consider a third factor for building emotional capacity. We must take clear and consistent action in the direction of building good patterns and habits. It's not enough to clean up a polluted water source and then leave it to the elements to become dirty again. It must be maintained and treated for sustainability. Removing destructive patterns that have depleted our emotional capacity is a good start. But we must build constructive patterns for productivity and resilience. This involves changing the things on which we focus our attention. Improving proficiency in any sport involves practice and focus on the fundamentals. Similarly, learning to play an instrument requires pattern-forming drills and exercises to create habitual motion. Great effort goes into skillful playing.

You may have heard it said, "love is an action." This certainly is true. We may think we value something, but if our actions do not move us to stronger devotion, we are not demonstrating love for it. For example, you may read about shame and vulnerability and think it worthy of your consideration, but if you make no commitment to practice vulnerability, your skill of using it to increase your emotional capacity will not be developed. A great book was authored by James K.A. Smith to help establish spiritual life. It is called *You Are What You Love: the Spiritual Power of Habit*. We live in a time when information is overabundant, but truth is hard to find. We do well to treasure truth, and practice it over and over again to develop skill for quality emotional response.

Great commitment is required to build and maintain emotional capacity. It is tough work, but it is worth it. It is worth it because each person's worth is "built in." Assurance of built-in worth gives a person "well power." Remember, well power is better than will power. Will power eventually runs out because of human frailty. For the God-follower, this is where God comes in. I believe God is willing and able to meet us in our toughest spots of vulnerability. We are wired for struggle, and our Creator wired in each of us our personal spirit as an access point to his divine power. Surrendering our power to his power is the deepest place of vulnerability, and provides for us the deepest, bottomless well (capacity) as a life-giving fountain. In fact, Jesus himself said, "… whoever drinks the water I give them will never thirst …" (John 4:14 NIV).

I believe Jesus is the ultimate solution to shame. His whole purpose for being is to restore our connection to Father God. Vulnerability is the path to finding Jesus. I'm not talking about religion. Religion tries to *work* its way out of shame. But a true Christ-follower yields to Jesus Christ's identity and worthiness as the Solution for the shame we are each born into. Our faith is related to the capacity we have to receive the love, peace, and joy he supplies.

Emotion Quotient

Emotion Quotient (EQ) is the measurement for identifying EC. As noted above we saw how emotional capacity (EC) is directly linked to perceived worth and value as a human being. We discussed how shame destroys emotional health and how vulnerability is necessary to chase away the shame. Two core elements of vulnerability are discussed next: honesty and humility.

> Forgiving an offense is not merely a mental decision.

As I researched the topic of forgiveness for three years as part of a seminary doctorate degree, I learned many amazing things about forgiveness that changed my life forever. I authored a book, *Escaping the Pain of Offense: Empowered to Forgive from the Heart,* to help people find the freedom that true forgiveness provides. The book is written from a Christian perspective, but principles apply universally. I continue to learn more, but the ironic thing about learning to forgive is that, at any given moment, I am only one offense away from my next lesson in forgiveness. The necessity to forgive is always preceded by an offense. Forgiving an offense is not merely a mental decision. Forgiving involves the emotional capacity (vulnerability) to recognize offense and take the necessary action to surrender ultimate judgment to a higher power. I discovered that most people do not truly understand and practice forgiveness because they do not understand the nature of offense and its negative impact on their emotional and mental health. Everyone needs to grow in forgiveness because everyone both offends and gets offended. At the core of offense are the bitter root judgments.

A person's reaction to offense is a primary indicator of EQ. Recognizing an offense, wrestling with the reality of loss, and facing the painful emotions takes hard work, but there are no shortcuts to building EC. When our heart is offended, our mind will usually try to cover it up as a self-protection mechanism. The first step to uncovering our mind's scheme is to be willing to admit our heart's offense. When negative thoughts and feelings produce anger and undue fear toward someone who has done us wrong, we must be willing to drill down inside our heart and discover roots of offense. It's not about the other person's actions, it's about our response to them. Some people believe a myth that they are harder to offend than others. The truth is, we all offend easily and that's where honesty comes in.

Self-honesty begins with awareness. Am I acting on truth or falsehood? Am I deceiving myself about the real motive behind my reactions? Am I merely numbing pain with some of the actions discussed above (overeating, overmedicating, using pornography, overstimulating with technology, etc.)? These questions should be asked of self when you feel disappointed, discomforted, displeased, frustrated, etc. to uncover the stronger feelings of rejection, shame, unworthiness, and the like.

Failure to recognize and handle offense adequately is the greatest block to building emotional capacity. It astounds me how frequently people declare, "I'm not really angry," but then constantly blame and condemn other people, justify their own bad behavior, and show obvious gestures of frustration and discontent about the situation for which they deny the anger. People claim not to be offended, but show obvious emotions of pain and discomfort and even lash out in slander and gossip of the person they feel wounded by. The anger usually points to a deeper root of bitter judgment linked to offense. These judgments are often so common they are difficult to recognize as offense.

Truth Wins

As we discussed earlier, the world operates under natural laws that shape reality. Breaking these laws (realities) produce consequences. For example, the law of gravity demonstrates disastrous results for jumping out a building on the tenth floor without a landing device. I believe God created these laws for mankind's benefit. Truth can be defined as God's view of reality. Each person has their own perspective of reality. When the perspective lines up with truth (God's reality), things go well. When things are not going well, it usually means that our perception(s) of reality are out of whack somewhere.

Being honest with ourselves about our true condition makes all the difference. For example, the law of sowing and reaping says that when a person does good deeds, good results will follow. When a person does bad deeds, bad will follow. When a person drinks too much alcohol and drives a car, they endanger themselves and others around them. If a person is charged with DUI, they are failing to be honest about the effects of alcohol and their ability to drive. When we are unable or unwilling to be honest about our true condition, this is an indicator of low self-worth and low EQ. When we have a poor image of self as evidenced by feelings of rejection, shame, and unworthiness, our perceptions of reality will cause self-defeat and self-destruction.

Accepting this truth also takes humility. Just behind honesty, humility becomes the second major demonstration of healthy vulnerability. Being humble is not a show of weakness, but it is strength. Being humble knows the difference between self-confidence and pride. Being humble puts other people's interests ahead of self. Life's true meaning and purpose is found in adding value to other people's lives. Maybe the most telling aspect of humility (and the most crucial to EQ) is the degree to which a person is teachable. Teachableness is not merely measured by receiving raw knowledge, but also the willingness to apply that knowledge appropriately. The writer of the ancient Proverbs called this wisdom. "The fear of the Lord is the beginning of knowledge, but fools despise wisdom and instruction" (Proverbs 1:7 NIV). The "fear" of the Lord is speaking of respect and honor of God as the source of truth and natural laws (realities of the way the world operates). A person shows humility when they receive and practice input from other people. Seeking and relying on truth from God's higher authority is the most solid foundation for building EQ and establishing a shame shield.

Most people follow one of two remedies to deal with hurt from life circumstances or relationships. People try their best to pretend things are better than they really are (denial), or they live to relieve it at all costs (addictive behaviors). Whether people deny or over-gratify, at some point they become more painfully aware of their desperate state of human weakness and inability to effect lasting change without higher power resources. For people to let go of denial or false refuge to face the truth about themselves is sometimes a fearful step. The tension in the inner person between God pushing truth up and a fearful mind pushing the truth down is a form of anxiety. Part of a person is wise and wants to know the truth. Part of the person is foolish and fears the truth. For the God-follower, as I write in my book *Escaping the Pain of Offense,* God's Spirit "reveals the difference, and will bring healing to those who humble themselves and are willing to be cooperative. As people give up their fear of the truth and choose to trust God to forgive them just as they are, then they can begin to surrender themselves and learn to rest in the salvation of God's grace."

The plumb line of Truth (God's view of reality) is the best "measuring stick" for emotional capacity. Only God knows the degree to which a person makes their heart vulnerable to truth. A truly honest and humble heart receives truth even when it hurts. The psalmist says, "Behold, You desire truth in the innermost being" (Psalm 51:6 NASB). Receiving (believing) the truth always involves giving up falsehood. For example, for a long time I've believed that God loves me. However, my thoughts about God's love toward me are much different now than five, ten, even one year ago. Why? Because intentional vulnerability has allowed me to root out a huge amount of falsehood from my heart. "God loves me," "My life has meaning," "I know who I am" have deeper meaning because there is less falsehood. The following falsehoods have less grip on my thinking: "I'm not good enough for God to love me," "I'm nobody," "I'm not worthy," "I'll never be good enough," and the like.

Sometimes pondering the answers to questions can help reveal our true beliefs. Some of the questions below may be tougher for you than others, but I encourage the reader to invite God into their secret place for some soul searching.

What do I think about vulnerability?

Do I allow myself to feel?

Am I afraid to be honest with myself? What do I fear?

Am I honest with myself about my mental and emotional condition?

What positive expressions would I like to see more of in my life (e.g., love, joy, peace …)?

How could being more honest with myself about my emotional condition produce better results?

Are any of my activities/behaviors numbing pain?

If so, what kind of help do I need to address the problem?

Am I truly willing to make the adjustments necessary for lasting transformation?

What is the next step for improvement?

Can I do it now? What is the date/time the step will be taken by?

My hope is that self-honesty and humility will guide you to some answers so you can find vulnerability for growth. Take action, and come back to questions like these in a week or month and repeat for building emotional quotient. I hope you are attempting to answer the questions in the back of the book for each chapter. I provide the questions so application can be made and action taken.

Growing as a person, parent, or leader requires more than intelligence, skill, and experience. Emotion cannot be measured in quantity, but in quality of expression. True meaning and purpose await a response.

Before we turn attention to cooperating with God in more significant ways for transformational living, the next chapter helps identify trauma as another element of our human condition.

Chapter 8

Trauma

Trauma can be a traumatic topic. Just the mention of the word can stir fear in the hearts of some. Others I have known who have lived through horrific events (from my perspective) wouldn't necessarily term them traumatic. Just to say, trauma is highly individualistic in nature. Trauma is not about the event itself, but our response to an event.

Trauma is a normal response to an abnormal event. The same catastrophe may be traumatic for one person, and not for another. Emotional Capacity (EC) may provide a shield, but not always. As an unusual, uncommon, or unforeseen circumstance, by definition, our response(s) cannot always be predicted.

Trauma is not a respecter of persons. When a natural disaster strikes, for example, everything and everyone in its path is affected. Disasters caused by human error or folly can sometimes be even more devastating. Man-made disasters seem to be more and more common in our world. This makes it less and less safe. Plus, the exposure levels (via technology and media) of potentially traumatic graphic visuals and print content make it increasingly difficult to escape secondary sources of trauma. Incidents of violence and personal injury spread through so-called entertainment, so-called news programs, and so-called social media have the effect of traumatizing people, many times without them realizing it.

Hence, regardless of our comfort level with the topic, it is important to give it some thought. Doing all we can to understand and prevent trauma is an important strategy for looking ahead to the future. The more understanding we have about trauma and its effects on our physical and psychological health, the more we can build our own resilience, and the more we can help those who have experienced trauma in their past.

Trauma adds a whole new layer to everything we discuss in this book. A great resource for understanding more detail is a book called *The Body Keeps the Score: How Trauma And Suppressed Emotion Affects the Brain* by Bessel Van der Kolk. As a psychiatrist and neurologist, Professor Van der Kolk explains in very understandable terms the workings of the brain and how trauma can pattern the brain into interpreting common realities into perceived life-and-death situations. Thus, the brain is sending red alert signals to the rest of the body (including emotions) causing adverse reactions. He attributes many psychological problems to specific areas of dysfunction in the brain. He has worked with many abuse victims, and explains why the earlier abuse occurs, and the longer it continues, the more damage that it inflicts. I like his emphasis on treatment models that try to get to the root, rather than just using medications to try to control behaviors.

A resource that addresses trauma recovery from a Christian perspective is a book called *The Life Model: Living From the Heart Jesus Gave You*. It is written from a clinical and pastoral perspective by five authors including James Friesen and James Wilder. They discuss trauma as two distinct categories—Type A and Type B. In their words, "Type A traumas are the absence of good things we all need. These traumas produce problems in relationships, so recovery requires a loving relationship to repair the Type A wound. Type B traumas are bad things that should never happen. They create fear. The 'bad events' need to be revisited and the fear needs to be deactivated, so that life can proceed without the fear."[9]

For years therapists have been helping people with Type B trauma. Many specific techniques have been developed with varying degrees of success. The key for healing is not necessarily finding the right technique for therapy, but understanding the nature of the wound and resolving the fears around it. The issues with Type A trauma have been discovered more recently and are much more common. In fact, to some degree, we are all affected by Type A traumas. I discuss Type A trauma here because it is part of every person's transformation journey to some form or another.

Type A Trauma

Recent discoveries are showing that Type A trauma (the absence of the good) is actually more damaging to us than Type B (bad things that happen to us). Children need love from their parents. The absence of love is very wounding. But the truth is, no parent, no matter how loving they are, can provide all the love a child needs to escape wounding. It is part of mankind's human condition to be born with a "hole" in the heart (emotionally speaking) that no amount of human love can completely fill. Even when parents try hard to meet their children's needs for love, the children's perceptions in receiving love will be deficient.

That said, parents must try. Most parents do try to love their children. But failures are common. Though wounding is unintentional, it's mostly what parents do NOT do that hurts the most. When love isn't intentionally expressed by parents, children doubt, despise, or outright reject their Inner Treasure. Neglect by parents creates a wall (described earlier) inside children.

---

9 James G. Friesen, et al., *The Life Model: Living From the Heart Jesus Gave You* (Pasadena, CA: Shepherd House, Incorporated, 2004), #.

As a child, we instinctively interpret love as time and attention. When ignored by parents, even if it is not true, we falsely believe we are not being loved because something is wrong with us. It is our fault. We are inferior. We are "not enough," "not lovable," or "unworthy of love." We feel the pain of shame and build the wall of self-protection to keep the pain away. We conclude we are the problem and condemningly judge ourselves. As time goes on we add brick upon brick to the wall as the pain grows with our parents' lifestyle and habits of care (or neglected care), as the self-judgment, self-condemnation, self-bitterness, and self-rejection take root and prevent us from loving the inner person God created us to be. Self-hatred ultimately steals our sense of self-worth.

It is very hard for us to see Type A trauma in ourselves. For one, there is not any single event to identify, as there is with Type B trauma. Type A trauma is more like the constant drip of a leaky faucet. We are not being loved right now and it hurts. Without love five minutes from now, it still hurts. And when love doesn't arrive later in the day, it still hurts. The love and attention seem never to arrive when needed.

A second reason Type A trauma is so hard for us to see is that we don't feel the pain anymore. The rejection of self compels us to shut off our conscious self from the source of the pain—our Inner Treasure crying out. The rejection of self was so painful that we needed to create defenses to avoid feeling it. The pain was too big to live with every moment of our life. Since relief in the form of love never arrived, our only way to avoid the pain was to build the wall inside. To the degree that we were successful in building the wall, to that degree we became unaware that there was ever a problem. Existing with the wall inside then feels "normal" to us, so we may not even be aware that something was wrong in our childhood.

Attachment

Research continues to explore the idea of attachment (or bonding as it sometimes is called in early years). Attachment is complex and has to do with a person's ability to have close relationships without becoming co-dependent. Bonding is a connection that occurs between a caregiver, usually the mother, and a small child. Bonding begins in the womb and continues for the early years of childhood. The most crucial period is from the prenatal time to about eighteen months.

Bonding events actually affect the physical development of a child's growing brain. Through these bonding events there are certain messages that become built into the child's brain. When bonding successfully occurs, the messages that become a part of the child are: "Someone is loving me, so I must be lovable," "My needs are going to be met," "Mom is here for me, and so it is safe." When bonding does not occur, the opposite messages become built into the child's brain: "Nobody is loving me, so I must not be lovable," "My needs are not going to be met," and "Nobody is here to protect me, so it isn't safe."

Since these messages have actually become a part of the child's brain structure, they constitute the way the child views the world. These perspectives then color all of his or her subsequent life experiences and relationships. An absence of healthy attachment is a very deep and pervasive wound, which only the Lord can heal. God can heal even this type of trauma through the journey of transformation he desires for each of us.

We All Need the Blessing

A great book that I wish I had encountered much earlier in my own parenting days is *The Blessing* written by Gary Smalley and John Trent. Through this book I was able to identify some of my own Type A trauma. I recommend the book for both understanding better how to give others needed love, and understanding the reader's own need for love (and where it may have been deficient). To the degree we were not given or were not able to receive elements of The Blessing, we were likely wounded with Type A trauma.

Though Smalley and Trent have focused their book on children, the truth is that we all need to receive these blessings throughout our whole lives. In addition, if we give these blessings to those who are important to us (spouse, children, friends), life's true meaning and purpose is greatly enhanced. When we give another person these blessings, they shine as though all the lights have been turned on inside them and they will always want to be around us. After all, we are giving them what they need the most—love. If we find this difficult to do, that is bad fruit, and we need to find the bad root so that we can be healed and begin to do this more naturally. Receiving love from others and giving love to others, both in greater and greater measures, is good fruit of being changed into the image of Jesus.

Smalley and Trent identify five elements necessary for The Blessing:

1. We need eight nonsexual meaningful touches in a day. For some of us, we may not feel like we need that. However, it could be that an unawareness of the need for these touches keeps us in denial. The denial can be protection from feeling the pain of not being actively loved.

2. We need positive spoken words. Spoken words tell us that the other person knows we are present and that they desire to communicate with us. Being ignored is the opposite of this. Children would rather be loved than abused, but they would rather take abuse than be ignored. Being ignored tells us that we are not even worth the other person's time and attention.

3. We need our parents (and, as adults, other people) to see high value in us, and to express it. When they genuinely appreciate, affirm, and compliment us, it makes us feel good. We think that because they are interested in us, we must be worthwhile. And they are telling us specific ways in which we are worthwhile. For instance, they might notice that we are good at communicating and will tell us something like, "You certainly have a gift of speaking. You are better at persuading people than I am." The opposite of this is negative talk, such as, "You are a lazy bum. You

should try harder." These negative statements have the effect of adding to our self-judgment.

4. We need our parents to picture a special future for us. When they do this, we feel optimistic about the future, and we feel worthy of such a future. Statements like, "You are so good at math. Maybe someday you can teach it." The opposite would be a statement such as, "You'll never amount to anything."

5. We need our parents to actively help us to pursue our special future, as much as it lies within their means. Even if they don't have many resources they can help us to find ways to achieve our dreams. Such actions tell us that our parents really meant it when they affirmed our gifts and talents; that they genuinely see these attributes as worthwhile; and that they see us as valuable enough for them to put forth effort on our behalf. The opposite of this would be to force us to do what they want us to do, regardless of our desires and talents. For instance, they may have a family business and want us to take it over someday. Because of their own desire they are blind to the fact that we have different talents and desires. Experiencing this tells us that our individual desires, and who God made us to be, doesn't matter, and that our needs are unimportant.

When we receive the five good things above, we are blessed and we prosper. Behind all of these elements of blessing is a huge boost to tapping our inner treasure. When parents truly relate to their child in these ways, it is abundantly evident that they are training their child "in the way he/she should go" (see Proverbs 22:6). They see their child as important enough to focus attention and energy on. Those parents then understand the unique person that God created their child to be, and are delighted with who he or she is. For example, an athletic father is willing and able to delight in his artistic and uncoordinated son. He does not try to push him into athletics, but enthusiastically promotes the son's artistic pursuits. This is sometimes a challenge for parents, and can require a sacrifice of their own dreams for their child.

When this sort of awareness happens, children know their parents are paying close attention to them, as well as being delighted in them. This causes children to conclude that they must be valuable and lovable just the way they are. Their parents love them, so they must be lovable. Children are thus enabled to obey God's command to love themselves, and so life has a better chance of going well for them.

Type C Trauma

Year 2020 brought unique challenges to most of the global population. A strain of virus known as COVID-19 caused disruptions in life for billions of people, a great degree of loss for millions, and grievous loss for untold numbers. With beginnings traced to a city in China, the virus spread through contact with people traveling around the world to become a global "pandemic." Institutions like government, education, healthcare, and commerce were impacted severely and traditional media outlets had a field day with their specialty—creating controversy. Fear-based reporting, for example, caused people to panic and hoard things like toilet paper so that retail shelves were empty for months.

So many conflicting reports about the never-before-encountered virus abounded. Circumstances and subsequent reactions and overreactions caused so much uncertainty and insecurity in individuals' lives that their usual coping mechanisms crumbled. My belief is that, so profound are the mental health effects, that at this writing, we have barely scratched the surface of discovering the cumulative impact of the damages. I call this a Type C trauma—Cumulative bad events. Maybe it could also be called Crisis.

Sometimes losses and trauma happen so closely in quantity and/ or intensity that the cumulative effect causes a trauma of its own. For example, the threat of acquiring a deadly virus is one thing, but when combined with facing it alone (because of quarantine restrictions), or being in a population identified as more vulnerable (by age, pre-existing health conditions, etc.), or already going through job or relationship loss, the toxic stress can build much more rapidly and more impactfully. Recovery from this type of loss or trauma may need more time and intentional treatment. Next, let's consider some things about recovering from trauma and loss in general.

Grief and Loss

In the scenario of 2020 events, looming as large as a pandemic of coronavirus outbreak, is a pandemic of grief. In my earlier life I thought of grief only in terms of an event like mourning the death of a loved one. But I've learned that loss creates needs, and in order to recover from loss, finding new ways of meeting those needs must be discovered. No matter how large or small the loss, the principles of adjustment are the same. The adjustment process is called grief.

Besides the obvious hugely impactful and difficult situations in life, grief also applies to the more generalized losses. These may include sudden illness, public safety, home safety, and losses like necessities of life (food and shelter), physical health, life routines, peace of mind, emotional security, employment, business ownership, career, trust in people, privacy, social interaction, faith in science, faith in God, self-image, self-worth, and a host of identity issues and beliefs questioning who we are and where we're going. There is no shortage of loss these days. For loss to be recovered (large and small losses alike), loss must be grieved.

When things feel so out of control, as in times described in Type C above, how should we respond? As a Christian, the obvious answer is to turn to God. But in our human condition, what does that look like? We see in the Bible that Jesus bears our grief and carries our sorrows for us (see Isaiah 53:1-6; Matthew 11:28-29). Jesus came to redeem us from our sin and to bear the pain of the consequences of sin in our world. Although Jesus accomplished this work for us, it is often very difficult for us as individuals to surrender to his way of working it out in our humanity. Processing grief can be hard work, but it is essential for our well-being. Grief is something everyone is going through in the midst of pandemic, whether they are willing to admit it or not.

Grief is the process of engaging loss, making adjustments, and recovering new hope for meeting life's needs. Let's briefly consider these three elements. I have greatly benefited by processing through adversity and trials in this way.

First, consider your losses. Identify them, and make a list. Name not only the tangible losses like job, finances, school, time, health, relationship, too much or too little personal space etc., but also name the intangible (emotional) losses that go with each tangible loss. Intangible losses may be things like confidence or competence level; sense of safety or security; degree of peace of mind; personal dignity; self-sufficiency; sense of control; beliefs about God, other people, or self; trust in people or institutions, and self-worth and values issues. Making this list may sound like a goofy idea, but it will have a huge payoff in the long run. If you don't name, you don't know what to reclaim. There's no recovery without discovery. It's that simple. An exercise in naming losses requires some time alone and free from distractions. It can be emotionally draining, so take a break if you feel overwhelmed.

With a written list, you now have something to return to as you go through making adjustments, which is the core work of grief. Making adjustments involves stepping through at least four phases of reorienting yourself to life. As many counselors do, when I explain grief, I usually draw an inverted bell-shaped curve on a blank sheet of paper. The curve slopes downward on the left side and back up on the right.

Beginning on the left, the first, initial impact phase is the shock of it all, likely including some numbness, denial, and maybe even some erratic emotional reactions. Second phase, wrestling with reality, is where the anger and fear may kick in with searching for answers, and sometimes some panic feelings with an incident of high impact. A third phase, dealing with the pain, is at the bottom of the curve. This is where the feelings and emotions need to be identified and worked through to resolution. Things like guilt, shame, fear, anxiety, loneliness, rejection, abandonment, powerlessness, depression, and confusion are normal responses and felt in varying degrees by different people. Resolving to a tolerable degree of pain may take time—hours, days, months, and years for deeper losses. Time periods for grieving losses are also unique to the individual.

This process is much too involved to completely describe here, but an important key is to permit yourself to feel. That might sound strange, but most of us have been taught to ignore, deny, or minimize, as much as possible, the emotional part of our being. Dumbing down emotions without first discovering the message they are trying to relay to us is a perilous mistake. Be honest with yourself and name the feelings and emotions. This is the phase of grieving where many people get stuck. Even if you give up (intentionally or unintentionally) on grief, grief will never give up on you. Grief is real. If not processed through, it can haunt you the rest of your life. If the unpleasant emotion is too hard to work through, seek out a good counselor to help you to recovery.

Recovery is on the way when you can start to look back and see your quality of life returning in a positive direction to what it was before the loss. Recovery is a process of re-organizing your life and finding new hope for the future. After job loss, for example, a person may develop a new skill, or discover a hidden talent that helps them find a more suitable job than their previous employment. Recovery is being able to say, "If I hadn't lost my job, I wouldn't be in a better place today." Things like new skills, new relationships, new beliefs, and ways of seeing things around you all provide hope. Hope is what keeps us going. The journey isn't always a smooth ride neatly progressing through the phases. There may be some degree of victory, and then another reminder, negative event, anniversary date, or trigger that raises more concerns or things to process. Reprocessing is not to be considered a setback, but growth. Growing involves periods of stretching and relaxing the stretch.

As believers in Christ, our true hope is in the Lord, as our Bible tells us. God is at the center of this entire process and as we walk with Jesus, he transforms our heart along the way. The inner person healing journey is very similar to working through grief. New understanding and practice of forgiveness is often a part of this. We are about to look at this next.

The process of grieving losses described above can be as reflective and prayerful as you choose to make it. The greater the seriousness you give it, the greater the potential blessing God has for you on the recovery side. Grief can be viewed as a gift to give us an invitation to press into God to know him more, and be known by him.

Whether you work with God to respond to loss or not, there is one more thing to consider. Unresolved grief produces high levels of toxic stress. When this stress becomes intolerable, very unhealthy things occur. One of three scenarios is likely—victim, survivor, or rescuer. A victim interprets life from a poverty mindset and acts out by rejecting (victimizing) self or others. A survivor stuffs the pain, and appears to have survived with a decent level of functionality, but losing control is always a threat. A rescuer turns to unwittingly helping others out of their pain to compensate for their own lack of pain processing. Examining ourselves to see where we may have tendencies of victim, survivor, or rescuer can make us aware of unprocessed pain.

There is much more to the topic of grief, but I hope you now understand that if you are struggling, you are not strange and you are not beyond hope. Reach out to someone you trust today. We all have grief to process, and I have my own to process too.

My prayer is that we are willing to do the hard work of grieving losses, to become more resilient and better prepared to help as help is needed in our communities.

Part 3

Cooperate With God in Surrender

Do not be anxious about anything, but in every situation, by prayer and petition, with thanksgiving, present your requests to God. And the peace of God, which transcends all understanding, will guard your hearts and your minds in Christ Jesus. Philippians 4:6-7 NIV

Once we have prepared our mind and heart with the truth that things are going to have to change to get better (part 1), and accepted the fact that we are desperately broken (part 2), we now explore the miraculous solution. God has provided the way for daily victory if we can only surrender to his way. His way is to turn from our way, and receive his forgiveness, and give his forgiveness away to others. His forgiveness transcends human understanding. Each step we take in further surrender to Christ's love strengthens our hearts and minds in the peace of God.

Chapter 9

Give Away the House

We turn now to the topic of forgiveness. By cooperating with God's spiritual laws revealing forgiveness, we are set free to see God, ourselves, and others the way he truly means for us to see. I studied forgiveness thoroughly for a three-year seminary research project and it changed my life forever. I then authored a book *Escaping the Pain of Offense*, but I still consider myself a learner on the topic. I encourage the reader to check out the book to delve deeper, but some highlights of forgiving and being forgiven are shared here.

Forgiveness is the solution for the sinful judging we do that was discussed in the previous section. Jesus is the only rightful Judge of all things. When we judge, we attempt to take his place. The blood of Jesus is the only cure for the bitter roots planted in our hearts by the sin of bad judging. We need his blood to wash away this sin of judging so we don't have to reap the resulting consequences that come about from the operation of God's laws.

Forgiveness can be defined as surrendering to God the right to judge. Forgiveness is God's idea, God's work, and God's way of getting us to collaborate with his work. Forgiveness is deciding to cooperate with God's way. Forgiving is relinquishing an offender from a "debt" he may owe. Unforgiveness says, "I've been hurt, he owes me, and I must make him pay." Forgiveness says, "Even though I am hurt, and am owed a debt, I am writing it off. It is not my place to make him pay, and I release him to the judgment of Jesus." He is the just Judge, and he will rightly decide the case. If there is any penalty, he will collect it.

Born From Above

For a Christian, forgiveness is centered in a "born again" experience. In John 3, Jesus instructed a religious leader named Nick that following God has nothing to do with a particular family of origin, religion, culture, or preexisting belief system. Scholars believe the term "born again" can be more accurately translated in English as "born from above." Jesus explains, "I assure you, no one can enter the Kingdom of God without being born of water and the Spirit. Humans can reproduce only human life, but the Holy Spirit gives birth to spiritual life. So don't be surprised when I say, 'You must be born again.' The wind blows wherever it wants. Just as you can hear the wind but can't tell where it comes from or where it is going, so you can't explain how people are born of the Spirit" (John 3:5-8 NLT).

As noted earlier, we exist in a physical (tangible) realm, and also a spiritual (intangible) realm. Though the spiritual is every bit as real, it cannot be understood in the same way as the natural. Heavenly Truth is not always understandable with earthly paradigms. The earthly paradigm of birth is event-driven, human-effort intensive, and is subject to natural laws of earthly existence. When a baby is discovered in his mother's womb, he is given a due date. Pregnancy is a labor-intensive process with a climax of the newborn breathing on its own. The new life is now part of the family of origin and human race made of the same stuff as the very first human created in the natural world.

The heavenly paradigm of birth from above, however, is much different. It has no earthly timetable, all effort is God's, and the changes are mostly in the inner invisible realm (likened to the wind). Each individual's response to God is unique in terms of a conversion experience. The Holy Spirit reveals the Light of Jesus to a darkened spirit part of our being. Being born from above is predicated on acceptance of God's love (forgiveness of sins) as demonstrated through Jesus Christ dying on a Cross and being raised from the dead. The Spirit of God continues to breathe life into our spirit to renew and re-create our being from the inside out. This inner change of heart comes as a result of surrendering the natural body, mind, and soul to the supernatural power of God. Spiritual growth occurs with an increasing compliance with this process of surrendering to the ways of God. Understanding and practicing forgiveness empowers this journey.

The birth of a baby is a wonderful reminder of God's handiwork. As I witnessed the birth of our three natural-born children, I was each time reminded of the absolute wonderment of God's gift of life. Natural birth is a miracle. How much more then is spiritual birth a miraculous (supernatural) process. Forgiveness is nothing short of a miracle.

We are each born with a personal spirit, but the spirit part of our being is not fully awakened until it is born from above (see Romans 6). When we surrender to God the right to rule our being, the rebirth of our spirit begins. In order to reach the maximum potential as the person we are meant to be, this rebirth process must continue all throughout our lives. We experience deeper and deeper revelation of God's forgiving grace and grant His grace to others.

If you've been around the Church for any length of time, you've heard someone talk about "decision for Christ" in reference to a *conversion* experience. But being born again is more than acknowledging a need for a Savior. A one-time decision of a natural mind is not enough to complete the ongoing aspects of salvation (to be discussed in the next chapter). You may also have heard someone talk about "accepting Christ into your heart." Although accepting the message of Truth in a conversion experience gives rebirth of spirit, Jesus is now released to grow the spirit part of being in a new way. The initial deciding and accepting may be a good starting point, but in order for the spiritual realm to intersect with the natural realm, it always requires yielding of the natural. Surrendering control of your inner person is the key issue.

What might surrender look like? The finer details of surrender may look different for each individual, but here are some possibilities. It means submitting beliefs and values to a higher power and being willing to realign to a God-defined standard of Truth. It means giving up control of the ability to decide for yourself right from wrong. It means letting go of a self-made identity in exchange for God reshaping who you are as a person.

The transformation is somewhat of a mystery, but over time the practice of surrendering control will become evident in the natural realm. For example, you may come to an understanding of family that includes a desire to grow your relationships closer without feeling like you are losing your identity as an individual. Your value for healthy life recognizes the harmful effects of smoking cigarettes, so you give them up without it becoming a sacrifice. Your concepts of love, happiness, and fulfillment become more in line with what God has already outlined in the Bible. Your employment, standards of sexual morality, living arrangements, or consumer habits may need to change, not simply because you made a decision to change your behavior, but change occurs because the "wind" of the Holy Spirit is working a change of heart. It is also not a result of "trying harder," but surrendering to and cooperating with God's work at a deeper level.

Forgiveness Beginnings

A person surrendering his or her heart in a born-again experience is like handing over the deed to a house as we saw in an earlier illustration. He gives his house (whole being) to God, and God's "wind" of change begins the reconstruction and re-creation processes. Surrendering sinful judgments (through forgiveness) allows God to brighten the dark areas and reshape the living spaces to be more useful for his glory. Some areas may be tweaked, some given a makeover, and some taken down to the foundation to start over.

We must let go of our demands for payment of debts caused by damage to our house by others. Our house now belongs to God, so it is his right or responsibility to collect payment as needed for the maintenance of the property.

Jesus shed His blood to take away our sin and shame. We acknowledge this by giving him ownership of our house. We need his blood to wash away this sin of judging so we don't have to reap the resulting consequences that come about from the way God's laws work. Even though God owns our house, our natural bodily existence exposes us to thieves, storm damage, deterioration, and normal wear and tear. The way to accomplish the work of repairs and re-construction is to be forgiven by Jesus (any part we had in the offense, including judging), and to forgive (from our heart) the one(s) who wounded us. When he forgives us, he pays the debt we owe in the spiritual realm, and we are set free from the consequences we would otherwise have to pay for our debt. If we don't forgive (from our heart), we won't be forgiven by God (though this sin may not send us to hell). If we are not forgiven by God, we will continue to do the things we hate (we will continue to experience the reaping from the operation of God's laws). Our house will continue to be a mess.

Forgiveness is a tool God uses for his makeover work. It is helpful to remember that God is doing similar work with others' houses. The one I am living in is in a neighborhood of believers. The transformation he is working in me is not just for my benefit, but for his glory, and the good of a community of believers (Church). He has designed and built a wider community of houses he's waiting to be given back to him for transformation (world). The makeover work God is doing in me is also similarly being done in those I relate to. Forgiveness is also a tool God uses for me to assist in the makeover work he is doing in the lives of those I relate to (see John 20:21-23). God's forgiveness of our debts put us in position to forgive others' debts (see Matthew 18). More on this is to come.

What Forgiveness is NOT

A key to understanding and practicing forgiveness is first understanding what forgiveness is not.

Forgiveness is NOT:

1. simple remorse - Being "sorry" is not enough. One can be sorry that something bad happened and still not be willing to change his heart attitude about it.

2. simply forgetting - One cannot forget what they haven't first remembered. Forgiving an offense involves first calling to memory the offender, the offense, and the hurt so that these all can be *intentionally* surrendered to God.

3. simply excusing - An offended person does not have to continually excuse an offender's bad behavior. Godly boundaries and confrontation are necessary elements of relationship.

4. simply trusting - Trusting another person involves the trustworthiness of the person's behavior. God can always be trusted, and his trustworthiness is not the same as peoples' trustworthiness.

5. letting *time* heal - Time can only complicate the issue if the root problem(s) has not been properly dealt with. "Moving on" often involves some form of denial which can only make matters worse from a long-term perspective.

6. letting go - For the Christian, forgiveness is NOT a mere choice to move away from something, but must involve consciously surrendering that "something" to God. The past cannot be changed, but it may need to be temporarily brought into the light so we can see what is being redeemed by Christ's blood shed to forgive the debt.

7. just a feeling - Most of the time a choice to forgive comes before positive feelings toward an offender. An offended person cannot wait on feelings to determine when to forgive.

8. reducing unforgiveness - Forgiving is not merely finding a way to reduce the effects of negative feelings (i.e., denying, minimizing, blaming, or dodging the hurt).

9. a one-time thing - Multiple offenses require multiple times forgiven. God forgives us as many times as we need it, and he asks us to do the same for those who offend us.

10. waiting for (requiring) the offender to behave a certain way – None of these excuses are valid for withholding forgiveness:
    - the offense was too great
    - he/she won't accept responsibility for the offense
    - he/she never asked to be forgiven
    - he/she will do it again
    - he/she did it again
    - he/she isn't truly sorry
    - he/she did it deliberately
    - I don't like him/her
    - if I forgive the offense, I'd have to treat the offender well
    - someone has to punish him/her
    - I don't feel like forgiving him/her
    - I can't forget what happened

Three Discoveries

Let's turn again to more on what forgiveness is. I uncovered three "take aways" in doing the research for the project that led to authoring my book *Escaping the Pain of Offense*. In my counseling with people over the years, these are three of the most striking revelations that prove to be "game changers" in people's lives:

1. Forgiveness is a Gift (of Jesus) to be received,

2. All the work necessary for forgiveness has already been accomplished by Jesus, and

3. Forgiveness is different than reconciliation.

First, forgiveness must be received from God. Knowing about forgiveness is not enough; one must experience forgiveness. To practice God-centered forgiveness, one must know the Forgiver. A cognitive ascent to the truth about redemption helps to prepare the way, but a personal relationship with the Redeemer affords the intimacy needed for the act of receiving the gift. For a gift to accomplish its intended purpose for being given, it must be received. An act of kindness shrugged off by a recipient does not complete the purpose for a giver expressing love. A $100 check may be given to a family member on a special occasion, but unless the check is cashed into a bank account, the gift cannot be discharged for its intended use.

The transforming power of forgiveness must be received and experienced in the heart in order for the "renewing of the mind" (Romans 12:1-2) to be accomplished. A Christian's conversion opens the door (deposits the check in the illustration above) to the Holy Spirit's power to appropriate the miracle of God's free gift of forgiveness as discussed earlier. Then, sanctification involves a cooperative effort between God and man (as God's Gift is assimilated). One of the gauges of maturity in a Christian's life is the ability to receive God's love and give his love away to other people.

Next, forgiveness is about Christ's work, not ours. The burden of forgiveness rests on Jesus, not us.

Recognizing both the volitional and emotional aspects of the suffering of Christ in accomplishing forgiveness creates increased awareness of the depths of God's love. Christ acted in accordance with the Father's pleasure. No greater love can be known. The type of suffering Christ endured had been prophesied by Isaiah and others hundreds of years before Christ came to earth. Christ knew precise details of the kind and magnitude of his sufferings, including the excruciatingly painful death He would have to experience.

An entire chapter of my book *Escaping the Pain of Offense* is devoted to discussing the theology of forgiveness. Chapter Three explains that in order to atone for the sin of mankind (to satisfy God's wrath),

Christ had to suffer. "let us also lay aside every encumbrance and the sin which so easily entangles us, and let us run with endurance the race that is set before us, fixing our eyes on Jesus, the [b]author and perfecter of faith, who for the joy set before Him endured the cross, despising the shame, and has sat down at the right hand of the throne of God. For consider Him who has endured such hostility by sinners against Himself, so that you will not grow weary [c]and lose heart." (Hebrews 12:2-3 NASB). In his humanity, Jesus suffered. He suffered temptation, rejection and betrayal, hardships in ministry on behalf of others, sorrow and remorse, and the struggle of accepting the suffering in the garden of Gethsemane.

Christ suffered extreme physical pain in the process of crucifixion. Though sinless himself, he suffered the judgment of God the Father for sin. In his death, Jesus accomplished the death of death. The work of Christ on the cross provides the basis of forgiveness of sin. Forgiveness of sin was the focus of the teaching of Jesus. Jesus demonstrated his power over evil, performed miracles (not being preoccupied with his own suffering), gave glory to whom glory was due (his Father), showed great patience in his sufferings, refrained from returning evil for evil, and maintained a sense of mission through it all. His suffering in death and his resurrection give meaning and hope in the midst of our suffering. The only work left for us to do is to believe (see John 6:29), and demonstrate our belief by cooperating with God.

Thirdly, forgiveness and reconciliation are two related but distinctly different journeys. Forgiveness involves first being reconciled to God. This can be termed "vertical forgiveness" and is not to be confused with reconciliation with our fellow man. Reconciliation between human beings is the work done to restore right relationship between the debtor and one to whom the debt is owed (which can be called "horizontal forgiveness"). Reconciling with God and yielding the debt (forgiveness) to him is an important prerequisite for restoring a relationship with the debtor (reconciliation). The debt(s) must be surrendered to God, and then right fellowship with God, self, and other persons has opportunity to be restored. This restoration and reconciliation process will be discussed in the next chapter. Some distinguish forgiveness and reconciliation by using the terms *personal* forgiveness and *interpersonal* forgiveness. It takes two people to reconcile. It only takes a relationship with God to experience true forgiveness in the heart (whether or not the other person is ready, or able, to reconcile).

In my estimation, dealing with offense and forgiveness is one of the most misunderstood and poorly practiced of human experiences. How can forgiveness be so frequently talked about, read about, studied, and attempted while at the same time the actual fruit of forgiveness (joy and peace of heart) so often seems to slip out of reach? The answer to this question still remains somewhat of a mystery to me, but knowing forgiveness is God's idea keeps me finding more answers in him.

Release from Prison

Racial equality advocate Nelson Mandela was a political prisoner for two decades in South Africa. His heart attitude led to actions which made a huge difference, not only for him but numerous people following his lead. When being released from prison he is quoted as saying, "As I walked out the door toward the gate that would lead to my freedom, I knew if I didn't leave my bitterness and hatred behind, I'd still be in prison." He understood how bitter roots are formed from the seed of nursing wounds and grudges that grow in the human heart. Left unchecked, bitterness will inevitably turn to resentment. Mandela also says, "Resentment is like drinking poison and then hoping it will kill your enemies." That is very true in a figurative sense, but it also holds true literally. Research points to the connection between unforgiving emotions and the development and spread of bodily diseases like cancer.

Furthermore, resentment often moves down the slippery slope to create an atmosphere of revenge. Josh Billings turns this around when he says, "There is no revenge so complete as forgiveness." When someone intentionally tries to cause harm but is answered with forgiveness instead of retaliation, a cycle of hurt and harm is immediately broken. Abraham Lincoln once asked, " Am I not destroying my enemies when I make friends of them?" Oscar Wilde remarks, "Always forgive your enemies—nothing annoys them so much."

Forgiving Injustice

So you genuinely want to forgive someone for the hurt they have caused you in the past. Maybe you've already tried to forgive, but it doesn't seem to work. Lack of results is usually not caused by failure of forgiveness, but failure to understand what forgiveness really is. Contrary to what many believe, forgiveness is not simply a choice. It is not simply forgetting. Author Louis Smedes writes, "Forgiving does not erase the bitter past. A healed memory is not a deleted memory. Instead, forgiving what we cannot forget creates a new way to remember. We change the memory of our past into a hope for our future." Forgiveness is not an exercise of the mind using willpower to shut off the emotions. The lasting fruit of forgiveness requires a person's heart to be involved.

Forgiving is Love

Forgiveness begins with love. Love is more than having feelings toward another. It is more than making a decision to care. Love is an action. True love is acting in the best interest of the other person. "Forgiveness is choosing to love. It is the first skill of self-giving love," says Mahatma Gandhi. In a book called *Sonship: A Journey into Father's Heart,* James Jordan writes a chapter titled, "Forgiving from the Heart." I recommend his book for further reading. Jordan explains how human beings are "wired" by their Creator for love and forgiveness. Jordan writes, "He wants us to progress from choosing to forgive, to forgiving with love, and then to the place where we *love* to forgive. Moving far beyond forgiving as an act of the will, to forgiving endlessly from a heart that *loves* to forgive."[10]

If you believe in God and you want a deeper relationship with Father, surrendering your heart to his love and forgiveness is essential. Father God is the source of all truth. The fact of the matter is, no human being will ever *fully* be able to grasp how huge this topic is from God's perspective. At some point, forgiveness comes down to trusting Father and his ways as totally right and just. Forgiveness is surrendering to God the ultimate rights of judgment on whatever matter is in question. The human demand to be a judge is surrendered to allow God to be Judge.

> Forgiveness is surrendering to God the ultimate rights of judgment.

Anger Unjustified

Some believe they are justified in holding anger against someone who does them wrong. "After all," they say, "If I forgive him, he will get off too easy," or, "He will just do it over again," or, "It doesn't seem fair." Again, this thinking stems from a misbelief about forgiveness. Feeling anger is not wrong, but allowing anger to turn into hatred creates the bitterness that causes wrong. Forgiveness does not mean you are giving up your right to hope for justice to be served, but it means you are giving up your right to be the "executor" of judgment.

I believe that a casual attitude toward unfounded anger (bitterness and resentment) is the primary root that keeps most people locked in their prison of unforgiveness. A person holding unforgiveness in their heart generally falls into one of two categories. The first is one who recognizes the bitterness or resentment he or she feels and knows

---

10 M. James Jordan, *Sonship: A Journey into Father's Heart* (Taupo, New Zealand: Tree of Life Media, 2012), p58.

s/he has to decide whether to take forgiving action or try to go on pretending things are okay.

The second is more difficult. In this case, a person may have no immediate awareness of a wound or wrong done to him or her, but symptoms hint of a problem. These symptoms may include troublesome moods like nagging frustration, irritation, annoyance, disappointment, discouragement, or depression. It may take the form of physical symptoms like persistent sleeplessness, loss of appetite, or body aches and pains. This second category is quite common and not to be despised or feared. The sooner you try to discover the root and take action toward forgiveness, the sooner a pace to peace of mind begins, and new freedom can be found.

If you wish to change the atmosphere of your home, workplace, church, and community, dare to lead in the practice of forgiveness and positive results you will see. The ancient Proverb states, "A man's discretion makes him slow to anger, And it is his glory to overlook a transgression" (Proverbs 19:11 NASB).

Forgiving Self

There is only one person who can cooperate with God to change your inner being. That person is you. What about the idea of having a relationship with yourself? It may sound strange to consider relating to yourself, but "judging" self is very common. In fact, we all do it to some degree or another. Remember, part of judging is trying to attach blame to someone. Some people are more prone to blame God, or someone else, but some are more prone to blame themselves. Thinking of self as a target to blame for disappointments or failures may help you identify where you tend to shame and condemningly judge yourself.

Self-judgment is often overlooked as a bitter root to a problem. If blaming yourself is your first reaction when an accident happens, there may be a deeper root that caused this tendency to take hold. If spilling a glass of water, burning food on the stove, or tripping over misplaced items in the hallway consistently causes great distress, it is likely a pattern that developed over time. Finding the source, and forgiving self, could be of great benefit.

Forgiving God

It may also seem strange to think we need to forgive God because we know he is perfect and doesn't even know how to do anything wrong. But the issue is not with God, but our own tendency to blame. And we have all charged God for bad things that happened at one time or another. If nothing else, it's part of the original sin of mankind perceiving God to be something/ someone worse than who he really is.

We may know and believe with our mind that God is not responsible for anything bad that happens. God cannot wrong us, but if we perceive in our heart that he is responsible for something we perceive as bad, we may make a condemning judgment that is sin. The sin causes a bitter root, and the bitterness must be forgiven in order to release the guilt (in the spiritual realm) of having held the bitterness.

Judging God is not unlike holding blame and bitterness against ourselves or another person. If we perceived rejection, for example, whether or not it was truly wrong that was done, becoming angry, casting blame, and condemningly judging a person creates a bitter root that gets planted in our heart. We may discover later that the rejection was not rejection at all, but the discovery of truth alone does not solve our need to forgive and be forgiven. Jesus is the one we must trust to remove the bitter root. As a child, blaming God for not protecting us from serious abuse (for example), may have gotten deeply buried in a dark corner of our house, but now that God owns our house, he wants it healed so we can make the house more inhabitable and productive.

Praying to Forgive

What has to happen to forgive and remove the bitter roots that get planted in our hearts? We must connect with God to access his power to forgive and be forgiven. Forgiveness is both a decision and an active commitment to cooperate with his process of restoring what was lost through the transgression.

The next chapter will look at some specifics. In general, we must first become aware of our sin, acknowledge our sinfulness, confess, repent, and renounce. Confessing involves simply speaking it aloud to bring it out of hiddenness. Repenting means to turn away from it and go in a new direction more in line with God's plans and purposes. Renouncing is committing to not going back to the old patterns of thinking and behaving, but instead remaining on a track of transforming, wholehearted living.

Chapter 10

Clean Up the House

Now that we understand some basics about forgiveness from the last chapter, we can explore more about how to "work out" salvation in daily life as the Apostle Paul wrote to the Church in Philippi. "So then, my beloved, just as you have always obeyed, not as in my presence only, but now much more in my absence, work out your salvation with fear and trembling;" (Philippians 2:12 NASB). Each person is responsible for their own life. No one can live off someone else's faith. Each must take his or her own responsibility for inner person change.

Sanctification

In considering a transformational path to peace in our inner being, it becomes important to consider theology regarding sanctification. God has done his part. The legal aspect of salvation (justification) once and for all accomplishes forgiveness for all who believe. With this understanding, continuing on the journey requires collaboration with God on the part of the human. God calls believers to "work out" their salvation through a process called sanctification. Here forgiveness becomes a "personal" matter, not personal in the sense of originating from within a person, but personal in the sense of God's truth confronting the person's sinful, rebellious, and broken nature of his creation.

Therefore, we must consider sanctification and the role of the Christian in appropriating forgiveness. Several acts of God occur in a person before sanctification begins: the gospel call (which God addresses to him), regeneration (by which God imparts new life to him), justification (by which God gives him right legal standing before him), and adoption (in which God makes him a member of his family). These events along with conversion (in which a person repents of sin and trusts in Christ for salvation) all occur at the beginning of a Christian's life. After discussing these topics in his treatment of systematic theology, Wayne Grudem then states,

> But now we come to a part of the application of redemption that is a *progressive* work that continues throughout our earthly lives. It is also a work in which *God and man cooperate*, each playing distinct roles. This part of the application of redemption is called sanctification: *Sanctification is a progressive work of God and man that makes us more and more free from sin and like Christ in our actual lives.*[11]

Grudem describes three distinct stages of sanctification. First, sanctification has a definite beginning at regeneration and brings a definite moral change. This initial step in sanctification involves a definite break from the ruling power and love of sin, so that the believer is no longer ruled or dominated by sin and no longer loves to sin.

Second, sanctification increases throughout life. This is the primary sense in which sanctification is considered in this book. Although Paul says that his readers have been set free from sin and that they are "dead to sin and alive to God" (Romans 6:11), he nonetheless recognizes that sin remains in their lives, so he tells them not to let it reign

---

11 Wayne Grudem, *Systematic Theology: An introduction to Biblical Doctrine* (Grand Rapids, MI: Inter-Varsity Press and Zondervan, 1994) #.

and not to yield to it (Romans 6:12-13). The task for Christians is to grow more and more in sanctification, just as they previously grew more and more in sin: "Just as you once yielded your members to impurity and to greater and greater iniquity, so now yield your members to righteousness for sanctification" (Romans 6:19). Paul also says Christians "are being changed into Christ's likeness from one degree of glory to another" (2 Corinthians 3:18).

Third, sanctification is completed at death for Christians' souls and never completed fully in this life. Because there is sin (dark spot, corner, closet) that potentially remains in their hearts even though they have become Christians (see Romans 6:13, 1 John 1:8), their sanctification will never be completed in this life (see Hebrews 12:23).

Sanctification requires cooperation between man and God. In explaining the nature of God's role and man's role in sanctification, Grudem states:

> It does not seem inappropriate to say that God and man cooperate in sanctification. God works in our sanctification and we work as well, and we work for the same purpose. We are not saying that we have equal roles in sanctification or that we both work in the same way, but simply that we cooperate with God in ways that are appropriate to our status as God's creatures. And the fact that Scripture emphasizes the role that we play in sanctification (with all the moral commands of the New Testament), makes it appropriate to teach that God calls us to cooperate with him in this activity.[12]

God's role in sanctification is a primary one. Jesus is our example. The Holy Spirit works in a Christian to change his life. The role that man plays in sanctification is both a *passive* one in which we depend on God to sanctify us, and an *active* one in which we strive to obey God and take steps that will develop our sanctification. Grudem states,

---

12 Grudem, #.

It is important that we continue to grow both in our passive trust in God to sanctify us and in our active striving for holiness and greater obedience in our lives. If we neglect active striving to obey God, we become passive, lazy Christians. If we neglect the passive role of trusting God and yielding to him, we become proud and overly confident in ourselves. In either case, our sanctification will be greatly deficient.[13]

Christians must maintain faith and practice diligence to obey at the same time. This book deals with some of the active human aspects of sanctification as they relate to finding a path to peace and rest for our souls.

Redeeming the Whole Person

Sanctification affects both the physical and nonphysical parts of the human being. Scripture teaches that sanctification affects man's intellect and knowledge when Paul says that we have put on the new nature "which is being renewed in knowledge after the image of its creator" (Colossians 3:10 ESV). He prays that the Philippians may see their love "abound more and more, with knowledge and all discernment" (Philippians 1:9 ESV). And he urges the Roman Christians to be "transformed by the renewal of your mind" (Romans 12:1-2 ESV). A person's knowledge of God (including an understanding that is more than intellectual knowledge) should keep increasing throughout life (see Colossians 1:10; 2 Corinthians 10:5).

Moreover, as Grudem notes, growth in sanctification will affect our emotions.

We will see increasingly in our lives emotions such as "love, joy, peace, patience" (Galatians 5:22). We will be able increasingly to obey Peter's command "to abstain from the passions of the flesh, which wage war against your soul" (1 Peter 2:11 ESV). We will find it increas-

---

13 Grudem, #.

ingly true that we do not "love the world or the things in the world" (1 John 2:15 ESV), but that we, like our Savior, delight to do God's will.

In ever-increasing measure, believers will become "obedient from the heart" (Romans 6:12) and they will "put away" deeds and thinking involved in "bitterness and wrath and anger and clamor and slander" (Ephesians 4:31 ESV).

Sanctification will also have an effect on the human *will*, the decision-making faculty. God is at work in a believer "to *will* and to work for his good pleasure" (Philippians 2:13 ESV).

Sanctification also affects the human *spirit*, the nonphysical part of human beings and a believer's physical body. The Apostle Paul says that a concern about the affairs of the Lord will mean taking thought for "how to be holy in body and spirit" (1 Corinthians 7:34 ESV). To the Thessalonians, Paul says, "May the God of peace himself sanctify you wholly; and may your spirit and soul and body be kept sound and blameless at the coming of our Lord Jesus Christ" (1 Thessalonians 5:23 ESV). Moreover, Paul encourages the Corinthians, "Let us cleanse ourselves from every defilement of *body* and spirit, and make holiness perfect in the fear of God" (2 Corinthians 7:1). As we become more sanctified in our bodies, our bodies become more and more useful servants of God, more and more responsive to the will of God and the desires of the Holy Spirit (2 Corinthians 9:27). We will not let sin reign in our bodies (Romans 6:12) nor allow our bodies to participate in any way in immorality (1 Corinthians 6:13). But we will treat our bodies with care and will recognize that they are the means by which the Holy Spirit works through us in this life (1 Corinthians 6:19; Acts 13:2).

Soul Cleansing

The biblical use of the term soul is primarily referencing the inner aspect of the person (see 2 Corinthians 4:16), in contrast to the outer person or the body. The Bible presents an anthropological view of human beings as being comprised of both body and soul; (Genesis 2:22) however, Scripture stresses the person as a whole, described ultimately in relationship with God and others (see 1 Thessalonians 5:23).

As mentioned earlier, neglecting the emotional part of a person's being can have damaging consequences. Pastor Peter Scazzero's book. *Emotionally Healthy Spirituality,* describes how even pastors and church leaders are susceptible to overdependence on intellect to solve problems. The jacket of his book reads, "... his church and marriage hit bottom and every 'Christian' remedy he tried produced nothing but more anger and fatigue. As he began digging under the 'good Christian' veneer, he discovered emotional layers of his life God had not yet touched—layers he had carefully tried to conceal from everyone. The resulting emotional immaturity had left him spiritually immature—and it nearly cost him everything."[14]

However, for Scazzero, realizing the critical link between emotional and spiritual health turned the failure of his dreams into the beginning of a journey that would forever change him, his church, and his relationships. Pastor Scazzero diagnoses why even intense spirituality and all its activity can still leave a person empty. Out of his pain-filled experiences and the seven steps to transformation detailed in these pages, he pointedly shows how one can escape the lifelessness of unhealthy spirituality and experience a fresh faith charged with authenticity, contemplation, and a hunger for God that leaves one filled up and overflowing instead of burnt out and exhausted.

Although this topic could be explored in much more detail, the purpose in this chapter is to introduce some of the dynamics within the soul (person) associated with cleansing the inner being, transformational healing, forgiveness, and the soul's Creator—while fully acknowledging the fact that the person as a whole is created, fallen, redeemed, and glorified. Scripture utilizes the term soul, especially in

---

14 Peter Scazzero, *Emotionally Healthy Spirituality: Unleash a Revolution in Your Life in Christ* (Nashville, TN: Thomas Nelson Publishing, 2006).

the Psalms, when focusing on the struggles within the heart and mind of the psalmist, though presupposing that the person, as a whole, is in relationship with God. One must also acknowledge the dynamic, inseparable interplay between body and soul, which is becoming increasingly evident in recent neuroscience and neuropsychological research.

Self-Honesty

A very often-quoted verse of Scripture is found in 2 Chronicles 7:14: "If my people, who are called by my name, will humble themselves and pray and seek my face and turn from their wicked ways, then will I hear from heaven and will forgive their sin and will heal their land" (NIV). Contextually, this verse is found in the midst of ceremonies to dedicate the greatest temple of its time. Why, during these holy acts of worship, would God remind his chosen people of the wicked ways at the core of their hearts? God uses the term wicked to describe his most holy people on the face of the earth. How can this be explained? God desires a radical commitment to heart transformation. Genuine transformation begins with an honest assessment of man's desperate need. At the same time that part of a person's heart may be seeking after God and submitted to his will to some degree, other aspects of his life may be influenced by evil and still need to be surrendered to God's will. As discussed above, sanctification has three distinct aspects: changed, being changed, and change completed at life's end. The dark parts of our fractured hearts are being transformed into the portions of light.

Although man is in right standing with God through justification, the sanctification process reveals a struggle to please God and do what is right. Paul describes it this way: "I do not understand what I do. For what I want to do I do not do, but what I hate I do" (Romans 7:15 NIV). Paul says to the Corinthians, "And we, who with unveiled faces all reflect the Lord's glory, are being transformed into his likeness with ever-increasing glory, which comes from the Lord, who is the Spirit"

(2 Corinthians 3:18). The first step toward genuine transformation is being honest with ourselves about the continual need of Christ's saving (sanctifying) power to change the heart.

Receiving God's forgiveness requires a realization of our need and inadequacy. But it must always be remembered that God required nothing of Adam and Eve before he initiated the reconciliation process. He came looking for them and questioned them about their fig-leaf covering before they ever acknowledged their sin and before they recognized their shame. God does the same for each person. Accepting the Gift of Jesus to cleanse from sins requires not only honesty of an unclean condition, but the humility to receive the help to become clean. That's where humility takes over in the process.

Humility

Honesty positions the mind (reasoning capacity) to receive from God, and humility positions the heart to receive in the inner being. The often-quoted verse in 2 Chronicles 7:14 might be summed up with the conditional phrase, "If my people … humble, pray, seek, and turn, then will I hear, forgive, and heal." The gift of forgiveness is free, but there must be a commitment to receive it. The commitment is demonstrated through repentance, which is also part of the conditional side of the phrase ("turn from their wicked ways").

If a person can humbly accept his condition as offender before God (and fellow man), then processing the offense of another offender in the same condition becomes more likely to impact the core identity of the person. The humble truth is that every person alive owes such a huge debt to his Creator, that a lifetime of trying to work it off cannot even pay a reasonable portion of the debt.

Jesus told a story to illustrate the enormity of debt, recorded in Matthew 18:23-34. Known as the parable of the slave's debt forgiven, a king decides to call for closure of the debt of one of his servants. The debt is about the equivalent of five billion dollars. Serving the king the rest of his life would not make a dent in the payments. This creates a legal dilemma for the king of not being able to balance the books because the note he holds for a debtor is worthless. Aware of this, the servant feels bad about the circumstances completely out of control. Totally humbled, he pleads for mercy. The king has compassion on him and forgives the entire debt. Legally and morally the servant is set free.

This story illustrates the condition of sinful man in the presence of a holy God. As Robert Jeffress (in his book *When Forgiveness Doesn't Make Sense*) explains, this story also shows how mistaken a person is to hold unforgiveness:

> Many people today are struggling with forgiveness because they are unaware that the "debt" they hold is really worthless. They mistakenly believe that there's some payment they can extract from their offender that will compensate for their loss. Understandably, they want vengeance. But the truth is that very few sinners have the resources to pay for their offenses. What satisfactory payment could someone offer you to compensate for…
>
> a child killed by a drunk driver
>
> a reputation slandered by a false rumor
>
> a marriage destroyed by infidelity
>
> a childhood innocence stolen by an immoral relative?[15]

Refusing to forgive is not just a mistake; it is sin. In another teaching prior to the parable of the king and the slave's debt forgiven, Jesus makes the connection and offers a solution. "You have heard that it was said, 'An eye for an eye, and a tooth for a tooth.' But I say to you, do not resist him who is evil; but whoever slaps you on your right cheek, turn to him the other also" (Matthew 5:38-39 NASB). Like the

---

15 Robert Jeffress, *When Forgiveness Doesn't Make Sense* (Colorado Springs, CO: Waterbrook Press, 2000), #

king in the parable, Jesus taught that forgiveness is the only way to break the cycle of hurt and unfairness caused by sin. For a person to accept the truth that he or she owes God a debt that can never be repaid takes great humility. For a person to accept the truth that other persons' offenses against them may never be properly accounted for (in this life at least) also takes great humility.

Proverbs 11:2 says, "When pride comes, then comes disgrace, but with humility comes wisdom" (NIV). A path of humility may not be the easiest path to take, but it is the wisest. The role of suffering and adversity will be explored more deeply in a later section, but it should be noted here that human weakness has a way of naturally creating an environment more conducive to exercising humility. Human weaknesses and inabilities have a way of deflating pride, and as such, make way for repentance.

Repentance

Some question whether repentance is necessary before forgiveness. To answer this, an important distinction must be made between *receiving* forgiveness and *granting* forgiveness. The issue of repentance is vitally important to an offender *accepting* the forgiveness of a victim (as part of reconciliation). However, an offended person *granting* forgiveness to an offender cannot place demands (such as repentance on the part of their offender) as conditions for obeying God and practicing forgiveness.

Although repentance is a necessary ingredient to experience forgiveness from God, one should never forget that God has made all the first moves to bring about that reconciliation with his creatures. That is why Christians should understand that sometimes the offended party must take the first step to restore a broken relationship. Repentance and confession (on the part of the offender) are necessary to receive forgiveness (from God). At the same time, they are not required prerequisites for *granting* forgiveness, from the perspective of an offended person needing to forgive an offense. A person can only repent for himself, but not for another person.

The parable in Matthew 18, mentioned above, also presents a second servant who owed the first servant sixteen dollars. The first servant mistakenly thought that imprisoning and torturing his fellow slave would somehow enrich him, or at least console him over the forfeited debt. Yet in the end, he collected no more of what was due him than did the king.

Those (victims) who think they can demand repentance (from their offender) before granting forgiveness are operating under the illusion that somehow their offender's repentance will be sufficient to cover the offense. The same is true in a person's relationship with God. Since every person alive is an offender, there is nothing one could ever do to earn God's forgiveness. Is showing remorse or even genuine repentance ever truly enough to erase the stain of an abortion, a divorce, an affair, or a broken vow to God? Jeffress answers, "How silly (and prideful) it is to think that we could ever repay our Creator for the hurt we have inflicted upon Him by any act of penitence, much less uttering a simple 'I'm sorry.' Mark it down, circle it, and remember this forever: we are not saved by our repentance but by God's grace."[16]

Nonetheless, repentance and forgiveness fit hand in glove in releasing an offender from his offense. The offended person's willingness to take responsibility for any part he or she plays in causing the offense demonstrates a true heart of humility, shows the love of God, and opens the door for reconciliation in the proper timing. When the offender is ourselves, and we need God's forgiveness, repentance opens the door for a reconciled relationship with God. The fellowship with God brings with it true inner rest, peace, and joy.

---

16 Jeffress, #.

Forgiving To Gain Health

Yielding to God in obedience to forgive is rarely an easy choice. In her book *Choosing Forgiveness,* Nancy DeMoss challenges her readers, "It's possible that even after reading the Scriptures and examining the concepts we've explored, you still find forgiveness too painful and difficult to contemplate. Or perhaps, truth be known, you'd rather keep nursing your wounds and savoring your resentment than to release the offense. Either way you're just not ready to forgive."[17] For those who fall into this category, she then warns, "Your unwillingness to trust and obey God in this matter—even if it's more from exhaustion and self-preservation than from rank hardness of heart—will keep the atmosphere of your life contaminated with the poison of bitterness. You may not be conscious of its noxious effects every day, but it will cut off the flow of God's grace into your life."[18]

It is possible to recognize offenses as terrible or horrific and still choose not to forgive. Part of the reason some find this difficult is because of myths they believe about forgiveness. Exploring what forgiveness is not helps in defining what true forgiveness is. DeMoss says, "Many people who genuinely want to find themselves on the other side of forgiveness have bought into myths and misconceptions that have defeated their best attempts at following through. They have misunderstood what forgiveness should look like, feel like, and be like. As a result, they've found their journey to freedom frustrated."[19]

DeMoss shares four common myths about forgiveness: 1) that forgiveness and good feelings always go hand in hand, 2) that forgiveness means forgetting, 3) that forgiveness requires a long, drawn-out process and cannot take place until healing is complete, and 4) that

---

17 Nancy DeMoss, *Choosing Forgiveness: Your Journey to Freedom* (Chicago, IL: Moody Publications, 2006) #.

18 DeMoss, #.

19 DeMoss, #.

forgiveness should always make things better. Forgiveness is first a choice and the feelings follow, whether good or bad. Wiping out hurtful memory is not the object of forgiveness. God's grace can redeem the afflicted memory. The Scriptures remind us that affliction not only allows us to receive deep, rich comfort from God, but gives us a basis from which to minister that comfort to others. By God's grace, a person can choose to forgive in a moment of time, to the level of his understanding at that point. And as he grows in his understanding of the circumstances that took place, as well as his understanding of God's ways, the forgiveness in his heart may likely go to deeper levels. Finally, not only may the results of forgiveness not feel better, but they possibly will not *be* better. Unfairness and mistreatment by others are never guaranteed to go away.

Recognizing Unforgiveness

Unforgiveness lodged in the heart generally falls in one of two categories. The first type carries with it identifiable negative feelings toward a person(s) or situation. The second type is not, at first, definable with specific feelings, but carries a deep, well-disguised wound. Prayers of forgiveness can bring release for immediately identifiable sources of unforgiveness. Healing prayer techniques of various kinds can be used to identify more hidden sources of unforgiveness.

Is there someone (in your family or circle of friends and acquaintances) you discover you would rather not meet up with, intentionally avoid, or hope bad things happen to? Is there an incident you cannot get out of your mind? Do you feel vengeful emotions, frustration, or anger toward someone?

If you answer yes to any of these questions, or if you have discovered "bad fruit" of unforgiveness through some means, it is probably time to proceed with this self-examination exercise.

Self-examination exercise questions:

Who do you need to forgive?

What did they do / say? (be specific)

How did this offend? Hurt? (list specifics)

When are you ruminating or making up speeches in your mind? (consumed with thoughts provoked by frustration)

Why are you ready/ not ready to release/ surrender/ let go of this?

Where do you stand with God on this? (what would he have you do?)

Where do you want to be/ go on this? (next step)

If you are ready to forgive and you need the help of a sample prayer, see the Appendices for some help.

The following is a list of some of the common effects of unforgiveness. If a number of these are apparent in your life, you may want to seek help from a trusted friend or counselor to pray and ask God to reveal a source (or root) and what to do about it.

Common Effects of Unforgiveness:

a. stress and anxiety

b. self-inflicted condemnation

c. lack of trust and love

d. anger and bitterness

e. perpetual conflict

f. building up of emotional walls

g. depression and hopelessness

h. physical problems (i.e. chronic illness)

i. sleeplessness or appetite loss

j. wilderness in spiritual condition or relationship with God

God wants ALL the parts of your heart, not just some and not just on your terms or in your timing. It's total surrender that he's after. He initiated the process of wholeness, completed his part of the work of salvation, and now only asks for your cooperation in transforming the heart into a tool to be used for his glory. Only through much prayer and reflection is the path to wholeness discerned. The Holy Spirit reveals truth to those who seek it earnestly. Now is the day of salvation. Seek God for your healing word. Intellect alone is not enough to discover, dislodge, or mend the sinful condition. Prayerfully consider questions and further study in this book. Practice "listening prayer" to hear what the Holy Spirit is speaking to your heart.

As you seek God for more revelation of his saving grace, I declare the spirit of Elijah to fall on you. Jesus said, "Truly I tell you, among those born of women there has not risen anyone greater than John the Baptist; yet whoever is least in the kingdom of heaven is greater than he. From the days of John the Baptist until now, the kingdom of heaven has been subjected to violence, and violent people have been raiding it. For all the Prophets and the Law prophesied until John. And if you are willing to accept it, he is the Elijah who was to come. Whoever has ears, let them hear" (Matthew 11:11-15 NIV).

Turning from your condition (repenting) and allowing the "violent" winds of the Holy Spirit to blow the darkness out of your heart is the preparatory work necessary for the peace and "rest of your souls" as you come closer to Jesus. This is the divinely masterminded strategy for cleaning out the dark areas of the heart, escaping the pain of offense, and finding true rest for the soul.

Practicing Healing Prayer

The practice of healing prayer is not a religious exercise as many would be inclined to think of when hearing the word "prayer." It is not an exercise of willpower, nor a spiritual discipline to add to a list of good works to make one more pleasing to God. Salvation through faith is a Gift of grace accomplished by the work of Jesus (see Ephesians 2:8-10). Jesus finished his work by living on the earth as a man, dying on a cross, and returning to the Father through resurrection life. His work now is in the hearts of those people who believe in him, to change them from the inside out in becoming more and more like him (Psalm 51:6, Romans 12:1-2, Colossians 1:22-23, 2 Corinthians 3:18, 1 Thessalonians 5:23-24, 1 Peter 3:4).

This transformation process is putting the hurt and wounded pieces (discussed previously) back in order, to make us whole and complete in God's original design. Healing prayer is a tool to help in this transformation process. It requires an enormous amount of self-honesty, humility, facing painful memories, and trusting God to see us through. Healing prayer can take many forms and vary greatly from person to person. Let's look briefly at the following five basic elements.

1. Acknowledge the beliefs of our inner heart, feel the emotions they stir, and identify the specific lies believed.

2. Ask Jesus to take us to the source of these ingrained misbeliefs (perhaps in a memory).

3. Confess belief(s) in the memory(ies), renounce their effects, and acknowledge inability to change without the help of God.

4. Ask Jesus to reveal his presence in our pain in whatever way he chooses, and receive the truth.

5. Engage Jesus' ministry of truth in the memory(ies), and respond with ongoing transformation.

First, we start with where it hurts. What are the specific sensations, feelings, and emotions causing pain (displeasure, discomfort, disruption) at the moment? Avoid trying to "figure out why" at this point. Many people start by identifying things their "inner voice" is telling them. Examples might be "I am not important, not loved, not needed, or unfit," "I am worthless, a mistake, a failure, or stupid," "I should have done something to stop the abuse from happening," "I am too weak, helpless, or defenseless," "I am bad, dirty, or shameful," "I am all alone and will always be alone," "I am incompetent, or I can't do anything right," "I am anxious or afraid," or "I am not _____ enough. or I don't have enough ____ ."

What are the feelings driving these beliefs? Be as specific as you can in naming the negative feelings (i.e., abandoned, rejected, deserted, forgotten, left out, don't belong, ashamed, failure, faulty, stupid, trashy, unclean, unfit, unworthy, anxious, desperate, fearful, nervous, scared, untrusting, confined, cornered, defenseless, frail, helpless, weak, damaged, flawed, ruined, betrayed, disgraced, inferior, insignificant, unappreciated, unloved, defeated, hopeless, tired, despair, disoriented, confused, or indifferent).

The next element is to invite God into the midst of the pain. Jesus is very qualified to identify with pain and suffering. In fact, the Bible says there is absolutely no type of human suffering he himself has not experienced (see Hebrews 4:14-16). Remember, Jesus is the Healer. He knows where the source of the pain lies. He wants to remove the bad root, not just the symptoms. Ask him to lead you to the origin of this pain in your life.

> We cannot change the past, but we can change the way we respond to it.

The next major element is acknowledging and confessing our own misperceptions, false assumptions, misinterpretations, misjudgments, and/or misconduct in the event(s) our memory(ies) lead us to. We cannot change the past, and much of what happened is out of our control, but we can recognize and change the way we respond to it. For example, maybe our pain leads us to remember our perfectionist dad or mom not giving us recognition or affirmation for significant achievements, but instead always communicating how our performance was lacking. Yes, maybe our parents were neglectful (or even abusive) is some regard, but blaming them for our reactions will not help us now. We must indeed admit we were hurt, and reacted negatively, and confess (speak out loud) what we thought and felt about this at the time. The list above may help here too. Again, focus on what it felt like in the inner most depths of your being as a child, not on what it would'a, could'a, should'a been like.

Longings for appropriate touch, acceptance, affirmation, and belonging are normal. When these longings are not met, it is also normal to react and believe things that are not true (critically judge) about those people in our life who should be supplying those needs. In the example of a perfectionist parent, our inner voice may be telling us things like "Dad doesn't love me," Mom is mean," "Dad cares about my sister more than me," "Mom doesn't understand," "I'll never be able to please Dad and Mom," or "They are not interested in how I feel." But because "normal" in this case, is sinful, we must be willing to renounce the misbeliefs, condemning judgments, and actions, and surrender these over to God in exchange for the truth.

The next major element is listening for what God wants to tell us. Listening is a skill to be developed. Our faith is often so oriented toward doing (for God), we have difficulty being in God's presence long enough to hear (from God) what he is saying to us. This seems so basic, but it needs attention as an element of its own because it is SO important. This involves quieting our spirit (complete silence is preferable) and asking questions like "Jesus, what truth would you like to reveal to me?" "What are you saying?" "What is the truth about my parents (in the example above)?" "Where were you, Jesus, when this happened?" or "What is the truth about who I am (and whose I am)?"

Shame is the greatest source of lies. Blaming ourselves for things out of our control is a form of shaming ourselves. God never condemns us. He sometimes condemns actions (that are against his will), but God does not condemn people he created in his image. Any voice of condemnation we hear against our identity as a child of God is from the enemy of our soul. Truth always affirms our identity as children of God.

God speaks truth through his written Word, the Bible. He also speaks truth through other means such as his creation, people, pictures, prophetic images, and imagination. Truth always affirms God's character as holy, righteous, all loving, and all powerful. Regarding other people, truth is able to separate their bad behavior from who they are as a unique creation of God. And regarding the self, truth affirms our identity as God's child, and his unfailing love is always accessible. Simply asking and receiving his love will connect us to it.

The last element to mention here is surrendering to the truth with our heart (not just with mental assent) and commitment to action for soul sanctification. Perhaps confession, repentance, and/or forgiveness is necessary, in addition to this type of work done in previous steps. Our hearts are made of many parts (chambers). Some parts may have been brought into the realm of believing, while other parts have work remaining to be done. Healing is God's work and in his timing. Remember, when Jesus says, "the truth will set you free" (John 8:32), there is a prerequisite. Jesus says, "if you hold to my teaching," that is how you will know the truth (John 8:31-32). Truth is truth. But truth that makes a difference (sets us free) is truth that we *apply*. The ongoing application of the truth of Christ's teaching restores us to wholeness. Not only are spiritual and psychological conditions restored, but physical conditions such as body aches, pains, and diseases can be healed as well.

God Is the Healer

Ultimately, healing is not merely for personal benefit, but to make more intimate our relationship with God, and become a more useful servant in his Kingdom. The practice of healing prayer can become a habit that produces a lifestyle of godly character. Journaling is a great way to record progress, and provide a way to look back and observe measurable improvements. Writing can also have great therapeutic value.

Some parts of our heart can be more resistant than others to healing prayer intervention. Severe trauma or abuse may complicate the process. Evil spirits can create another layer of bondage. Family history can also be a factor. It may be wise to attain the help of an experienced healing prayer warrior or counselor to guide steps in the journey. When practicing the steps above, a feeling of unusual fear, anxiety, or of being overwhelmed should be cause for halting the practice and seeking help right away.

Leaders should be leading in regularly practicing the transforming power of healing prayer. I recommend all leaders practice healing prayer with a competent practitioner on a regular basis to guard against blind spots and areas of unawareness the enemy of our soul tries to exploit. People helpers can only help people overcome to the degree they themselves have overcome. Charismatic gifting and people skills are not a healthy substitute for the deep heart work of inner healing prayer.

In my own life, I am so thankful to John and Paula Sandford and others from whom I have learned much over the past several decades. I have found the practice of healing prayer invaluable in removing shame, false guilt, powerlessness, anxiety, depression, controlling behavior, and so many more unwanted thoughts, feelings, and behaviors. I haven't arrived at complete wholeness, but my hope is secure in trusting God for transformation in his timing, without needing to understand all the details. When I practice healing prayer, my heart is at rest in Refuge (see Matthew 11:28-29, Psalms 34, 46, 62 and others). The sooner I can get to Refuge, the more empowered is my pace to peace. My house is cleaner, and made a more livable dwelling for God (Isaiah 30:15, Isaiah 32:18, Psalm 84, Psalm 132:14, Deuteronomy 12:9).

Caution

The earth is subject to earthquakes, hurricanes, floods, and all sorts of natural disasters. When these occur, houses get damaged and things shaken up. Walls may crack, roofs may get blown off, water damage may destroy contents, and so forth. Combat zones and military conflict can also cause human suffering of unimaginable proportions. These natural world examples can illustrate how our heart gets hurt. Circumstances in life can create damage and shake our sense of safety and security. Like we discussed in another chapter, tangible losses create needs and all sorts of intangible consequences.

Sometimes a catastrophic event in life can cause a "shaking" of our inner world so severe that we lose our ability to function. Feelings of dread and of being overwhelmed crowd out any sense of hope that things can ever return to a manageable condition. That kind of crisis or trauma needs a different kind of attention than what is discussed in this book. This book tries to help the reader in areas where comfortability with dysfunction is keeping them from being the best person they can be. Instead of disturbing the comfortable, recovery from catastrophe involves comforting the disturbed.

The reality is, we live in a world that makes us vulnerable to potential life-altering events at any time. We may not have a history of mental health problems, but that doesn't make us immune to serious mental health concerns when disaster strikes. Instead of living in fear of disaster, we do well to trust God and strengthen our resilience through transformational living. In working with people in counseling ministry, I acknowledge that some people have more difficulty with combatting this fear than others.

I want to add a disclaimer for those with more serious mental health concerns. I realize there may be a small percentage of people who read the material in this book who have tried as hard as they can to choose and practice the better way, but feel, for whatever reason, they are unable to do it. Please do not feel condemned for trying and failing. Seek help from a trusted friend or counselor, and remember that human flesh may be weak, but God is strong. God only asks of us what he knows we can handle. Never give up! God never gives up on us.

Chapter 11

Care for the Neighborhood

As a person allows the house cleaning in their heart to take place, he/she becomes more readied to help others in their process of giving their houses to God and experiencing peace in their lives. God's reconstruction and re-creation work (inner transformation) makes a more peaceful person, and interpersonal relationships are improved as well.

Making Things Friendly

Forgiving means surrendering to God the right to judge. Forgiving restores relationship with God, whereas reconciliation restores relationship human to human (the offender with those offended). The good news for the offended is that the freedom of forgiveness is not tied to the offender's ability (or willingness) to reconcile. Another important thing to learn is that trying to reconcile before forgiving may actually cause more harm to a relationship than not attempting to reconcile at all. Forgiveness (from the offended person's view) prepares the heart and helps make a person's attitude more responsive rather than reactive.

Let's define reconciliation. According to Webster's dictionary it is "the act of causing two people or groups to become friendly again after an argument or disagreement." Reconciling is often not an easy choice. It may require humility and vulnerability to let other people see who you really are on the inside. It usually requires confrontation. The self-confrontation involved in forgiving can be difficult, but confronting another person because of an offense can be even more scary. The lack of willingness to confront is often the greatest barrier to reconciliation.

Like forgiving, reconciling is not an option for a Christian. It is a mandate. We must take very seriously the responsibility of attempting to "set things right." The Apostle Paul's letter to the first-century Corinthian church states that Christ himself "has committed to us the ministry of reconciliation" (see 2 Corinthians 5:15-20). So, what might the results of this ministry of reconciliation look like? I encourage you to read the entire fourth chapter of Ephesians to get a good snapshot of an answer to that question. Some of the phrases that jump out are these, "live a life worthy," "be completely humble and gentle," "be patient, bearing one another in love," "keep the unity," "speaking the truth in love," "grow and build up," "put off your old self," "put on the new self," "be made new in the attitudes of your mind," and "do not let the sun go down on your anger." Summarizing the chapter, "Do not let any unwholesome talk come out of your mouths, but only what is helpful for building others up according to their needs, that it may benefit those who listen. https://www.blogger.com/null ... Get rid of all bitterness, rage and anger, brawling and slander, along with every form of malice. https://www.blogger.com/null Be kind and compassionate to one another, forgiving each other, just as in Christ God forgave you" (Ephesians 4:29-32 NIV). Reconciling is meant to benefit not only the offended, but the offender as well. When relationships are restored and functioning well, the community at large will also benefit. Church, business, government, and other organizations thrive on healthy relationships between individuals.

It takes at least one party to initiate reconciliation. It takes two parties to obey the mandate for completing reconciliation. One of the most common reasons for relational breakup and disunity is a disagreement, disappointment, or offense that has never been processed through to an adequate resolution. It is not okay to walk away from a relationship, group, or situation just because you become angry or hurt by things that didn't go your way. It is okay to have desires, preferences, and high expectations of character (remembering that no one is perfect), but it is not okay to avoid healthy confrontation of brokenness that causes relational separation and division.

Remember, surrendering *your* right to judge doesn't mean you are surrendering your rights for justice to be served. In fact, when the "heart work" of forgiveness begins to produce its good fruit, it requires the action steps (toward reconciliation) to deliver the results to the world around you. Forgiving an offender does not mean the offender is relieved of due consequences to be paid for an offense. For example, in the case of abuse, forgiving an abuser is different from holding the abuser accountable for his or her actions. The safety of the victim must be established and if the abuser's actions are criminal behavior, the laws must be enforced to protect from further victimization and give the victimizer an opportunity to turn away from the sin of abuse and be restored as a person with worth and dignity. The abuse victim may or may not ever be reconciled to the abuser, but the power of forgiveness can free the victim of inner losses created by the victimization. The more completely forgiveness is achieved, the greater the degree of freedom to be lived.

Resolving Offense

It is also true that the more completely forgiveness is achieved (the more an offense is surrendered to God), the more prepared an offended person is to attempt reconciliation. It only takes one party to forgive. It takes two parties to reconcile. Remember, there are two sides to every offense (the offender and the offended), and you may find yourself on either side at any given time in a relationship or circumstance. If the offense seems unintentional on the part of the offender, forgiveness may be exercised by the offended, but for reconciliation to be complete, the offender may still need to become involved. Perhaps, for example, a minor miscommunication of traveling directions by Jane causes John to be late for an important appointment. John may forgive Jane and decide it's not worth mentioning Jane's mistake to her. John may even hold himself responsible for not double-checking or using a different source to find the information he needed. But then another similar incident occurs between Jane and John, and John has a harder time to forgive and the need to reconcile becomes more evident.

The teaching of Jesus addresses the issue of repeat offenses among brothers and sisters in Christ. One reference is in Matthew 18:15-17. I'll not go into detail here, but when reconciliation is attempted by the person offended, and the offender wants nothing to do with reconciliation or justice, it is time to get help from a friend or advocate. Forgiveness, without pursuing reconciliation or justice, may only make the situation worse for everyone.

Relational Integrity

Sometimes offensive behaviors get excused as personality traits, styles of leadership, attributes of professionalism, or "everybody does it" generalities. They may even pose as necessity to keep the peace, tolerable as long as no one is getting hurt, or as a short-term loss to achieve a long-term benefit. An example might be an internal culture of a company making a product (or performing a service) that doesn't quite meet the qualifications of its advertised outcomes. Employees are expected to put a spin on (hide) the deficiencies in order to keep their jobs.

However, the truth often requires pain with gain. There are no short-cuts to relational integrity. Frequently needed is confrontation to achieve inner peace, and trustworthy character to facilitate trust. Leaders can fall into the trap of offense as quickly as anyone else. Look at Moses for example. One of the strongest leaders of the ancient Israeli people witnessed an incident of severe injustice against a kinsman. Although his intentions were good in trying to help his fellow

Hebrew brothers and sisters, his attitude and behaviors that led to killing an Egyptian slavedriver backfired. Moses had to escape and live in hiding for forty years as a result of his mistake. Attempting shortcuts, when it comes to forgiving and reconciling, often erect negative relational walls that create confusion, erode authenticity, prohibit collaboration, and ultimately destroy trust and trustworthiness.

People are not the enemy. The real enemy is the enemy of our soul trying to trap us in shame. People's condemning judgments and actions (causing the offenses) are part of the enemy tactics. When offended, it is important to distinguish between personhood and the behavior. Remember, we discussed earlier how bitter root judgments form when we cross over from discerning actions, into condemningly judging the person themselves. We have a great Enemy who uses offenses (people's transgressions) in an attempt to divide and conquer. We must be wise to this tactic and vigilant to resist the trap of offense. People align with the enemy when they refuse to reconcile. An ever-deepening problem in American culture today is the division between individuals and groups not taking reconciliation seriously.

Refusing to reconcile is at the root of a practice that has come to be known as "cancel culture" (as an example of this refusal). This practice says it is okay (and even politically correct) to cut off or marginalize people with beliefs not in alignment with the party line or trendy movement. Instead of finding a way to agree to disagree in order to maintain a relationship, total rejection of a person (or group) becomes the way to deal with differences. Although "cancelling" people is an ungodly practice, it has become more common among Christians (alongside nonbelievers as well). It is obviously in direct opposition to a Christian's calling to be a "minister of reconciliation" (see 2 Corinthians 5).

Another violation of relational integrity I have noticed popping up more frequently is misuse of the concept of "boundaries." Proper use of boundaries is meant to facilitate and enhance relationship. However, when so-called boundaries are used as unhealthy self-protection and control techniques, they become more like the unhealthy walls discussed earlier. If friends, for example, have a disagreement about how to decorate their apartment, and Friend A decides to move out and have nothing more to do with Friend B, Friend A has more than a boundary violation issue going on. Another example is Spouse A refusing to discuss a topic and threatening Spouse B with divorce if they violate a boundary of not bringing up that topic. Spouses need to be in agreement on child training to some degree at least, but if one spouse is trying to shut down discussion just to get their way, it is not about boundaries, but it is all about control. A legitimate boundary might be *when* to talk about it (e.g., when not angry), or volume (e.g., not too loudly), but avoiding potentially uncomfortable or confrontational matters altogether is not valid for a married couple. A marriage relationship requires an especially close attention to forgiveness and reconciliation for relational integrity.

Individual Integrity

Sometimes a person can become an "enemy" of himself. A person's perception of low self-worth and poor self-concept (shame) is at the core of all human problems. God gave his only Son Jesus as our saving grace to reconcile us back to the Father. Father creates worth and value into each child born into the human race. The broken pieces of the human heart are reconciled back to Father through Jesus Christ (again see 2 Corinthians 5:15-20). A person's true value is based on who God made him to be as his son or daughter. It's not based on what he or she has done or failed to do. Believing in Jesus and surrendering the heart to God means a person is relying on Christ's completed work of reconciliation. It does not mean they have to come up with the strength to forgive and reconcile, but rely on the strength God gives them (see Matthew 11:28-29). Each has a choice to rely on the power of God every time he is offended. Why not do it?

Some offenses seem more difficult to forgive and reconcile than others. Examples might be infidelity of a spouse, murder or other crime against a family member, or severe injustice of a tribal nature. When God's power is invited into the situation, hope is much more free to win over a hopeless cause. After reconciling with God (receiving his unconditional love), reconciling with our fellow man becomes more tolerable. This is a continual process. Christ's work is complete, but our work of cooperating must be ongoing.

It seems the world is dealing us more opportunities for relational breakup than ever before. The recent Covid outbreak elicited some deep-seated responses in great numbers of people. People questioned whether to wear a mask or not, whether to inject a vaccine or not, whether to comply with mandated behaviors or not, and so on. Matters of trustworthiness of individuals and organizations were brought into question. Institutions of government, education, healthcare, and media were riddled with confusing messages and lack of clear direction. I realize the issues involved are multifaceted and complicated. Opinions abound, but how many of these are rooted in critical judgments? It's okay and necessary to have an opinion, but examining our own heart to keep it free of shaming and condemning judgment is essential for inner peace and peace with our neighbors.

Stepping Toward Reconciliation

May I encourage you to take the following steps toward deepening a commitment to reconciliation as a more common practice in your life. First, identify an area of unforgiveness or unreconciled problem you have toward another person. Next, if forgiveness is not complete, make a list of all the actions that caused offense (hurtful words spoken, mistreatments, negligence, transgressions). Be as specific as possible. Pray, confess, repent for any of your own reactive judgments, and forgive. Next, (if you believe you have surrendered your judgments to God), pray and discern strategy to address the offense with the offender. Go in a spirit of humility and empathy, recognizing the flip side of offense is in your own life as well. Keep the circle of people who know about the offense as small as is necessary to bring resolution. Do not engage in slander or gossip to make yourself become an offender. After completing the actions you believe are necessary to bring resolution, and there still is no resolution, commit to following the path of asking an advocate to go with you (as outlined in Matthew 18:15-17) if the offender is a brother or sister in Christ. Otherwise, pursue the matter with the appropriate systems of justice to bring resolution. Obviously, in cases of abuse or endangerment, the above steps should be abandoned to seek help immediately, outside the inner circle of the problem.

If you believe you've tried the steps outlined above and you still feel "stuck," it is probably time to get the help of a trusted friend or counselor. Try going back to step one and examine forgiveness. Be willing to allow God to show you a deeper level of forgiveness. God is most glorified when we allow him to lead us through this process. If there are numerous situations in your life that need to be reconciled, start with a small one, work it through to success, and don't become overwhelmed by trying too many, too soon.

One more tip is to discern whether the offender needs to be involved at all. The offense may be small enough for you to simply need to forgive. If you are 100% sure of what you are letting go, and totally certain the efforts of attempting to engage the other party would outweigh any potential benefits, let it go. Misunderstandings, errors, and accidents are just part of our broken human condition. Take the Beatles' advice and "Let It Be!"

When it must be, be a reconciler. A real friend will want to be reconciled. Be a friend, and make things friendly again.

The Great Commission to Forgive

When you hear the term "Great Commission" in the context of the Bible, what do you think of? The first four books of the New Testament are narratives written about the life of Jesus. Jesus gave his followers specific instructions about continuing his ministry when he left the earth. Christ's Great Commission is described similarly by

Matthew 28, Mark 16, and Luke 24. Most people focus on evangelizing and discipleship to categorize the activities described by the Great Commission. "Go and make disciples of all nations, ... teaching ..." (Matthew 28:19-20).

John's Gospel narrative is very different from the other three in many ways, and particularly in describing the Great Commission. John records this, "Again Jesus said, 'Peace be with you! As the Father has sent me, I am sending you.' And with that he breathed on them and said, 'Receive the Holy Spirit. If you forgive anyone's sins, their sins are forgiven; if you do not forgive them, they are not forgiven'" (John 20:21-23 NIV). His view of evangelism and discipleship takes on an inside-out perspective.

In contrast to the other three, John describes the Great Commission as a lifestyle of modeling forgiveness. Understanding and practicing forgiveness is central to the Christian faith; however, too few Christians make it a central part of their lives. Consequences of this deficiency include relational conflict, mental health problems, and lower quality of life. For many, instead of fulfilling the Great Commission of representing Christ's forgiveness to the world, they fall to what I would call the Great Omission, neglecting the role of forgiveness in their faith.

A common omission is failing to allow God to be the Lord and final Judge of people and circumstances in our lives. In becoming a Christian, the conversion experience includes recognizing the need for a Savior (Jesus) and receiving God's forgiveness into a new birth. At that point forgiveness is not finished, but it only begins. The forgiveness received from God by a believer (at conversion) is now to be given to others. The initial surrendering to God grows into an on-going relationship that involves deeper surrender and should involve greater and greater capacity to forgive and be forgiven.

When we are on the guilty side of an offense, desiring to be forgiven may come to our thoughts more quickly than when we are offended with our thoughts first turning to trying to find someone *else* to blame. Sometimes guilt is difficult to ascribe to one party or another.

Pre-judgments, misjudgments, and critical judgments make it even harder, but surrender is always an essential element of forgiveness. Surrendering *your* right to judge doesn't mean you are surrendering your rights for justice to be served. God is a perfect Judge, executing perfect justice and perfect mercy simultaneously. When you surrender to God the final rights of judgment, it puts your heart in a condition to focus on a hopeful future instead of a hopeless past. For both the offender and the one offended, a journey of redemption is possible.

Ministry of Reconciliation

In many cases, forgiveness sets the stage for reconciliation. The New Testament Apostle Paul describes the Christian life as a "ministry of reconciliation." He says, "And he [Jesus] died for all, that those who live should no longer live for themselves but for him who died for them and was raised again. ... Therefore, if anyone is in Christ, the new creation has come: The old has gone, the new is here! All this is from God, who reconciled us to himself through Christ and gave us the ministry of reconciliation: that God was reconciling the world to himself in Christ, not counting people's sins against them. And he has committed to us the message of reconciliation. We are therefore Christ's ambassadors ..." (2 Corinthians 5:15-20 NIV).

> God is a perfect Judge, executing perfect justice and perfect mercy.

First, let me comment on the phrase "the old is gone, the new is here." Some interpret this to mean Jesus has accomplished forgiveness of sins, and therefore the practice of forgiveness is no longer necessary (after we make a decision to believe). Yes, Jesus has completed the work of forgiveness by dying on the Cross and being resurrected to dwell with the Father. No, it does not mean our part is done. Surrendering our hearts to Jesus at a conversion experience is only the beginning of the journey in forgiveness and transformation. Jesus uses the illustration of occupying a house to show how our life with him progresses. In buying a house we receive the legal title and deed, but we still may have to paint, hang curtains, move furniture, and make it a home. Even after habitation, some rooms may need work and remain "projects" for some time. So too, in our hearts, our understanding and practice of forgiveness must continue on a path of cooperation with God to make our being a more inhabitable dwelling for his presence, and useful tool in his hand for the ministry of reconciliation.

A second thing to note is that "he has committed to us the message of reconciliation." Both being reconciled to God through Jesus and being reconciled to one another as human beings reinforces John's perspective of the Great Commission. If Christ-followers aren't modeling forgiveness and reconciliation, who will? The symbol of the cross gives us a picture of the vertical and horizontal connection of relationships. As we receive God's forgiveness to restore our relationship with him (vertically reconciled), he empowers us to forgive and reconcile with fellow human beings (horizontal reconciliation), and help some find their own relationship with God restored and freed to help others as well. This is the eternal purpose and perspective for our lifespan on earth.

Guilt and Shame

Guilt for sin has traditionally been recognized as the main thing standing in the way of this reconciliation. I have recently come to view shame as an even greater hindrance. Guilt and shame are two different problems. While guilt links a person to their behavior, shame attacks the person for who they are. Guilt focuses on the "doing," while shame focuses on the "being." Guilt says, "I did a bad thing." Shame says, "I am bad." Guilty actions can be amended with restitution, but pronouncing shame condemns irreparably. Whether true guilt is present or not, shaming the *self* results in self-condemnation, self-bitterness, and self-rejection. Shame creates condemning judgments, magnifies feelings of low self-worth, and separates our heart and mind from God as the master Designer of our being and the loving Father relationship he desires for us.

God never shames his sons and daughters. When you feel shame it is not from God. Shame tells you that you are not worthy of receiving God's forgiveness (as an offender). When you are on the other side of forgiveness as the one offended, shame tells you the offender is not worthy of your forgiveness or God's forgiveness. This shaming often disguises itself in some form of critical judgment. When you are tempted to think of someone else as a jerk, loser, or good-for-nothing, you must surrender to God the right to judge that person or situation and repent for any wrongful attitudes and actions you may have already taken. Our bad reactions toward other people are often rooted in the shame residing in our own inner person. Reconciling our relationship with Father God must include identifying the shame we carry by allowing God to show us where it may be hidden and surrendering it into His care.

Trading Offense for Peace

God is looking for followers who will allow the Son Jesus to carry the offenses of this world for them. Our world is a broken place to live. We cannot escape offense, but we can escape the pain of offense. The distinguishing mark of a Christian in this world should be to view offense as an opportunity for God's love to pierce the power of offense, and allow his Son Jesus to redeem the offenses one by one in our lives. Forgiveness is God's idea and plan to accomplish his purpose for his people. Facing offense head-on may cause some temporary pain. Allowing yourself to feel the pain affords you an opportunity to experience God in a more meaningful and peaceful way. That can never be a bad thing. We must practice receiving God's love in greater measure so we can give his gift of love to others as part of the Great Commission. We must grow in our capacity to receive God's love and become the person he intends for us to be. His love grows in our hearts when our judgments are surrendered to him. God's pace to peace becomes ours.

It's time the Church deals with her offenses. The brokenness that offense causes is evident all around us. Why can't we admit offense for what it is? Have we adopted a "religiously correct" speech similar to "political correctness"? I like to think of what would happen if instead of using the term "church split" we would call it a "garbage heap of unresolved offenses." Much of what we call "disunity" is in reality a lack of willingness to work through offenses. Granted, there are many other real problems contributing to our proneness to offense such as unhealthy perspectives of conflict, lack of communication, and lack of trust and trustworthiness. But the greatest impact to be made on our corporate offenses is for each individual to examine his own heart in honesty and humility before God to expose and correct offense as the Great Commission mandates. This also fulfills the vision of the ancient psalmist who wrote, "Great peace have they which love thy law: and nothing shall offend them" (Psalm 119:165 KJV). We all want peace of mind and heart, but it comes with conditions. These are not overbearing, but conditions for which our loving Father stands with open arms ready to receive our participation.

When someone offends you, you must be careful not to confuse their guilt with shaming the person (or persons). Condemning judgment toward God, yourself, or other people must be recognized as a chief enemy of forgiveness and reconciliation. Think of someone you believe has judged or offended you. Are you willing to release judgment of the person(s) who has done you wrong? Whether intentionally or unintentionally on the other person's part, the grip of the pain is in your power to release. Are you willing to surrender it to God right now for his judgment? I guarantee this will be the most freeing thing you can do. I can make this guarantee because I try to practice this regularly, and I help many other people do the same. In doing so you are fulfilling the Great Commission and helping to prepare others for finding their guilt and shame surrendered to God. I encourage you to read/study Psalm 32 for a wonderful expression of how this works.

Part 4

Engage Inner Change
as a Lifestyle

*Therefore I urge you, brethren, by the mercies of God, to present
your bodies a living and holy sacrifice, acceptable to God, which
is your spiritual service of worship. And do not be conformed to this world,
but be transformed by the renewing of your mind, so that you may prove
what the will of God is, that which is good and acceptable and perfect.*
Romans 12:1-2 NASB

The declaration to "be transformed by the renewing of your mind," requires a commitment to inner change. It has been said, "Ideas have consequences; bad ideas have victims." The default mode of the world is a declining condition. Conformity to the world in our thinking leads to our destruction. Rather than victims of the world system, we can be victors through the transforming power of God. Constant renewing of thoughts, mindsets, and beliefs into conformity with God's ways of thinking and believing paces our lives to peace. Peaceful hearts guide us into peaceful actions.

Chapter 12

Remove Blockages to Peace

The first step in treating a broken part of our physical body is cleaning out any dirt in the wound and setting things in order to prepare for the healing to take its course. So too, the first things we must look at for pacing to peace are the obstructions and factors that get in the way of our progress.

Previously we looked at how our heart governs our personhood. We discussed two distinct realms of being. Part of us is spiritual. Part of us is physical. Another part of us connects the two, and presents our identity and uniqueness as an individual. The spiritual part of us connects to God and as Christians we grow in our faith by surrendering more and more of our being to God.

If you are like me, I'm sure you struggle at times with allowing the spirit part of your being to become greater, and the physical taking a lesser role in the soul. Our soul is the intersection of the two realms, the spiritual (supernatural) and physical (natural). Our personhood is designed by our Creator for these two realms to work together to make the journey of life more complete and successful.

However, many of us spend a significant portion of our lives in "brokenness." First of all, we are all born into a broken world, so we are born broken. The spirit part of our being is made alive when we believe in Jesus. Following Jesus begins a process of change in our soul, whereby the spirit part of our being should influence the physical part in greater and greater measures. The process is given terms like transformation, sanctification, healing, and inner person change. If we are designed for relationship with God, why doesn't this process of change come easier for us? As part of this world's brokenness, there is a battle raging for every human soul. There is an enemy of our soul that uses roadblocks to keep us as far from God as possible. Let's examine some of these blocks and see how to engage them.

Four Types of Blockages

Sometimes this process of engaging inner change becomes especially difficult. I have found in my personal journey that simple is better. The simpler I can make things, the easier the journey becomes. Volumes have been written about each of the following four obstacles. Hopefully you may find some thoughts here that assist in the direction of simplifying. Quality of life is determined by how well these four barriers are navigated.

1. Sin

Sin is an ugly word. Whether you call it transgression, wrongdoing, offense, or rebellion against God, sin is the ugliest barrier that keeps us from experiencing connection to God. We are created for eternal connection, but sin formed a disconnect. God sent his one and only Son Jesus into the world so that whoever believes in him is saved from the eternal damnation (see John 3:16). For those who believe, life on earth is a constant process of change to be governed more and more each day by the Holy Spirit whom Jesus announced when his work on earth was completed. The Holy Spirit works with our personal spirit and soul to accomplish this change through repentance and forgiveness.

All sin offends God. There is no such thing as "big sin" and "little sin" in terms of how much it offends God. There may be differences in consequences, and some more obvious than not-so-obvious sin. But each one of us is born with a sin barrier.

The Bible calls the devil the "father of lies." Deception is a key factor we'll talk more about a little later. Even the most discerning people sometimes have difficulty allowing hidden heart issues to be exposed. Jesus consistently through his teaching identified the heart as the source of sin. The contents of our heart determine our actions (good or bad), and people around us see our actions and not our heart. Although our wrongful actions cause us to appear guilty, when we offend, it is God whom we offend the most (because of our resistant heart condition).

Many definitions for sin have surfaced, but a simple way to discover it is anything within our being that resists God. It's not a sin to have a bad thought. It's sin to grow (harbor, explore, expand, etc.) bad thoughts. A bad thought is any thought that condemns yourself, God, or another human being. Bad thoughts produce bad feelings and attitudes of heart, which produce bad actions. When we accept Jesus as the solution for our brokenness, we agree to allow God to break down the walls of our resistance piece by piece. He then reshapes our parts so they fit together (with the other parts of our being) as a better functioning "whole" person.

2. Legitimate Unmet Needs

In crisis situations, meeting immediate physical and emotional needs is of primary importance. However, in the day-to-day physical world, too much "stuff" can create distraction. A TV or the latest technology device is not a "need." Getting by with less stuff simplifies life. So too in our psychological and emotional world, expectations that are set too high will set us up for deeper disappointment. For example, it's okay to expect people to treat you with respect and dignity. When you feel like you are treated without respect and love, taking the hurt to the Lord and asking him to fill your need for love and respect may be the answer. Depending on the relationship, this need may indicate more work to be done in communication and acceptance. A spouse, for example, though no spouse is perfect, should be providing for needs of love and respect at the deepest level possible in a human relationship. Working things through to have legitimate needs met is very important.

3. False Beliefs

The more whole we become, the more free we are to be who we were created to be. Believing falsehood is an obstacle to freedom. Jesus declared, "If you hold to my teaching, you are really my disciples. Then you will know the truth, and the truth will set you free" (John 8:31-32 NIV). Many people quote the second sentence and conclude that knowing the truth sets a person free. Knowing truth does not necessarily mean you believe truth. In the verse quoted above, the word "then" makes it true only when the preceding condition is true. Being a disciple of Christ, as evidenced by holding to his teaching, is the Truth that sets a person free. Mentally agreeing with Christ's teaching isn't enough to overcome engrained patterns of bad thought and destructive habits.

Practicing Christ's teaching is the measuring stick for belief. Jesus simplified the Ten Commandments into two. "Jesus said, 'Love the Lord your God with all your heart and with all your soul and with all your mind.' This is the first and greatest commandment. And the second is like it: 'Love your neighbor as yourself'" (Matthew 22:37-39 NIV). Loving God with your whole being and showing it by loving yourself and other people is the core of Christ's teaching. To the degree we hold to this truth, we demonstrate that we really believe it. Love (acting in the best interest of another) is a solution to removing barriers.

The problem is that the broken world we grow up in forms our core belief system with only bits and pieces of Christ's truth, at best. Our default natural condition forms beliefs about God, ourselves, and other people which are false (and unloving). Chief of these false beliefs is that we can decide for ourselves which beliefs are true or not (good or evil), and we don't need God's help to decide. We also conclude things like "people don't like us if they don't give us what we want," and "I'm not worthy of love" if someone criticizes something I do. Most of these beliefs come from our sinful reactions to our parents (or primary caretakers), but we cannot blame them for how we behave as a result of adopting false beliefs.

Correcting our misperceptions caused by believing things not true is a bit like putting on new glasses (with new prescription lenses) for better eyesight. We may still have "blind spots" and not see perfectly. Our glasses still become dirty (creating distortions) and need regular cleaning. But the pair of lenses is the tool to be used for focusing on our surroundings. The tool we need for focusing on Truth is the Bible. It is called God's Word because it is the final word. The Bible is the recorded history of God's people living out the combination of the natural and supernatural realm (see also Hebrews 4:12). It is the lenses through which all our beliefs need to be filtered for complete vision.

4. Psychological Pain

The two distinct categories of pain I wish to mention here are: self-inflicted pain and pain inflicted by others. Self-inflicted pain means it comes from within self. Your own personal sin, unmet needs, and/or false beliefs are the primary source. The most common types of feelings of pain are rejection and shame. Sin creates guilt for behavior which can be corrected. Guilt then is a positive motivator. Shame, on the other hand, is based on a false sense of guilt and produces condemnation. Guilt says, "I did bad," whereas shame says, "I AM bad." Shame causes rejection of self and the God who created the self. Self-rejections fuels bitterness, resentment, and blame in the deepest part of your core being. Wherever condemnation is felt, shame is at its root. Shame is the ugliest of bad roots and dark spots in the soul.

The pain of shame can be very hard to identify, but this obstacle is common in every human being. Shame is impossible to resolve without finding the source where a person has rejected self. Remember, resisting God is sin. Resisting who God made you to be is resisting

God. Dissatisfaction, discontent, and rebellion against who God made you as a person is an offense against God. So, self-inflicted pain may require repentance and forgiveness to become free and return to wholeness.

Pain inflicted by others causes different kinds of issues. Examples are emotional damage caused by abuse, violence, traumatic injury, or some type of injustice for which a reason cannot be explained. Injustice is part of our broken world, but our broken soul has no way to justify it. Jesus came not only to save the world from sin, but to heal the world from the pain of the consequences of sin (see Isaiah 53:1-6 and 61:1-3). Jesus can heal the broken heart caused by injustice.

> God is not accessed through religion, but through relationship.

To remove the barrier of emotional pain, we must discern the message it is trying to send us. As we examined earlier, negative feelings and unpleasant emotions are carrying messages that clue us in to bad roots. Instead of running, denying, merely managing, or quitting, we must commit to earnestly engage. Jesus came to be our pain bearer.

In summary, God does not expect you to remove these four barriers before you can have his favor. In fact, he implores us to come to him for help on the journey. He says, "Come to me .... and I will give you rest" (see Matthew 11:28-30). His "rest" includes rest from trying to perform your own way around these barriers. So, I sometimes ask, "Why is it so hard to make/ keep things simple?" I haven't come up with a good answer, but I know the enemy of our soul wants nothing more than to have us believe the way to God is about working instead of resting.

God is not accessed through religion, but through relationship. Religion can become a barrier of its own that hinders a relationship with God. Religion can encapsulate all four of the barriers listed above.

A simple cry of the psalmist's heart is,
Search me, God, and know my heart;
 test me and know my anxious thoughts.
See if there is any offensive way in me,
 and lead me in the way everlasting. (Psalm 139:23-24 NIV)

May this be our heart's cry to God. I can speak from my experience that as I surrender more of my heart to God's searchlight, I encounter less resistance from these barriers.

Religious Barriers

Could it be possible that religion is a barrier to finding God? Can religion hinder a deeper or more meaningful relationship with God?

We all have a distorted view of God. The filters or imperfections in the way we see God sometimes creates a barrier of its own, complicating the sin, unmet legitimate needs, psychological pain, and false beliefs as barriers to a better quality of life. In some ways it may seem like "religion" is an answer to overcoming these barriers, but let me explain a little more of how religion can skew a genuine relationship with God.

Religion tends to direct more focus on the human than on the divine. Religion is about human effort. Religious practice is based on self-effort to achieve a self-imaged perception of the divine. It's about becoming good enough, strong enough, or worthy enough to please God. No matter how well we perform, however, our human limitations cause us to eventually "miss the mark." The mark is placed ever higher or further along with every skirmish or race on life's journey.

Take "good enough" as an example. Relationship of any kind is based on trust. Although many are affected by evil things in the world, and sometimes blame God for allowing them, God is not responsible for bad things that happen. God has proved himself trustworthy. Everything God thinks and does is for the good of people. Anything "bad" has nothing to do with God. Reframing our perceptions of God toward his goodness is part of trusting God more and improving relationship. God is good, all the time. Not trusting him is our problem, not his.

Somehow we think that in order for God to accept us, we must attain a certain level of goodness to qualify. Some err by giving up on God completely, and others (calling themselves religious people) try way too hard. If we try to "relate up" to God's goodness, we will fail every time because his goodness is inexhaustible. The bar will always go higher and we will get more and more frustrated with trying harder to be good. Religion does not see this deficiency, and tries to produce good rather than surrendering (yielding) to God's ways.

Jesus came to solve this dilemma and tear down barriers that keep people from relationship with God. Isaiah the prophet spoke of Jesus the Messiah's mission:

The Spirit of the Sovereign Lord is on me,
  because the LORD has anointed me
  to proclaim good news to the poor.
He has sent me to bind up the brokenhearted,
  to proclaim freedom for the captives
  and release from darkness for the prisoners (Isaiah 61:1 NIV).

Christ's earthly life, crucifixion, and resurrection restored the path to Father God (in fulfilling the Isaiah 61 prophecy).

- Our sin produces guilt that leaves our heart broken and wounded.

- Our unmet needs may leave us in needy (poor) condition.

- Our psychological pain holds us captive to inner turmoil.

- Our false beliefs filter out the light of truth, leaving us in a dark prison.

Believing in Jesus (Not Religion) is the Way through all the Barriers

Church background, family practices, and cultural norms may all factor into our filtered perceptions of who God really is. Some of our views may line up with what the Bible tells us about God's ways, and some may not. Although a Christian since boyhood, my own personal journey is sprinkled with sin, unmet needs, pain, and misbeliefs. Take misbeliefs for example. I recently encountered a different interpretation of a Bible story I had known since childhood.

The classic Bible story of David and Goliath highlights a small shepherd boy defeating a heavily armed, giant of a man taunting the armies of ancient Israel. A common interpretation is that God strengthened the underdog David to battle Goliath; God can strengthen us to defeat giants in our lives. While it is true that God strengthens his people to do great things, that is not the point of this story. In the story (see 1 Samuel 17), David is to be interpreted as a type of the Messiah Jesus. Jesus came as the Savior. Jesus has conquered the giants. Jesus defeated the enemy of our soul and all evil. Now we (as representative of the armies of Israel in the story) battle from a position of the final outcome having been determined. But fight we must. And the cleanup of conquered territory must continue. I recently discovered this insight about the story by watching a sermon online called "Goliath Must Fall" by Louie Giglio.

By incorrectly inserting ourselves into the story as David, we reinforce the idea that somehow we can become good enough, strong enough, or worthy enough to conquer bad things in our lives. We can add religion into the mix and say, "God wants me to conquer _____" (fill in the blank with your personal struggle). But the truth is, by surrendering to Jesus as our Savior/ Messiah, our relationship with God and access to his power is restored. Our giants are not conquered by our own efforts (religion), but through the relationship Jesus made possible.

The largest giants in our personal stories are not the financial struggles, relational struggles, or health concerns. The big giants are inner-person issues like anger, fear, guilt, shame, and rejection. These giants are too big. Jesus is the one who conquers giants. I've been following Jesus for about half a century now, and I still need to be reminded of that truth! I'm dependent more than ever on my relationship with God to repeal the bad and replace with the good—the sins, unmet needs, pain, and falsehood in exchange for the righteousness, abundance, peace, and truth for better living. God is the one who initiated removing the barriers and he accomplished barrier removal. Our part is not to try harder to remove barriers on our own, but to surrender to what God has done.

The Gospel of John records the details of the intimate fellowship the Son Jesus demonstrated with Father God. At the very end of John, the very last words he recorded as spoken by Jesus are "follow me." Becoming a follower of Jesus means you commit to grow your relationship with him as life moves on. Following Jesus is not just a concept, principle, prayer, going to church, remembering a stained-glass picture on a wall, or relying on a deeply spiritual experience in the past. Following Jesus is an active pursuit of discovering more of the person of God and putting your whole trust in him.

I'm not encouraging anyone to sever all ties to religious practices and traditions. My hope is for people to discern between religion and relationship with God. One more thing to point out is mankind's vulnerability to false religion. We must recognize that some people in our world hold to ideologies which pose as religion, but are more aligned with forces of evil than good. False religion can become extremely dangerous. Blaise Pascal has stated, "Men never do evil so completely and cheerfully as when they do it from a religious conviction." Without naming them here, I'm sure we can all think of examples of this in our world today. May God deal with this kind of giant as well.

My prayer is that everyone reading this will see through barriers of religion, to find the authentic relationship with God that fulfills their true purpose and destiny. My prayer too is that as you read the material in this book, the Holy Spirit will reveal truth that removes blockages and prepares your heart for the deeper life he has for each of us.

Repentance and forgiveness begin a process of transformation. Some change may be immediate, but transformation requires a longer-term commitment. The longer-term mindset is too seldom taught and practiced in the Body of Christ. Sinful behavior is the barrier most focused on. Sometimes unmet needs are addressed. But belief systems and pain relief are rarely addressed in an adequate manner. That's why I focus on these in the book.

Cognitive Distortions

False beliefs and lie-based thinking can take many forms. There are a number of deficiencies, discrepancies, disconnections, and discombobulations in our thinking processes that the field of psychology refers to as cognitive distortions. A cognitive distortion is a thought that is not based in reality.

Our thoughts are powerful things. What we choose to allow ourselves to think about determines our feelings and behaviors that influence future outcomes. Have you ever been fooled by an optical illusion? Sometimes what we "see" isn't the reality, but only a superficial representation. In a similar way that optical illusions misshape our visual perceptions, we can develop mind illusions that can misshape our mental perceptions. We can sometimes develop subconscious grooves of thinking that do not match up with reality. Our brain can fool us into concluding something that is not actually true. When untrue or twisted thoughts are repeated, they form inaccurate, unhealthy, or even dangerous pattern for precedent.

Examples:

- All-or-nothing thinking – Everything is thought of in terms of black or white extremes. It omits balanced perspectives. Thinking goes like, "I won't go to the doctor for help to treat my sickness, because all doctors are bad."

- Overgeneralizing – One negative experience or interaction is overlaid onto the entire relationship or situation. Thinking is, "John/Jane doesn't love me," when their spouse does something by accident that irritates them. Or it could involve jumping to conclusions by thinking about quitting a job after a boss corrects a small detail for improvement.

- Minimizing or magnifying – Making too light of good things and dwelling on bad things too much. This could be thinking of yourself as unworthy of a compliment someone gives you (after a job well done), or falling apart emotionally when someone says something bad about you.

- Mind reading – This is assuming something negative about a person or situation without a confirmation of truth. This might look like assuming a friend is ignoring you at a party without finding out why they are preoccupied for a legitimate reason.

- Disaster predicting – Fortune-telling of events toward the negative. This is about thinking in worst-case scenarios like concern for losing a job following an excellent review. Or it could be worrying about losing a close friend over a small disagreement.

- Catastrophizing – This is the proverbial "making a mountain out of a molehill." A small mistake becomes an insurmountable problem.

- Emotional reasoning - This amounts to feelings being allowed to rule, feelings leading over facts, or grossly confusing feelings for thoughts. This may explain how a person abandons a relationship with a friend or family member because they didn't "feel heard," or "feel understood." It may also explain abandonment of a successful job or business venture simply because it didn't "feel right."

- Consuming regrets – Dominated by would'a, could'a, should'a scenarios. Focused on stories in the past for which nothing can profit the future. This is staying stuck on past event (perhaps an accident that could have seemingly been avoided) which steals vision and hope for the future.

- Victim – Thoughts creating a *victim mindset*. This can develop into oversensitivity in feelings of impoverishment, underprivilege, or being part of an oppressed class of people. Common losses in life are turned into one of two extremes: inward to perpetual self-pity, or outward toward aggression (e.g., when an abused person becomes an abuser).

- Labeling – Stereotyping is common expression of this distortion. This is unnecessarily categorizing another person (or yourself) by singling out an unwelcomed characteristic. You then overlay your assumptions and perceptions onto interactions with other people (or yourself) to "confirm" negative traits like unintelligent, awkward, disrespectful, or unloving.

- Personalizing – This is taking things personally without an objective reason. This is when you take on too much responsibility for another person's negative reaction(s).

- Projecting – This is transferring thoughts from memories of negative experiences in the past. It may present in things like difficulties relating to a person of the opposite sex because of repeated ill-treatment by people of that sex in earlier years.

- Over-spiritualizing – This is when God is used as a rationalization for something inconsistent with the Bible or common sense of morality. It may look like "God told me __x__" being used to justify something others may find disagreeable. Yes God speaks, but people's mental processing sometimes distorts God's speech.

- Trauma-related – Irrational thinking may sometimes accompany the initial impact of a traumatic event. The initial distortion is normal, as it reflects the brain's function in trying to suddenly deal with "abnormal" circumstances. But much later, getting stuck in the grieving process of the loss in tragedy, it may become a problem. This could be unintentional unawareness of a state of denial, for example, or an intentional remaining stuck as part of a victim role.

- Defying logic – This is a sort of "catch all" for twisted thoughts not fitting in categories above. It may also be irrational thinking for the sake of being reckless or contrary and can become dangerous. This may include vindictive thoughts or thoughts meant to harm oneself or someone else.

Thinking patterns create outcomes of behavior and habits for an individual's interacting with other people. Distorted thinking may shape a person's expectations for other people to think and see their world, to match their own distortions. Instead of healthy differentiation, they seek to control. They think everyone should think with the same distortions and agree with them in the same distorted conclusions they have drawn. They impose a distortion(s) on others' minds. For example, this happens when a third party is involved, and a person distorts (misinterprets) Friend A's failure to say hello as disrespectful when they entered a room, and then gets mad at Friend B who doesn't agree that disrespect was shown by Friend A's actions (regardless of the fact that Friend A had an emergency situation to deal with).

Another example of how a person can impose distorted thinking on another person is with mind reading. This can occur when a person takes offense at a relatively small unintentional action from a friend or family member, and then expects the "offender" should have known that would hurt them. Refusing to reconcile without the perceived offense being recognized and confessed to, without the distorter thinker telling them what caused the offense, is an irrational expectation. Most conflict in relationships is caused by one or both parties' distorted thinking.

Cognitive distortion is a huge topic, again not allowing for detailed discussion here. I recently encountered two books each devoting a chapter to the topic, for reading more about cognitive distortions. One Is Frank Viola's *Hang On, Let Go: What to Do When Your Dreams Are Shattered and Life Is Falling Apart*, and the other is Debra Fileta's *Are You Really OK?*

A common thread running through most of these distortions is *overthinking*. Getting too much into the mind, and not acknowledging the heart leads to cognitive constipation. As discussed earlier, knowing "why" and knowing the *right* things is not enough. However, "distorted knowing" (believing the *wrong* things) can be even more destructive. This condition can contribute to a wall (barrier) that keeps the heart from being able to receive truth. Cognitive distortions are usually the raw material for bitterness and condemning judgments discussed earlier. They happen frequently and so automatically we rarely notice until we intentionally trace the "fruit" to the "root." The way to combat these distortions of healthy thinking is to focus on truth, which will be discussed in a later chapter.

Mental Health Concerns

I wish to address mental health concerns and the mental health system as a potential barrier. One of two extremes presents issues. On the one extreme, the word "mental health" engenders a negative stereotypical image of anything related to the topic. Images of "shrink," Freudian psychoanalysis, and electrical shock treatment creates fears of being termed "crazy" or demented in some way. For some, mental health concerns are a reality of life, and seeking help from a counselor or medical professional is an important step in their journey to wholeness. Stigma surrounding mental illness still is alive and well, but this is part of a shame-story that needs to be broken.

Then there is the opposite extreme. For many, the mental health system itself becomes a barrier to wholeness. Much of modern psychology leaves God out of the equation. Mood- altering drugs have been developed to manipulate the brain's chemistry. Pills are dispensed as "treatment" for common maladies that were not considered problems until recent decades. Americans love their pills. Americans consume mental health drugs at a much higher per capita rate than other nations of the world. Even among professing Christians, pills often trend toward leaving God out of their healing.

Besides turning to a pill before turning to God, what is wrong with this picture? In order to dispense pills, professionals use the DSM (Diagnostic & Statistical Manual) to create a label for a condition. The book categorizes symptoms to come up with a label such as major depression, bipolar, or anxiety disorder. There is little science to the labeling since the diagnosis is determined merely by symptoms disclosed by the patient. Margin of error for interpretation of behaviors to qualify as symptoms is huge.

But the real problem is the potential identity of the label taken on by the patient. I have encountered numerous clients in my counseling who have grabbed a hold on a label and allowed it to become a definition for their behavior. For example, a person labeled with depression is more prone to using depression as an excuse for not getting out of bed, or for isolating instead of keeping an appointment with a friend. When asked "why" they couldn't get out of bed, the answer is, "I'm depressed." Their identity becomes depression. It becomes a convenient way to describe behaviors for which they likely do not want to change.

Misdiagnosing or overmedicating is another problem on the part of professionals. For about ten years I worked alongside a medical doctor in a clinic where we treated mental health and addictions. A team of Christian counselors prayed and counseled people in the exam rooms (amidst the medical equipment) of the doctor's office. We discovered many patients that were labeled as bipolar had symptoms which made other conditions more acute. Bipolar is commonly misdiagnosed because the symptoms are often caused by a more significant undetected problem. Up and down swings in mood do not make a person bipolar, necessarily. Whether officially diagnosed, or self-acclaimed, the bipolar label can be very self-defeating in its grip on a person's identity.

And then there are the mental health gurus. There are some activist medical and mental health so-called experts trying to use their influence to reshape society in the wrong direction. For example, recently the *Diagnostic and Statistical Manual of Mental Disorders* (DSM-V) removed transgender as a mental problem. In my opinion, this is a slap in the face to people who are genuinely struggling with gender identity. It seems mental health professionals who support this change have abandoned their commitment to core common-sense principles of human nature and divine providence. Sometimes they seem too quick to label people for whom a label is the last thing they need. But in the case of gender confusion, a proper label may help reveal thoughts and behaviors that need transformed rather than accepting and assimilating misperceptions as normal. Not accepting the reality of biological gender is pathological (sick), and has root causes that need to be discovered, worked through, and transformed into a life-affirming direction.

I encourage the reader to beware of labels. Do not allow a label to steal the truth that is set forth in this book. Inner peace is for everyone, with or without a man-made label. A diagnosis of bipolar, major depression, anxiety disorder, or PTSD for example (even if it is a legitimate and correct diagnosis) does not disqualify someone from the heart transformation by the power of God that improves their quality of life. There is always hope. God's grace is always sufficient. God can make a way where there seems to be no other way. Sometimes professional treatment (including medication) may be part of the way, but as with everything in life, putting God first establishes the first step in a pace to peace.

Chapter 13

Garden the Soul

The Bible uses the word Garden to describe the place of fellowship with God that Adam and Eve enjoyed from their creation until their choices to turn against God's ways. The curse they brought on themselves included being driven out of the Garden and being presented with barriers so they could not return (see Genesis 3). Jesus came to earth to redeem the situation.

Redeeming the Garden

Evangelism is commonly thought of as an activity of saving souls. A conversion experience is wonderful. God reveals himself to the heart of a person and the person responds by believing in Jesus as Savior. The first hole is poked in the barrier (wall) which is keeping us out of the Garden (place to walk with God). But what's next? Jesus must become Lord (Master) of our life through a journey of discipleship. The journey involves continuous heart change as we learn to relate to Father God like Jesus did while on earth (see John 17:15-19). Not to take away from the fact that Jesus was already God to begin with, the human nature side of his being needed to grow as any human does (see also Luke 2:52).

Becoming a follower of Christ looks a little different for each person, but the more radical the transformation, the closer the walk becomes with God. Therefore, saving souls also involves "gardening" souls. God plants a seed of love in the soil of each of our hearts as a part of our humanity. A revelation of truth awakens the seed to its surroundings of the soil (conversion experience) in which the garden filled with plants (our life) can flourish and fulfill its God-given purpose for being. Being "saved" is not just the opening of the seed into a sprout, but includes the entire life of the plant until harvesting occurs.

The example of a physical garden may help with understanding. My wife and I have been growing a vegetable garden each summer for years. We usually grow things like tomatoes, peppers, turnips, radishes, onions, carrots, beans, melons, squash, lettuce, and potatoes. Each year, the growing season brings new experiences and learning for best practices. New revelations for spiritual application also abound. Although the fundamentals are always the same, conditions vary. Each season, the soil is prepared, the seed is planted, natural elements such as water and sunlight call forth the sprout, the plant matures into the type of plant imprinted by the seed, fruit (vegetable) grows according to its kind, and the gardener harvests and enjoys the "fruit" fit for harvesting.

There are numerous environmental conditions along the way that factor into the productivity of the garden. Beginning with the soil itself, providing and maintaining the correct balance of nutrients can be a challenge. For example, some plant varieties tolerate more nitrates and fertilizer elements. Some like it more sandy than clayish. The amount of water and sunlight can also affect whether some types of plants grow well or not. Then there are the weeds. Oh, the weeds! Pulling weeds is necessary all through the growth season. Some types of weeds are more annoying than others. Bugs are similar. Some bugs attack the leaves for their own food. Some attack the roots and stems of the plants. A gardener has a challenge of figuring out the best environmentally safe ways to protect the plants from destructive forces like weeds and bugs. The harvest can also be stolen by birds, deer, groundhogs, rabbits, or other animals trying to grab a quick dinner for themselves. Extreme or harsh weather conditions (e.g., wind, hail, or drought) can also disrupt plant growth and harvest.

God is the Gardener

Many spiritual parallels show God's hand at work in our lives as the garden. God as the Gardener plants the Seed of the gospel of Jesus Christ into the soil of our hearts. Jesus himself tells a "garden story" of four different types of soil receiving the seed (see Matthew 13 and Mark 4).

All through the growth season the garden must be watered, weeded, and protected against the intruders like animals, insects, storms, and thieves. All through our lives God is our Provider and Protector. God provides our spiritual food and water, and protects us from the enemy's theft to "kill, steal, and destroy" (John 10:10). He heals our afflictions (physical health), binds up our wounds (emotional health), liberates us from captive unbelief (mental health), and sets us free from the imprisoning circumstances holding back healthy growth and harvest (Isaiah 61:1).

God also determines our identity. Just as each kernel of corn produces a corn stalk with an ear of corn, God creates individuals with a unique stamp of gender, ethnicity, and personality. Corn doesn't grow on a tomato stalk, and tomatoes do not grow on a corn stalk. As each seed produces fruit of its own kind, God created diversity into the human race so that the variety adds spice to life. Sometimes a whole field is planted together for the purpose of harvesting at the same time. For example, an entire field is planted with wheat so a combine (harvester) can be used when harvest time comes. God puts his people together in families and organizations to accomplish his purposes together as one.

In order for the garden to produce a good crop, it takes a lot of effort on the part of the gardener. Sometimes sacrifices have to be made to complete the seemingly endless tasks of watering, weeding, protecting, and providing for the best garden conditions. Here is where this metaphor trips up many people. They take the work of the garden seriously and try to do all it takes to produce good fruit (behavior). Tending the garden and producing results as a "good Christian" may include behaviors like loving God, loving others, keeping the Ten Commandments, sharing the gospel, fulfilling the Great Commission, resisting evil, praying for one another, and so on.

Does God call us to do these tasks? Be careful not to answer too quickly. The answer to this question, for me, has changed over the years, and it keeps changing. I now think the answer is, maybe. A better question might be, "How does God ask us to do these tasks?" Of course there are "commands" in the Bible, but God does not require us to accomplish them in our own strength and willpower alone, as one extreme would teach us how to obey commandments. The other extreme would ignore commandments, or replace the commands with their own false interpretations.

I believe clarifying ownership will help answer these questions. We grow up in a broken world and our garden is not in the best of condition. We realize we need help (Savior) and surrender our life to God. At conversion, the ownership of the garden changes. We are no longer the gardener for our own soul. God becomes the Gardener of our soul. In business terms, we are no longer running our own business, but working for a new Master. We remain a partner to carry out some tasks, but we discern and follow the orders of the new Owner. It becomes a lifelong process of learning our new role. Our calling is now to cooperate with production, rather than to produce. We yield ourselves to the growth (gardening) process, but responsibility for the results is not on our shoulders.

Does that sound freeing? It should because that is what transformation and sanctification is all about. It is healing to our soul. It gives us peace and rest because that's what Jesus said it would do (see Matthew 11:28-29). The gospel of Jesus is a gospel of being freed (from sin and shame) and being made ever more free (from the burden of sin and shame).

Well-intentioned preachers often present the message as "Come to Jesus, and change yourself into a person of service to God." As I've come to see it, a more true message is, "Come to Jesus, and surrender yourself to a lifelong process of change from the inside out, making you more and more fit for service with God."

The first message places the emphasis on performance and self-effort and it fosters self-righteousness. The latter not only recognizes that God is the one who changes hearts, but commits to ongoing change for deeper cleansing. The former often views storms and struggles as a nuisance, hindrance, or even a sign of unbelief or sinfulness. The latter sees difficulties as opportunities for God to show himself strong (2 Corinthians 12:9-10) and develop us into lasting treasures for his glory. The former only plants in the garden, but the latter adopts gardening as a way of life.

My prayer is that each person reading this will invite God to be the Gardener of a lifelong process of soul-saving gardening. If you are struggling because you were led to believe Jesus would take care of all your problems (but the problems still linger), take hold of your heart and give it to the Master Gardener. Working through relationships (marriage, family, or cohorts), health concerns, unemployment, pandemic, and other life challenges are part of the gardening process. Jesus already accomplished all of the work of the garden. He invites you to cooperate with him in shepherding your soul into the beautiful garden you were meant to be (Isaiah 61:3).

Esteeming Jesus

To esteem is to attach worth or value to something. For followers of Jesus reading this, I have a question, "How much of your life demonstrates the value of what Jesus did for mankind?" As we grow in God's garden as committed believers in transformational living, we should be able to identify greater degrees of our lives showing esteem (value) for Jesus as the King of Kings.

Let us consider the response of his very first followers when he came to the earth. Yes, even though they had about three years hanging out with Jesus face-to-face, saw the raw miracles with their eyes, and with their own ears heard Jesus explaining the prophetic writings (from the Book), they were unable to understand and value the Kingdom of God unfolding in their midst. Near the end of Jesus' time with them Luke records, "Jesus took the Twelve aside and told them, 'We are going up to Jerusalem, and everything that is written by the prophets about the Son of Man will be fulfilled. He will be delivered over to the Gentiles. They will mock him, insult him and spit on him; they will flog him and kill him. On the third day he will rise again.' The disciples did not understand any of this. Its meaning was hidden from them, and they did not know what he was talking about" (Luke 18:31-34; NIV). They could not accept the idea of a "suffering Messiah," even when the Messiah himself told them plainly part of his reason for coming was to take on himself the sin and pain of the world. Jesus came to redeem the guilt of sin, and suffer the pain of the shameful consequences. For every person who believes in him, he restores sonship with Father God.

Jesus is referring to messages foretold hundreds of years prior like this one in Isaiah,

Who has believed our message
and to whom has the arm of the Lord been revealed?
He grew up before him like a tender shoot,
and like a root out of dry ground.
He had no beauty or majesty to attract us to him,
nothing in his appearance that we should desire him.
He was despised and rejected by mankind,
a man of suffering, and familiar with pain.
Like one from whom people hide their faces
he was despised, and we held him in low esteem.
Surely he took up our pain

and bore our suffering,
yet we considered him punished by God,
stricken by him, and afflicted.
But he was pierced for our transgressions,
he was crushed for our iniquities;
the punishment that brought us peace was on him,
and by his wounds we are healed.
We all, like sheep, have gone astray,
each of us has turned to our own way;
and the Lord has laid on him
the iniquity of us all. (Isaiah 53:1-6 NIV)

The phrase in verse 3 "and we held him in low esteem" is worth a closer look. Obviously the people who were bent on killing Jesus held him in low esteem, but the twelve disciples he was talking to in the Luke verses above also failed to esteem Jesus. Luke says, "they did not know what he was talking about" (Luke 18:34). They were not able to fully comprehend the message Jesus was sharing with them, at least in part because of the earthly mindset (belief system) of how things should turn out. They thought, for example, the Messiah (whomever that was) would be the one to deliver them from the oppression of the Roman government. The Romans were the ruling power over the Jews, and all the first believers in Jesus were of Jewish origin. For a Messiah to redeem the Jewish people, they were looking for a literal overthrow of the regime. But that was not in God's plan. God's plan was laid out in the verses of Isaiah above. Even after these verses were fulfilled and the gruesome trauma of the crucifixion of Jesus took place, the disciples still didn't understand. In the days following his resurrection, the Bible records a number of times that Jesus appeared to his disciples to encourage them and give them the Holy Spirit and their Great Commission before he ascended to the Father (see Luke 24:36-49).

When Jesus appeared to two of them on the road to Emmaus, for example (Luke 24:36-49), they were clearly not in a state to bring esteem to what Jesus had endured on their behalf. They were downcast, depressed, and likely a bit traumatized. They were likely guilt-ridden for not being able to protect Jesus from the cruel and unjust treatment he received. One of their members betrayed Jesus. In betraying Jesus, Judas also betrayed each of the disciples as team members. They were all scattered, alone, fearing for their own lives, with their leader dead (or so they thought), and no purpose to continue what had consumed the last three years of their lives. Their pain was too great to bear, and Jesus had to appear to them to bring them back from their strayed condition.

Like the first disciples who had suffered great loss and needed to be reminded that Jesus came to bear their grief and pain, we too have a similar opportunity to show that we value what Jesus did on the cross to bear our sin and pain. Jesus didn't only die to wash away the guilt of our sin, but also was tortured to bear the pain of the consequences of sin. The pain may be from an accident with no one at fault (i.e., a natural disaster, financial crisis, illness, or physical problem). It may be inflicted on you by someone else intentionally or unintentionally (i.e., prejudgment, misjudgment, mistreatment, slander, rejection, betrayal, abuse, injustice, etc.). Or pain may be self-imposed (i.e., shame, self-condemnation, self-rejection, bitterness, resentment, etc.).

"Come to me," says Jesus

Whatever the source of emotional pain may be, we (like the very first disciples onward) fail to esteem Jesus when we fail to give Jesus our pain. You may ask, "What does it mean to give Jesus our pain?" Inner hurts and wounds from past and present are common. Acknowledging hurt and offense is the first step to allowing Jesus to bear it for you. After that, it is responding to his invitation to come. He says, "Come to me, all you who are weary and burdened, and I will give you rest. Take my yoke upon you and learn from me, for I am gentle and humble in heart, and you will find rest for your souls. For my yoke is easy and my burden is light" (Matthew 11:28-30 NIV). It seems too simple to be true. Yoking up with Jesus makes all the difference. The "yoke" as mentioned here is a term for the instrument that controls a team of work horses, enabling them to work together to accomplish a task. Relief from the pain of an unrested soul, comes through surrender of control. No matter how good we think we are at controlling things, God always does better.

This surrender continues the rest of our lives, so that greater and greater degrees of control are yielded to God. As we "draw near" to God (see Hebrews 10:19-31), his power changes us in a way that goes beyond our natural abilities to change ourselves. We esteem Jesus by surrendering to this ongoing change process. Instead of "going astray" and "turning to our own way" (as described in Isaiah 53:6 above), we allow God to satisfy our deepest longings and needs. Instead of depending on "self" to determine our fate, we cooperate with God's plan and ways of doing things. Or, instead of turning to a counterfeit like alcohol, drugs, porn, workaholism, etc., we permit our hearts to be contented in gratitude for what Jesus has done to accomplish our rescue.

How much of your struggles, disappointments, failed expectations, worries, disagreements, concerns, criticisms, conflicts, etc. do you quickly take to Jesus for him to bear? The more you take to him and the quicker you respond demonstrates the degree to which you truly value (esteem) Jesus. And if right now you are struggling to value Jesus, no condemnation. Do not listen to the enemy of your soul who tells you things like "you're all alone," "no one cares," or "you're beyond hope." Perhaps you need some help from a counselor to sort out the effects of some very difficult events in your life.

Sometimes I find it a challenge to practically esteem Jesus. Relinquishing control is hard work, and it's too easy to justify a self-focused "need" to remain in charge. But may we be found faithful in esteeming Jesus. May God grant us the rest our soul craves. May we be freed to help others find their freedom in Christ Jesus. And may God be glorified and greatly esteemed!

Pain Evangelism as Discipleship

Some think that pursuing healing of the inner person and becoming a more devoted disciple selfishly puts the follower of Christ at odds with the commission to evangelize the world. I do not believe that. The loss and pain (everything from failures and disappointments to serious abuse) are experienced as a result of the broken world we live in. Loss and pain are common to both the new believer, *and* the most seasoned disciple of Christ alike.

Healing is part of Jesus' ministry of evangelism. Jesus says of himself, "For the Son of Man came to seek and to save the lost" (Luke 19:10 NIV). Jesus spoke these words in reply to religious people accusing him of hanging out with people of undesirable social status and the needy. God wants to meet people in loss and pain. Whether in small losses, moderate failures, or full-blown hopelessness and despair, hope for healing is available for the asking.

The best way to help people recover from their losses and find freedom from their pain is the way Jesus himself helped people when he walked on earth. He found people in loss and pain and offered salvation to them. We must be like Jesus, and offer Jesus as the only true Savior. Generally speaking, people who responded in greatest measure were people in the greatest need, with the most losses and most ready for change.

We must also be people who are open to admitting our own needs. If we wish to recover from loss and pain, we must stop trying to hide it, and allow it to be found by Jesus. Breaking through denial and positioning our hearts for healing involves three things discussed earlier (when the topic of loss was considered).

Consider the purpose of pain. Physical pain in the body is meant to signal a warning of disrupted functionality. And consider what governs our actions. Reaction of the physical or tangible (outer man) is determined by the nonphysical or intangible (inner man). Jesus taught us that the sinful actions we take part in have their source in our heart (see Mark 7:20-23). And consider what lies at the root of painful feelings. From our conception in the womb, our own brokenness, and the brokenness of people around us, creates critical judgments, bitterness, injustices, and wounds of soul and spirit. These are the "weeds" in the garden of our soul.

So if, 1) our bad behavior is undesirable or destructive (sinful), which is, 2) caused by a heart full of pain, which is 3) caused by un-resolved bitterness and woundedness, then doesn't it make sense to go after the "bitter root" to bring healing to the problem? This is ac-tually commanded in Hebrews 12:15, "See to it that … no bitter root grows up to cause trouble and defile" (NIV). Why is this so difficult? It is hard because it cannot be done with mere knowledge or sheer willpower. It requires surrendering to the power of God for transfor-mational healing.

Only Jesus can truly redeem the broken condition of the human heart. He has given us the gift and power of the Holy Spirit to accom-plish this in our heart.

Healing Is a Process

Healing is a process. We must embrace the process. As John and Paula Sandford (founders of the Elijah House ministry) teach in a book called *The Transformation of the Inner Man*, healing is the pro-cess of evangelizing the soul. It is evangelizing believers in unbelieving areas of their lives. Everyone is in need of some kind of healing and many times healing is painful because of the weakness of our flesh (2 Corinthians 12:9). Healing involves transformation. The Sandfords define transformation as "that process of death and rebirth whereby what was our weakness becomes our strength." Transformation is still needed after our initial conversion experience (Philippians 1:6 and Hebrews 12:1-2). As we discussed earlier, knowing our problem does not set us free, but only the Cross of Jesus (applied to our problem) can set us free. Our goal then is to discover unbelieving areas of the heart and invite God to minister to them. Hebrews 3:12 says, "See to it, brothers and sisters, that none of you has a sinful, unbelieving heart that turns away from the living God" (NIV).

Continued evangelism is necessary for discipleship, and discipleship thrives on pain evangelism. The healing we receive also makes us better evangelists. The more of Christ's salvation we receive into our own being, the more we understand and identify with others. Compassion and empathy for loss and pain are more effective tools than condemnation of people for sinful behaviors. Again, as Jesus taught, the *being* (heart) supersedes the *doing* (behaviors).

Pursuing God's help for healing your own setbacks, losses, and hurts can be one of the best ways to help others. By becoming a better person on the inside, others around you will surely be blessed.

Again, as in the earlier chapter, let me encourage you to take inventory of your heart. What might remain lost (and waiting to be found by Jesus) in your life? Is there a behavior, habit, or pattern of reaction that may indicate some degree of unrest in your soul? Is there a root of bitterness and unforgiveness you already know about, but haven't surrendered it to God for him to be the Judge? Are there ashes of loss, failures, discomfort, uneasiness, restlessness, confusion, doubt, worry, anxiety, or depression that need to be turned into beauty of pain-free circumstances?

Repentance and forgiveness is the path to a garden with fewer weeds, and the pace maker for a heart of peace.

Champions Are Made Through Change

When Olympic competition takes place, the top medalists take gold as their prize. Great effort and sacrifice precede a slot to compete. Olympians and professional athletes do not just show up at an event and expect to do well. Athletes understand the need for practice in order to change an unconditioned body into a body fit for Olympic competition.

Mental and spiritual transformation requires similar conditioning and change to live a fruitful life. Jesus told many stories that illustrate the need for conditioning our soul. At conversion we are given a new personal spirit. The need for change in our mind and heart continue through our whole life. The more we welcome and pursue this change, the closer we arrive at championship living.

In the book of Matthew chapter 22, Jesus compared our life in the Kingdom of God to a person preparing himself for a banquet feast at a wedding. It reads, "… and the wedding hall was filled with guests. But when the king came in to see the guests, he noticed a man there who was not wearing wedding clothes. He asked, 'How did you get in here without wedding clothes, friend?' The man was speechless. Then the king told the attendants, 'Tie him hand and foot, and throw him outside, into the darkness, where there will be weeping and gnashing of teeth.' For many are invited, but few are chosen." (Matthew 22:10-14). Wow! This seems like a harsh treatment for a seemingly minor offense of not dressing properly. Although additional interpretations may apply, "dressing" in (changing into) proper clothes seems to indicate the necessity of proper heart attitude toward preparation and conditioning for our life's journey.

> **The healthiest thing we can do is admit our need for further change.**

Remember, this is a parable (story) Jesus used to make a point. I believe his primary point is that he is interested in having disciples committed to a process of genuine change of heart and not just showing up for an exciting experience.

Pious people also asked of Jesus, "'Why does he eat with tax collectors and sinners [*the undesirables of the day*]?' On hearing this Jesus said to them, 'It is not the healthy who need a doctor, but the sick. I have not come to call the righteous, but sinners'" (Mark 2:16-17 NIV). Doctors are called on to diagnose health problems of sick people. Jesus uses this picture to show that he heals the "sickness" of undesirable behavior (and sin). I believe we can also infer from this that unless we consider ourselves "sick" (unprepared and unconditioned for life's finest), our hearts are not in a place to receive the completeness of the healing Jesus has for us. The healthiest thing we can do for ourselves is admit our need for further change and conditioning to live a more abundant life. This involves examining inner attitudes and motivations without falling into a trap of being overly introspective.

All throughout the teachings of Jesus, he connects the physical (tangible) condition with the psychological and spiritual (intangible) condition. "Nothing outside a man can make him 'unclean' by going into him. Rather, it is what comes out of a man that makes him 'unclean.' ... He went on: "What comes out of a man is what makes him 'unclean.' For from within, out of men's hearts, come evil thoughts, sexual immorality, theft, murder, adultery, greed, malice, deceit, lewdness, envy, slander, arrogance and folly. All these evils come from inside and make a man 'unclean'" (Mark 7:15-23). The point of this list is not as much to try to identify specific behaviors where we may fall short, but to reveal that each person has an "unclean" heart that needs to be reconditioned by a process to clean it up.

Heart Conditioning

Most people think of preparation, conditioning, and change in terms of behavior. Examples might be bad eating habits changed to good nutritious eating, negative talk changed to positive speech, or an addiction/bad habit totally wiped out. However, behavior is merely an indicator of a belief system. Bad behavior (fruit) comes from bad thoughts and beliefs (root). If you really believe using illegal drugs are wrong and bad for your health, you won't use any. It's that simple. Changing behavior requires a change of beliefs. Trying to justify smoking weed in "recreational" situations demonstrates double-mindedness, and threatens any positive steps you've made toward reconditioning your thoughts and beliefs (in overcoming a condition of constantly being stoned). For another example, if you use pornography, you really don't believe in the dignity of women (or men), nor the value of purity, fidelity, and loyalty. A change of heart is needed to realign behavior with a healthier growing value system. (Note: I am generalizing here, and please understand that trauma and serious mental health conditions may create exceptions).

Behaviors reveal beliefs, and beliefs reveal who you are on the inside. Who you are on the inside is the *real* you. The only way to change and condition yourself is to change your thoughts and core beliefs. If you claim to be a disciple of Christ, you will "dress" for the banquet with him, let him treat/heal your "sickness," and surrender your "unclean" core being to him for him to change. This is the miracle of salvation. This is the progressive work of salvation. This is essential in receiving the full impact of, and valuing, what Jesus did for us through his death and resurrection from the dead.

Change and heart conditioning is what we are called to as Christians. It won't work to show up in heaven one day unprepared. When Jesus taught us to pray that Father's will would be done "on earth as it is in heaven," could it be that he had the conditioning of our hearts in mind? Honestly ask yourself a few more questions to help you live a championship life. Am I "dressed" as a champion? Am I "dressing" (readying myself for the banquet) so my inner being is prepared for greater things? Where could my heart be more given to "cleaning" and surrendering to the progressive work of change and conditioning? Do I have a habit or pattern of behavior that needs to go? Might there be something destructive in my life that I have been excusing as a "part of my personality"? What thoughts and beliefs may be keeping me from further surrender? Do I need to ask God into my heart to show me the need for surrender?

God designed you to be a champion. Let the change begin, and continue, until your gold medal is presented in heaven! And, let the heavenly results begin now while you live out champion lifestyle here on earth!

Chapter 14

Lead with Transformational Living

This chapter discusses some transformational living themes from a perspective of leading. Leadership begins with the understanding that leading "self," especially in regard to soul care, is the greatest contribution that can be made in caring for others (those being cared for, led, influenced, pastored, managed, parented, etc.). With "servant leadership" being the best type of leadership, the best service to be given to anyone is a God-transformed inner person. A better "you" is always better for everyone you interact with. Taking the topics in this book to heart and diligently applying them is a great first step.

Understanding and practicing inner transformational living in yourself is the only way to truly understand other people. We have nothing to give another that hasn't first been given to us by God.

Every person alive is on their own transformational journcy. Everyone may be at a different place, but the dynamics are the same. In leading, it is important to recognize that the "leader" (authority figure) often becomes the direct target of peoples' untransformed "stuff." People at the beginning stages of a transformed life typically do a lot of blaming. The person "in charge" is a favorite target. Leaders can become a "scapegoat." Worse yet, if not wise to the luring, they can get drawn in and become part of the problem, instead of the one to offer solutions. A good book I found that discusses this dynamic and how to avoid it is *Sacrifice the Leader: How to Cope When Others Shift Their Burdens Onto You* by Paul Cos.

The demands placed on leaders by other people can be very stressful for the leader. The leader often tries harder to meet the perfectionistic standards others expect. In working harder, they stay busier and fail to give enough time and consideration for their inner well-being.

New Horizons

Failure to balance work with appropriate rest is one of the most common reasons people in leadership and service professions are forced to quit. It doesn't have to be that way.

In a book called *The Life God Blesses*, Gordon MacDonald tells the story of an expert sailor named Michael Plant. In 1992 he set out from the US east coast to cross the Atlantic Ocean in a sailboat with the best equipment available and the experience of having done this routine many times before. About two weeks into the voyage, his boat was found floating upside down in the sea with no signs of the man. MacDonald tells this story to point out that "we're all in the same boat" (pun intended), and that success in our life's journey is much like the metaphor of sailing.

Have you or someone you know experienced a hard-to-explain sailing accident or shipwreck? By wreck or serious accident I mean burnout, psychological breakdown (depression, anxiety, etc.), addiction, moral failure, suicide, homicide, or other criminal actions. Demands of life seem to create stressors in greater numbers and intensity than ever before in history. Professional achievement, accumulation of wealth, and outwardly happy marriage and family life do not automatically translate into a successful voyage. Hard work ethic, good friends and family, latest technology, and even strong faith are sometimes not enough to navigate the storms and trials of life. Storms happen. Disruptions occur. Only foolishness makes us think we are immune to bad things destroying our lives.

Plant's boat capsized mainly because a four-ton weight had detached from its keel. MacDonald mentions, "I discovered this much about sailboats as I read about Michael Plant's tragedy. I learned that in order for a sailboat to maintain a steady course, and in order for it not to capsize but to harness the tremendous power of the wind, *there must be more weight below the waterline than there is above it.* Any violation of this principle of weight distribution means disaster."[20] Although not visible, the boat's keel beneath the waterline is the most important part of the boat. Plant's sailboat was found upside down because of failure of its keel. Our lives get turned upside down when we fail to maintain our keel (soul) beneath the waterline (unseen inner person).

A sailboat must be properly maintained to ensure it can withstand the stormy seas. Over time joints crack, bolts rust, wind-driven structures shift, and the salty sea water requires reconditioning and replacement of parts. The only way to do the necessary repairs is to dry dock the boat. Dry docking is removing the boat from the water so the parts beneath the waterline can be accessed. Without dry docking, safety is compromised, and the boat is guaranteed to fail at some point, likely at a most inopportune moment in stormy seas.

Sailing to new horizons in our life requires occasional "dry docking." Depending on a person's circumstances and type of work this may mean vacation, debriefing, extended time off, sabbatical, personal retreat, retraining, rehabilitation, or a major reevaluation of your current path. Sometimes life above the waterline gets too busy keeping the business, church, organization, service, or ordinary roles and expectations moving along. Concern for positive image and good appearance may become a higher priority than genuine soul care. Our inner being beneath the waterline, so to speak, is overlooked. When

---

20 Gordon MacDonald, *The Life God Blesses,* (Nashville: Thomas Nelson Publishers, 1997), 4.

our reliance, rewards, and relationships are only at a surface level, we are in great danger of "cracks" developing in our soul.

Cracks expand into compromised life structures. For example, an unhealthy habit may turn into an addiction. A "difficult person" to deal with may trigger old forgotten wounds making it impossible to feel at peace. Or a stressful situation may turn into a traumatic event because it is the third major stressor in a short period of time. Cracks in our soul will eventually break us, likely in the most inopportune time, wrecking our lives, and often, many lives around us. Dry docking our activities, specifically for the purpose of inspecting the condition of our soul, is a necessary part of a leader's life.

A Proverb says, "Above all else, guard your heart, for everything you do flows from it" (Proverbs 4:23 NIV). The core of human experience is the inner being. Most of the actions people take spring from the hidden subconscious level. Relatively speaking, very few decisions are made at the conscious level. Humans are creatures of habit, always preferring the familiar over the unknown, even if the familiar is unwise, treacherous, or dangerous. Gaping cracks develop in our soul (and remain unseen beneath the waterline) because we tolerate the small cracks which make us increasingly vulnerable. Most people who have an affair, for example, don't set out to have sex with someone other than their spouse. The "play around" with flirting and one emotional attachment upon another sails them on a voyage of no return. Things like pornography, drugs, and workaholism happen the same way. Sometimes the only way to "guard your heart" (as the proverb says) is to dry dock and discover excesses (or omissions) in your behaviors.

Keel Care

The invisible keel of your personal life (whether you call it your soul, heart, core-self, inner person, spiritual center, or whatever), guides the course and quality of your entire existence. Are you giving your keel the attention it needs? Are you feeding your soul a healthy diet? Are you protecting your heart from as much harmful influence as you know how? Are you dry docking long enough to ask these kinds of questions? Are you being transparent with someone close to you for evaluation and assessment of your true condition?

You may be a great "sailor" (skillful leader or well-qualified manager), have a great sailing "crew" (staff and volunteers), and even have successfully navigated difficult "voyages" in the past (persevered through trying circumstances). The fact remains, to keep your "vessel" (personal life) seaworthy, you must make "dry dock" (rest and reevaluation) a regular and intentional part of your "sailing" (life journey) experience. Taking a respite from your primary work or service project is not a sign of poor leadership, weak resolve, or lacking in mental, emotional, and spiritual stability. Making a choice to dry dock is your only hope to develop resilience needed for the long haul.

It's even okay to admit you need help repairing your keel. There are people who specialize in repairing of cracks, realignments, and recalibration of the soul. Good counselors help people live psychologically healthy lives from a whole-person perspective.

Recently I have become aware of at least a half dozen significant leaders in our community who have wrecked their lives and many lives around them. Their offenses even include murder and other actions that have taken them to prison. Through my counseling I am indirectly connected to dozens more similar cases. Sometimes the most difficult thing to grieve in these losses is the surprise element. Many are so-called "good people" and well-intentioned, giving no indication that their deepest struggles are about to burst a bubble. Successfully sailing the seas of life takes much more than good works and strong willpower. Dry docking our sailboats must be taken more seriously. If we are going to sail far enough to see new horizons, we must first look into the hidden parts of our being for new strength and vitality.

God has done his part in providing a Savior for us to experience rebirth and spiritual renewal. It is up to us to surrender our hearts to him for his inspection and periodic dry docking for spiritual health.

Spiritual leaders are particularly prone to the perils of sailing without adequate attention on the keel. My prayer is that dry dock (down time) becomes more an accepted practice for the journey.

Sailing to Rest

There are many aspects of soul care which contribute to a healthy quality of life. Sailing a boat requires knowing how to harness the power of the wind to navigate in a particular direction. So too in life there are truths and principles that create predictable results. Good ethics, character development, life skills, and virtuous living all help for things to go well in life. Our performance-based culture rewards our focus on these kinds of activities. But a truth frequently forgotten is that good performance is predicated by how well we "perform" in our private thoughts and inner world.

As we noted, the main purpose of the keel, beneath the waterline, is to balance the boat. When the keel is weakened or broken, the ship is in severe danger of losing its balance in the slightest storm conditions, causing the ship to capsize with no chance to survive. Balancing the time a ship spends sailing on the sea with time spent in dry dock to maintain its seaworthy condition is crucial for survival. Balancing the time we spend pursuing our duties in life (as a parent, employee, leader, member, friend, etc.) with time spent temporarily putting those duties aside for rest is imperative for life to go well.

True rest is the balance that keeps your sailboat sailing. Proper rest is designed to renew and restore life. There is no way around it. Rest is the activity that keeps you active, creative, and productive. Let's briefly consider four types of rest. To help us remember these four types, let's unpack an acronym to sail (S-A-I-L). The S is Sleep. The A is Activity. The I is Inspiration and Inspection. The L is Listening intently.

1. **Sleep**. Sleep is the activity that completely shuts down our conscious mind for about one third of every day. Yes, we sleep about one third of our lives. Sleep is a huge and fascinating topic too big to ex-

plore here, but two points are worthy of mention. Although opinions may vary as to how much sleep is enough, making the decision and commitment to do what it takes to get enough sleep is the only way you will get enough sleep. You must decide your sailing vessel (body and soul) cannot sail without it. Secondly, sleep is not just for the body to rest, but also for the psyche to rest. Especially for those involved in people-helping activities on a daily basis, sleep is important to maintain psychological sharpness and stability.

2. **Activity**. In order to maximize the rest factor, consider better management of your daily activity. Make the most of the types, durations, flows, and intensities of routine tasks. Avoid extremes and practice moderation. Maybe the people you serve, or your employer, control a great deal of how your time is spent on the job, but you can limit stress by making time for sports, hobbies, music, reading, playing games with family, and other things you find relaxing. Make "play" an intention practice in three areas: physical (e.g., sports), spiritual (e.g., worship), and psychological (e.g., reading). Be aware of circumstances that sap your "emotional energy," and counter them with something that fills your "emotional tank."

3. **Inspiration and Inspection.** This type of rest is meant to "feed" the spirit part of your being. Humans are designed as spirit beings, and thus need spiritual food to nourish the personal spirit as desperately as they need physical food to nourish the physical body. A dictionary definition of inspiration is, "a divine influence directly and immediately exerted upon the mind or soul." Spiritual food may include time spent alone with God (getting to know him better), pursuing God together with other people, or anything with the goal of inspiring faith, hope, and love with divine qualities.

Inspection works hand in hand with inspiration to keep us honest about our true spiritual condition. We need self-evaluation and input from other people to stay true to our core identity and purpose in life. Our natural tendency is to try to make life work without God's help.

Even those who consider themselves God-followers have a leaning to "do life" under, over, from, or for God, as compared to living "with" God. For an explanation of how this works, see Skye Jethani's excellent book called *With: Reimagining the Way You Relate to God*.

4. **Listening intently.** The fourth type of rest, and the most engaged form of dry dock, is listening intently. Listening could be thought of as an extension of both inspiration and inspection described above. I use the term listening to emphasize an active receiving mode. It is not merely "hearing," or passive intellectual or emotional stimulation. The goal of listening is to transform (for the better) who you are as a person. It is not to evaluate performance as much as it is to uncover and strengthen your inner being. The ultimate response of listening involves surrender. The real secret to rest is complying with an exhortation that was given about 2000 years ago in Christ's words, "Come to me … " (Matthew 11:28-29).

Noise is so commonly tolerated that it's hard for some people to imagine an experience in life without it. Sheer busyness (over-scheduling) is a huge source of noise. Noise is somewhat dependent on background and culture. A New York City dweller is adapted to noise more than an Amish farmer in Lancaster, Pennsylvania. A hearing-impaired person is more likely confused by background noise when holding a conversation in a crowded room. An example of psychological noise may be your inner voice telling you lies about who you are (or are not) as a person because of past hurts or wounds. This kind of baggage noise causes excess weight to make sailing your ship even more difficult. Whether it be circumstantial, physical, or psychological noise, the more noise, the less listening is possible. Less listening means less rest. Without the dry dock of rest, your ship (life) is more likely to break down when storms rage like job loss, close relationship loss, health loss, or financial loss.

To the degree that you practice dry dock (these types of rest) you will be best prepared for the stressors of life when they come. Your ship is made ready to S-A-I-L.

In the Christian community, statistics are huge for burnout among church workers, pastors, missionaries, and leaders. A variety of things may contribute to a shipwreck incident, but one of the greatest failures is the lack of dry dock. I am committed to the value of rest in my personal life, and I want to see others become better sailors as well. Personal retreats, sabbaticals, debriefings, or extended times to focus on inner strength should be considered normal procedure in the concept (and constructs) of ministry. There are resources available to help. If you're not taking care of yourself, it's only a matter of time until you won't be taking care of anyone.

Vacation Reflections

Have you ever planned a trip for business or ministry and then said, "While I'm there, I may as well take a few extra days and visit some sites in the area?" Combining vacation time with business travel is common. But what about combining vacation time with reflection time?

What is meant by "vacation" may be different for all of us. It may mean beach, mountains, or forests. It may mean inclusion (with friends) or seclusion. It may mean outdoor or indoor activities. It may mean ocean cruise or land automobile, or so many other things. Vacation is supposed to be "down time," bringing rest, relaxation, and rejuvenation. But how many times have we returned from a "vacation" only to feel like we need a vacation from our vacation.

One solution might be a vacation for self-care. Engaging in down-time activity to give your body rest is one thing, but evaluating and discovering new ways of improving your mental, emotional, and spiritual status can take vacation to a higher level. Especially if your job or ministry is in people-helping business, the everyday wear and tear and built-up stressors can be weighing much more heavily than you, or even people in closest relationship to you, can recognize.

In 2012, I discovered a model of personal debriefing for Christian missionaries that has helped thousands find new vitality and meaning for their work. The Le Rucher model of debriefing is a guided five-day rest for personal reflection, sharing your story, and finding new perspectives from God. It is not only for missionaries, but works well to unpack stressors for any type of Christian leadership. This is a proven method of assessing events of life and ministry in a safe and supportive environment. It is a structured progression through stressors, associated losses, adjustments, and recovery of hopes and dreams. The result is fresh vision and energy for reengagement.

My wife and I benefited as participants in this model ourselves. I was so impressed with the results I've seen in participants that I trained and became a certified debriefer in the model. I began to offer the debriefing as a package with a stay at our Blue Rock Bed and Breakfast. I encourage all Christian pastors, missionaries, ministry or business leaders to consider something like this for making the most of a vacation or rest time. Taking these five days of debriefing is a perfect way to begin a several-month sabbatical or scheduled down time. Whether this model, or some other similar setting, guided retreat can be relaxing and very productive at the same time.

Rest Qualifies

The cost of neglecting self-care is much too great. We continue to hear of too many "big name" leaders falling to corruption, immorality, allegations of abuse, and even walking away from their faith. While the circumstances may be different for each individual, the qualifications for leadership are the same. First Timothy 3 is often cited as a source in the Bible for qualification of Christian leadership. Although biblical qualifications are important, we must never forget that leaders are first followers. We are all followers of Christ. A great book I read some time ago is Joseph Stowell's *Following Christ*. Becoming a transformed disciple of Christ involves putting aside our personal agendas and surrendering completely to God's plan and purposes.

So we all think we're pretty good at that stuff, right? After all, that's what makes us a good leader. That is, until an unforeseen temptation, trial, or drained human energy catches us off guard. Healthy leadership requires being proactive about psychological rest, building emotional stamina, and intentional transformational renewing of the mind.

Jesus says over and over throughout the Bible that following him means applying his teachings to our lives. Our faith in Jesus must be demonstrated with actions in keeping with his actions. Jesus also teaches that our actions spring from our heart. We are not called to merely act like Jesus, but to surrender our hearts to the heavenly Father as Jesus surrendered his heart to the Father. In my view, surrendering to God's transformation process is the most important qualification for leadership. An important question to be asking ourselves is, "Does the quality of my vacation time (down time, sabbatical, rest, relax time) truly replenish the reservoir of my heart, so that a potential storm ahead would not destroy me?"

An automatic "yes" answer would be tempting for most of us. But maybe we should give this question a bit more consideration. The beginning of a New Year is often a planning time. But any time is a good time to plan, not just a vacation, but a time of rest and rejuvenation. A healthy inner being is essential for healthy leadership, relationships, and all aspects of life.

May we give similar attention to our heart condition as King David did as expressed in Psalm 139, "Search me, God, and know my heart; test me and know my anxious thoughts. See if there is any offensive way in me, and lead me in the way everlasting" (Psalm 139:23-24 NIV). If the thought of letting God search your heart scares you, think again. Who knows you the best? Who loves you the most? Who cares the most that you fulfill your God-given purpose in life? The answers to these questions are found by reading the remainder of Psalm 139 and resting in the truth of our value in God's sight.

Jesus speaks, "Are you tired? Worn out? Burned out on religion? Come to me. Get away with me and you'll recover your life. I'll show you how to take a real rest. Walk with me and work with me—watch how I do it. Learn the unforced rhythms of grace. I won't lay anything heavy or ill-fitting on you. Keep company with me and you'll learn to live freely and lightly." (Matthew 11:28-30; Message)

Chapter 15

Choose God Daily

Coach John Wooden is credited as saying, "The true test of a man's character is what he does when no one is watching." I would add that the true test of a person's commitment to God is measured by the degree to which he or she embraces inside-out, heart-level, cleansing change on a daily basis. Sanctification is a big word, but there is no more biblical way to describe the process of being "transformed into the image" of Christ (see 2 Corinthians 3:18).

Little by little, step by step, we change "from glory to glory" (as the Bible says). One weed after another is pulled. One more dark corner of the house is brought into the light. One bad root of sin after another is left at the Cross for Christ's blood to wash away. Salvation lives on, and breathes more and more life into our earthly being.

Sanctification Stepping-stones

Earlier we touched on the topic of sanctification. It is not just a theological term, but should be the daily guide for the Christian life. Let's look a bit closer at the definition and why it makes all the difference in our quality of life.

The Webster's 1828 dictionary defines "sanctify" as the following: to cleanse, purify, set apart, separate, prepare for divine service, ordain and appoint to the work of redemption, cleanse from corruption, purify from sin, render productive of holiness or piety, make free from guilt, and secure from violation.

We may have differing perspectives on which of these meanings is most important or most relevant, but they all have one thing in common. Salvation through Jesus is the thread through all. Jesus came to complete the work of sanctification. Jesus as Savior includes Jesus as Sanctifier. Salvation of the human soul comes through sanctification. The path to deeper fellowship with God is through sanctification. Pacing to peace is through transformation and sanctification.

Each of us needs a Savior because the first man God created (Adam) turned away from God. Believing in Jesus as Savior, we activate salvation and the sanctification process. We noted earlier that theologians talk about sanctification from three angles: past, present, future. That is, "I am saved," "I am being saved," and "I will be saved." In legal terms, God has pronounced a judgment of "requirements fulfilled," "requirements being fulfilled," and "requirements yet to be fulfilled." Belief in Jesus is our initiation into a new covenant with God (see Luke 22:20, Hebrews 8). Requirements for our salvation are complete, they are in process, and they include a promise of future completion, all at the same time.

If that seems like too much to wrap your brain around, it's okay. It is for me too. But this I know. God is good, so I can trust the future to him, and I'm sure that part of sanctification will be glorious. I see that as heaven, and I'm looking forward to it. As far as the past, Jesus accomplished all that is needed, so by believing in Jesus, I am saying "yes, I'm in" to this sanctification thing. So, what remains is the middle part, or "being saved." This is the part that plays out the rest of my life on earth. The "process" part (in the present) is the part that begins with my conversion experience and continues until the day I die. Let's consider some more things about this process.

The ongoing work of sanctification in life creates a real battleground. The battle for our soul is not finished with a conversion experience.

The real battle for our soul intensifies at conversion. The battle for a completely sanctified soul is won by continually surrendering oneself over to the work of inner life change (sanctification as described in Webster's definition above).

Failing to understand this can lead to false hopes and expectations about what the "Christian life" should look like. Changing who we are on the inside is at the center of the battlefield. The struggles of life are real. The struggles are not meant to defeat us, but to sharpen our skills to become a better spiritual warrior. Many examples of this are written in the Bible for our encouragement.

A model for us is the ancient Israelites who were given a "promised land" by God upon exiting Egypt. They had to invade, conquer, and possess that land in order to enforce the "promise." Egypt represents the life of sin we are exiting when we convert to following Christ. Christ Jesus is the promised Messiah as the "promised land" for our existence. We must get past the resistance, fight the good fight, and rest in the completed work of Jesus, in order to inherit Father's promise to us of the sanctified life.

Eleven Stones

Each of the following "stepping-stones" corresponds to one of the eleven aspects of Webster's definition mentioned above. Are you living a sanctifying life? Which of these areas might God have you focus on for change?

1. **Cleansing** - (Psalm 51, Hebrews 9:11-13) To make room for the new, sometimes the old must be cleaned out. Old belief systems, thought patterns, habits, etc. may need to be cleansed for the new beliefs, commitments, and surrender to take a firmer hold. Too much electronic media, video games, movies, or activities like lying, cheating, flirting, or exposing your mind to internet sites that exploit human sexuality (porn), muddy the real thing. Cleansing of thoughts and activities are part of sanctification.

What needs cleansing in your life?

Are there particular vices (i.e., occult practices or sexual sin) from your past (or your family of origin's past) that need to be brought to the Cross for cleansing?

Are there friendships you need to let go because they are having too much negative influence in your life?

Do you give too much time or attention to TV, Facebook, alcohol, or something else?

2. **Purifying** - (Psalm 12:6, James 4:8) A precious metal like gold is valued by its degree of purification. The less impurities, the greater the value. Truth purifies. The Bible is the authoritative Word of God. That means it is the supreme source of Truth. Wisdom is gained from instruction in God's Word (Proverbs 1). We live in a world of information overload. Purifying may mean giving more attention to the real source of Truth.

Are you reading your Bible to relate to God and get to know him better?

Is the Bible worth more to you, and respected more by you, than any other book or influence?

How so?

Do the things you allow to influence your mind need stricter filters?

3. **Set apart** - (Psalm 4:3, Romans 1:1) "Fitting in" should not be our goal. Fulfilling our unique God-given purpose for being should be our goal. Comparing ourselves to other people or so-called "normal" standards, can keep us from growing in the skills, talents, relationships, and environment we need to flourish in fulfilling the call on our lives.

Are you comparing yourself to others too much?

Does it bother you that others appear more capable, more good looking, or stronger than you think you can become?

Is your concept of self based more on what you do than who your God created you to be on the inside?

4. **Separate** - (2 Corinthians 10:2-6) We are in the world, but we should not allow the world to dictate how we think and act. As we grow in being a Christ-follower, we develop an ability to discern right from wrong. Good must be separated from evil. Evil is real and it needs to be uprooted from all aspects of our life. We must be aware of enemy schemes to deceive us into believing lies. Refrain from dabbling in "questionable" practices. Stick to what can be confirmed true to Bible standards.

Do you "play around" with things you know are wrong?

Are you growing in your ability to discern (and distance yourself) from things you know are wrong?

What might you fear the most about taking a stand for truth?

Will you commit to trusting God more to overcome the fear?

5. **Prepare for divine service** - (Leviticus 20:24, 1 Corinthians 6:18-20) We are to demonstrate how much we value Jesus and the salvation he purchased for us with his own life blood. We do this by surrendering our entire being to his service (see Romans 12:1-2). Life is not about us. It is about God's Kingdom, his rule and reign as a sovereign King. We are to be at his service, and not the reverse.

What is most important in your life? Is God no. 1?

What is in the way of God being no. 1 at *all* times?

Is pleasing God more of a passion than pleasing people? Why or why not?

6. **Ordain and appoint to the work of redemption** - (2 Corinthians 5) To redeem is to purchase back or to deliver. Our sinful condition from birth made us a prisoner in slavery to the enemy. Jesus delivered our soul from this condition. Christ's deliverance gives us more freedom as we surrender more of our heart to the process. But it doesn't stop there. God makes us part of an army sent out to deliver others. God sanctifies our life so that our focus does not remain on our own welfare, but the welfare of others.

Are you able to explain to someone else what Christ's "redemption" means?

Are you growing in your understanding and practice of forgiveness and reconciliation? How?

Are you able to extend grace to close friends (in their imperfections), and can you give your trust to God for him to do his work, with his timing and methods, in their lives?

7. **Cleanse from corruption** - (Proverbs 20:10, 2 Peter 2:17-22) "People are slaves to whatever has mastered them" (2 Peter 2:19 NIV). Sometimes we need deliverance for something that has a particular stronghold on our thinking and behavior. Addiction would be an example of this. Or corrupt activity may be in our family line, producing destructive patterns. We may even need outside help to become free.

Is there a bad habit in your life you have tried to kick, but you can't get victory over it? Explain.

What desires (that lead to bad deeds) seem hardest to control?

What undesirable habits exist in your family line, and what is the impact in your life?

8. **Purify from sin** - (Mark 7:17-23) Sin is not about wrong actions as much as it is about a corrupted condition of heart. Allowing your heart to be reconditioned and purified by Jesus removes the desire to sin. Change from the inside out produces more lasting results. Turning bitterness and resentment over to God will free the heart of rage, leading to an action that may harm another person (or yourself). The Bible calls them "bitter roots" (see Hebrews 12:15). Anger is often a sign of a bitter root. Bitter roots are created by routine critical judgments we make (so common we are not even aware of them).

What is your anger trying to tell you about your heart condition?

Are you "seeing to it" that no bitter root is given space in your heart (see Hebrews 12:15)?

What part of your belief system is causing you to allow skewed perceptions, create untrue assumptions, form critical opinions, harbor bad intentions, make wrong decisions, and thus hold condemning judgments about people?

9. **Render productive of holiness or piety** - (1 Corinthians 7:1) God is holy. No man can be holy in the way God is holy. However, Christians are to represent God's holiness as best as is possible for mankind. We are to give God the "glory due his name" (Psalm 29:2). Jesus commanded us to "love the Lord your God with all your heart and with all your soul and with all your mind" (Matthew 22:37 NIV). We are to treasure nothing on this earth as more important than transformational life with God.

What does it mean for God to be holy?

Do you love him with all your being? Explain.

Is there an idol that might stand in the way of loving him more?

What steps might you need to take for God to regain first place?

10. **Make free from guilt** - (Hebrews 10:22) Repentance prepares the way for sanctification. Guilt is a good thing, and should lead us to confession and repentance (turning away from wrongdoing). Don't confuse guilt with shame. Shame condemns who you are as a person. God does not condemn people for who they are. God condemns wrong*doing* (sin). God provides forgiveness for wrong*doing*. Shame comes from condemning self (rejecting self) as not worthy of God's forgiveness. Along with any actions that offend God, we can repent for the guilt of shaming ourselves, and thus be free of shame as well! God works forgiveness and sanctification. Our good works can never take the place of that for which we must rely on God. Are there sins for which you have not repented and asked God's forgiveness?

> Come to Jesus, and surrender yourself to a lifelong process of change from the inside out.

Are you trying to "work off" (perform your way out of) a guilty conscience?

Are you feeling condemnation (shame) that is holding you back from the freedom Christ has provided you?

Are you willing to repent (turn these things over to God) and receive his forgiveness? Why not go ahead and do it right now!

11. **Secure from violation** - (Psalm 91) "Whoever dwells in the shelter of the Most High will rest in the shadow of the Almighty. ... With long life I will satisfy him and show him my salvation" (Psalm 91:1, 16 NIV). God is our salvation. Our "good works" do not save us. In fact, our attempts to get good enough for God end up driving us farther away. Going to church, practicing spiritual disciplines, and progress made (past experiences) in the areas mentioned above cannot be relied on for salvation. We must surrender (hand over) the steering wheel and let God be the Driver for our remaining journey on the sanctifying life.

Is God the place where your security lies?

To what degree are other people, places, or things in the way of God being a greater Refuge, Salvation, Sanctifying Life?

Is he your Source (is your full trust in him) for all the good change mentioned above?

Cooperative Effort

There is a verse in the Bible that people often misinterpret, and thus rely too much on self-effort for the sanctifying life. "Work out your salvation with fear and trembling" (Philippians 2:12) is to reinforce living out the previous verses with honor and respect for God. The verse before it summarizes, "every tongue acknowledge that Jesus Christ is Lord, to the glory of God the Father" (Philippians 2:11). "Work out your salvation" is not a license to trust in your own efforts to be saved, but an admonishment to cooperate with the work of God in our lives. This is explicitly stated in the next verse, "for it is God who works in you to will and to act in order to fulfill his good purpose" (Philippian 2:13 NIV). The work of sanctifying life is mainly to surrender to, and cooperate with, the work of God in this world.

Are there things in your life you want to see improved a year from now? Do you want to be a better person? Do you want to lead, speak, parent, teach, or work with more authority and influence? Unfortunately, most people aren't willing to make the changes necessary for sanctifying life, but if you are serious about this, I have a challenge for you. For each of the next eleven months, take one of the areas above and make it a focus for positive change in your life. Study the Bible on the topic. I gave some Scripture references for starters. Pray about it. Ask God to show you areas that need changed (sanctified) and allow him to show you how to make it happen. He is more than willing to meet you where you are and sanctify your life beyond your present condition. Ask yourself more questions specific to your circumstances. Let God speak specific answers to you. Take the twelfth and final month as an evaluation and planning (rest) month. Evaluate with questions like the following: Am I more comfortable with the process of change? What is the hardest part? In what areas do I see the greatest improvements? How can I help others and join with others in transformational living and sanctifying life?

Once a person starts reaping the fruit of a sanctifying life journey, a desire for more devotion to the process sets in. A satisfied hunger makes for true peace and rest in the soul. The old counterfeits to satisfaction generally have less and less appeal. Real relationship with God is much better than any fake idol. Relationships with other people are much more fruitful as well.

A Baptism of Repentance

Just the mention of the word "repent" can be offensive, but it's a very important word. Here are a few thoughts that I hope will help you see why. If you are a Christian, and you think you've already repented so you can move on to other things, be careful, since refuge and healing depend on repentance.

Isaiah 30:15 says, "In repentance and rest is your salvation, in quietness and trust is your strength" (NIV). Remember, salvation is an ongoing process, and this verse (and others) puts repentance at the heart of the process. By letting go of your own ability to control people and situations, and resting in what Christ has accomplished through his death and resurrection, your spirit quietly trusts God to give you the strength to receive the gift of salvation in Christ. This is not a once and done event. It is an ever-continuing occurrence that spawns growth in the depth of your relationship with God.

A verse struck me in a new way reading the first chapter of Mark's Gospel. John the Baptist is described here as a forerunner for Jesus preaching the message that the Savior was about to appear on earth. "John the Baptist appeared in the wilderness, preaching a baptism of repentance for the forgiveness of sins" (Mark 1:4 NIV). The word *baptism* caught my attention. Not only did John preach repentance, but he preached a baptism of repentance. A baptism of repentance speaks of an initiation, introduction, beginning, and launching into repentance. Not merely dabbling with repentance, but immersion into it, fully engulfed by it, and totally engaged. This is how Jesus is to be received (when he came to earth, or in your heart on a daily basis).

So, what is repentance? One of the Webster's 1828 dictionary definitions states, "Repentance is the relinquishment of any practice, from conviction that it has offended God." Some describe repentance as turning around to the opposite direction. Repentance is turning away from whatever takes us away from God, and turning toward the things that bring us closer to God. This is a journey of continually engaging God in worship and prayer, listening and watching for God's revelation on the path of life.

For our life in God to flourish, we must become aware of those things we do to offend him, and turn away from them. We are much like Israel, the people of God in the Old Testament. In calling Israel to repentance, Isaiah (as God's representative), demands that she forsake her thoughts and ways, because they are not his ways—which he sets over against theirs. Instead, God insists she must begin thinking his thoughts after him and walking in his ways (Isaiah 55:9). These "higher" thoughts and ways have been revealed in the Bible (Isaiah 55:10-11). Repentance is turning from one's own sinful thoughts and ways to biblical truth and holiness. Acknowledging and confessing our sins to God releases his forgiveness. "If we say that we have no sin, we are deceiving ourselves and the truth is not in us. If we confess our sins, He is faithful and righteous to forgive us our sins and to cleanse us from all unrighteousness" (1 John 1:8-9 NASB).

In the similar manner that repentance and confession are keys in reconciling oneself to God, repentance and confession are critical in reconciliation with our fellow man. Sorrow, remorse, and regret may accompany repentance, but neither can ever be equated with it. A weeping offender in the presence of an offended person does not necessarily identify true repentance. Repentance is not a feeling. A person may regret his words or actions, but not be repentant. Regret and remorse come from many causes and may be mixed with true repentance, but real repentance comes only from the honest acknowledgment of wrongdoing. Repentance is real when the offender feels more pain for the hurt he caused the offended than the inconvenience he inflicted on himself.

Until we die, we all offend and are offended against. There's no escaping offense. Therefore, repentance as a lifestyle is a matter for growth and maturity as a disciple of Christ. As John prepared the way for Christ coming to earth, a baptism of repentance prepares our way for freedom with Christ.

Holy Spirit Baptism

When I use the term "baptism of the Spirit," I realize a host of different kinds of meanings and images come to different readers' minds. The church I grew up in is a Pentecostal Assemblies of God. The seminary I graduated from is theologically in what could be called "reformed" persuasion. My wife and I have lived most of our lives in a community dominated by Anabaptists since the 1700s. Most of the church experience of my wife and I as adults has been in nondenominational settings with a "charismatic" bent. I say all that to say, my background runs a broad spectrum of theological views. I have observed that the topic of how the Holy Spirit works in a believer's life and what the work of the Holy Spirit looks like in our fellowship together is a major divisive issue in the Church at large in America. So, may I ask the reader to put all preconceived ideas on the shelf for a moment?

The Holy Spirit is a person. As Jesus finished his mission on earth and was returning to the Father in heaven he said, "'Peace be with you; as the Father has sent Me, I also send you.' And when He had said this, He breathed on them and said to them, 'Receive the Holy Spirit'" (John 20:21-22 NASB 20). This was the plan from the beginning. The Godhead, three persons in One, transferred anointing to the Holy Spirit for his work on earth through believers in Jesus. The Holy Spirit empowers us to do his work. But his work in our hearts is more than empowering—it is absolutely transformative. The work of the Holy Spirit transforms a heart of unrest into a heart of rest and peace. The Holy Spirit is a Person. The Holy Spirit is our Pacemaker. The Holy Spirit is a Peacemaker. The Holy Spirit is the Person who paces our heart to peace!

Earlier we looked at a passage in the Gospel of John as the Great Commission. The next verse after the one quoted above (John 20:23) is Jesus telling his disciples to go show the world how to receive God's forgiveness and become a forgiver themselves. We also saw earlier how Jesus came to be the Gift to accomplish the work of forgiveness in our hearts. Before Jesus left the earth, he sent the Holy Spirit to be the Gift working in our hearts. Do we realize how huge that is? The Gift of the Holy Spirit is God's very presence inside us!

In the book of Acts and in Paul's letters to the New Testament churches, the "gifts" of the Holy Spirit are discussed. The Holy Spirit works through people in a variety of ways that show his work for the advancement of God's Kingdom (see 1 Corinthians 12:4-7). In the Church today, there are many different viewpoints on the operation of these gifts. However, we must keep in mind that the Giver of the gifts should be our primary focus. The Giver of the gifts is the real Gift. The Holy Spirit is a person we can relate to. He is someone we can get to know, and be known by. As we get to know him, our hearts warm more toward him, our trust builds, and his peace expands. The Holy Spirit transforms our hearts in deeper and deeper surrender to Father's will. We relinquish our will for his, moment by moment, day by day, changing from the inside out. There is nothing more satisfying a human can experience than getting to know the Holy Spirit in this way.

This work of surrender, at the core, is a work of receiving God's forgiveness for demanding our way and sitting in the seat of Judge. Forgiveness is God's greatest gift. The gift of receiving God's forgiveness in our hearts and extending forgiveness to other people in our relationships (at the moments of offense) is every bit as valid, real, filling, baptizing, empowering, equipping, transforming, etc., as any of the manifestations (identified as "gifts") listed in the Apostle Paul's letters written to the churches in the New Testament.

A Baptism of Fire

The anointing of the Holy Spirit being placed on Christ's disciples before his ascension was foretold by John the Baptist when water baptizing Jesus. At the beginning of his ministry, John says, "The axe is already laid at the root of the trees; therefore every tree that does not bear good fruit is cut down and thrown into the fire. As for me, I baptize you with water for repentance, but He who is coming after me is mightier than I, and I am not fit to remove His sandals; He will baptize you with the Holy Spirit and fire" (Matthew 3:10-11 NASB). Reading this in context, John is speaking to religious leaders of the day whose actions were not in keeping with repentant hearts. It strikes me that the words "and fire" accompany the foretelling of the baptism in the Holy Spirit. What might this mean?

Fire is a process that changes the consistency of substances. It is used for purification (e.g., precious metals). It alters chemical structures. Fire consumes things. This reminds me of the sanctification process. The Holy Spirit comes to live inside when we believe in Jesus, and then the fire continues to purify and continues to change the substance of our being. The composition of our character is altered to reflect the image of Jesus (2 Corinthians 3:18). Thus we become Christ's "hands and feet" to carry out God's purposes on earth.

Noteworthy too in these verses is how baptism in the Holy Spirit is linked to the timing of Christ's water baptism. Baptism in the Holy Spirit is illustrated by the physical immersion of water baptism. The soaking-wet saturation of our whole being is God's way of reminding us of our need for repentance and converting our ways to his. Having participated in the event of water baptism, a believer now has a reference point to remember a transition to new life. Immersing our hearts in the Holy Spirit makes the likeness of that baptism experience real on a continual basis. With each step in sanctification, our life is made more and more new and whole. In that sense, baptism is an ongoing process as well.

Speaking of experiences, I think we must be careful not to confuse sanctification with brief encounters with the Holy Spirit's work in a moment of time. So-called charismatic believers can be especially vulnerable to confusing a single Holy Spirit encounter with lasting fruit that is born out over time. Alter prayer ministry, a deliverance session, a prophetic word, or some other deeply felt experience should not be given too much weight in determining evidence of the Holy Spirit's work in a person's life. I do not mean to devalue these experiences completely, but there must be "fruit in keeping with repentance" (Matthew 3:8).

A true commitment to following Jesus includes forsaking our old ways of trusting our own works. It's a process. As we saw in our garden illustration, "fruit" is produced by process. It doesn't just appear on a tree, without the unseen inside workings of the plant. The unseen nutrient transfer from the roots, through the plant, to the fruit, and creates the results. The outer part of the plant/tree that can be seen does not produce the fruit. Our cooperation with the Holy Spirit's work in our lives (with the nourishment he provides) is what produces the good fruit.

In the earlier house illustration, our cooperation with the Holy Spirit's work of reconstruction is what makes our house (inner being) a more inhabitable place for him to dwell. Our house also becomes a shelter and resource for others around us to fulfill the Great Commission. Jesus himself makes reference to this when he says, " But this He said in reference to the Spirit, whom those who believed in Him were to receive; for the Spirit was not yet given, because Jesus was not yet glorified" (John 7:39 NASB 20). This is a specific mention of the Holy Spirit's work in a believer's life to show the results of continuous inner-person change.

Jesus says a little later, "If you continue in My word, then you are truly disciples of Mine" (John 8:31 NASB). Here is the word "continue" again. It's a process. Jesus came to earth to be our Gift of salvation. He also came to give us a Gift in the person of the Holy Spirit. We receive the Gift by continuing to yield to his Word, and surrendering to change from the inside out. As we give more and more control to the Holy Spirit, we are empowered to be influencers, and our authority grows. Holy Spirit presence and "baptism" is our primary PACE to peace.

Chapter 16

God Is Altogether Good

Some of life's most difficult questions center around the theme of God's goodness in contrast to the apparent bad things that happen in the world. This chapter shares some of my reflections and hopefully increases the reader's sense of awe and wonderment of God. To understand how good God is, it helps to understand how suffering fits in the big picture. We will also discuss the role of suffering, but if I gave the chapter a title like "The Role of Suffering," it would probably get skipped by many. But how we view and respond to adversity makes *all* the difference in how well we pace to peace.

God Is Love

The depth of God's love is unfathomable. In Christ, God's justice and his mercy are reconciled. "Lovingkindness and truth have met together; Righteousness and peace have kissed each other" (Psalm 85:10 NASB). These two attributes of God have been reconciled. God has reconciled sinners to himself. All who truly believe in Jesus are forgiven an unpayable debt, not because we deserve it, not as a reward, but solely on the basis of what God himself has done for us.

Love is at the heart of God's redemptive story. It is God's grace that opens our minds and changes our hearts to respond to the agape love of

God. Though mankind turned his back on God in rebellion, the Bible explains how God initiated a way to return. "But God demonstrates His own love toward us, in that while we were yet sinners, Christ died for us" (Romans 5:8 NASB). God's love is not just an imaginary notion, but a personal guarantee of covenant partnership. "God is love" (1 John 4:8). When our choices are completely surrendered to God, there is absolutely nothing that can remove us from that love. "Who will separate us from the love of Christ? Will tribulation, or distress, or persecution, or famine, or nakedness, or peril, or sword? ... But in all these things we overwhelmingly conquer through Him who loved us" (Romans 8:35, 37 NASB).

The Christian life is all about change: change in behavior, in perspective, in attitude, and most importantly at the root, in affections (Colossians 3:1). Divine love contends for the soul as it battles sin and stirs the heart toward holiness. All throughout the journey of sanctification, God's conforming love brings about increasing Christlikeness in the redeemed soul. Upon conversion, the full beauty and power of divine love enters and embodies imperfect vessels wracked by the effects of sin. Love is powerful and is somewhat mysterious in how it impacts the soul. Love has the power to untwist, shape, and mold that which has been distorted and perverted, mysteriously and uniquely bringing about beauty from brokenness (Isaiah 61:3). Furthermore, love has a way of healing deep wounds and restoring life and vitality to a weary and withered soul. God's perfecting love undertakes the reformational work of reshaping the soul so that the hatred of unrighteousness and the love for righteousness increases in intensity (1 John 4:12; 1 Corinthians 13:6). This redemptive work is completed in both body and soul in the consummation of history.

So much more could be said about divine love's purpose in the human soul—creating anew and conforming the heart to God's created design. Even though the love of God works at the individual level, there is a much bigger handiwork taking place in redemptive history. The eternal motion of divine love is at work knitting together and building up a people for his own possession—the body, or bride, of Christ. Love is relational, exists only as it is shared, and does not diminish by being shared.

The love of God not only binds his children into community, but also builds up the body (Ephesians 4:16). A healthy physical body grows in stature and strength, as does the body of Christ. Every aspect of building up the body involves love. Therefore, the building up of the body is understood as the building up of love within the body for God and for one another. Love is the foundation, the building material, and the building itself. Considering that love is the supreme grace and is the ultimate end—since God is love, this communal building up of love is the culminating purpose of love.

Father Loves You

Father God is a source of hope, strength, and comfort, but sometimes it is difficult for us to open our human hearts to his love. Ancient Israel's King David and other ministers of the time wrote the book of Psalms in the Bible. Many of the 150 Psalms include a phrase something like this one, " When I was in distress, I sought the Lord ..." (Psalm 77:2 NIV). However, as often occurs in the Psalms, the psalmist goes on for several verses to express an inability and unwillingness to receive God's comfort. By the end he realizes a greater measure of God's love, but the path to this revelation was filled with darkness, distress, and disappointment. Do you think your refusal to receive God's love has made for some miserable days in your life? I know mine has.

Father God's power, might, rule and reign are also spoken of frequently in the Psalms. Throughout the Bible his standards (laws) are revealed. In relating to God, consideration must be given to our behavior and choosing actions that align with his purposes. We have looked at some of the spiritual laws earlier, and how attitudes and motivations of the heart must be examined to see how they line up. Discovering what is on God's heart and yielding our hearts to his will change the world. Love is on God's heart. Love is the chief motivation. God is love (1 John 4:16). Love is all the things described in the so-called "love chapter" of the Bible (1 Corinthians 13). Our loving Father God loves on his beloved (you and I). When God's love flows through the heart of a person, it changes lives. It causes growth in the life of the lover, and it enriches the life of the loved.

Father God's heart is bigger than you could ever imagine it to be. He has wonderful rooms (realms, places) prepared for his children to dwell (John 14:1-3). The Bible speaks of Jesus as his firstborn Son among many to follow. A disciple of Christ is welcomed into the family of God as a "son" (including both male and female gender). God's sons (and daughters) are adopted into an inheritance of provision, safety, and identity unmatched by anything a human being could discover or develop on his own. This place in Father's heart was provided for by what Jesus did through his crucifixion and resurrection. Before Jesus went through this, he described to his closest followers what was about to happen. They found it hard to believe it would happen this way, so Jesus was comforting them in their grief when he said, "Do not let your hearts be troubled. You believe in God; believe also in me. My Father's house has many rooms; if that were not so, would I have told you that I am going there to prepare a place for you? And if I go and prepare a place for you, I will come back and take you to be with me that you also may be where I am. You know the way to the place where I am going" (John 14:1-4 NIV).

The disciples were still confused about how and where Jesus was going so he clarified, "I am the way and the truth and the life. No one comes to the Father except through me. If you really know me, you will know my Father as well. From now on, you do know him and have seen him" (John 14:6-7 NIV). Jesus is the way to experience the limitless, unfailing, unconditionally accepting, matchless, amazing, wonderful, never ending ... love of Father God. Jesus, speaking of himself as the way, truth, and life, physically demonstrates God's love as directive, truthful, and life-giving. Just a short time later (from the verses quoted above), Jesus reemphasizes the path to peace in saying, "I leave the gift of peace with you—my peace. Not the kind of fragile peace given by the world, but my perfect peace. Don't yield to fear or be troubled in your hearts—instead, be courageous!" (John 14:27 TPT). Jesus reminded his disciples, and we need reminded often, that true peace is not found in anything this world has to offer. Peace is found in knowing God and being known by him.

No Need To Wait For Heaven

Father God has provided for his children the way to experience life on earth to its fullest. We don't have to wait for heaven. We can enjoy his presence now. Jesus made the way to know Father now. We can experience Father's love the way he intends for it to be experienced.

God is all about heart connection. Remember the ancient proverb, "You can lead a horse to water, but you can't make him drink." God gave us a mind to direct us to the well, but drinking water from his well involves engaging our heart to quench our thirst. Knowing about his love doesn't have the impact of knowing his love. Knowing Father's embrace changes a person's life—gives the person identity, security, and protection to confidently face any obstacle. A number of childhood experiences remind me of this. For example, as a child when my father picked me up and carried me across a stream on the hiking trail, or put his arms around me when sensing I was fearful of an intimidating pet dog or bull in the pasture, my response was relief and calm. Perhaps I could have stumbled across the creek, but wet shoes and a miserable rest of the journey was avoided by stronger legs and arms than mine. Maybe the bull would have wondered away on his own, but my father's presence created an authority hedge the bull was used to submitting to. The bull knew my dad very well. The bull had to respect my small size because my dad and I were in the pasture together. My identity was one with my father's in his presence.

Do you know Father God as your "dad"? You can. Jesus made it possible to know Father God as your personal dad. You can feel his security. You can be confident in the identity he has given you. You can rest in knowing that whatever you have in terms of resources will be enough, because he is your provider. These are the kinds of "rooms" Jesus is referring to in John 14 above. You can have places (rooms) of peace, joy, and rest when you remain securely in Father God's presence. He will carry you if you allow him to do so. He will embrace you if you let him into the deeper parts of your heart. He will stand up for you if you let him. He will chase away the bull (bullies) if you let him.

Many people have had negative experiences with their earthly father growing up. Their image of "father" is perhaps tainted or even difficult to think about. If this is you, let me encourage you that even the most well-intentioned earthly father makes mistakes and cannot live a perfect model of father. My wife and I raised four children, and although I was committed to the process of becoming the best father I could be, I realize my fathering had many weaknesses. Even for those of you who have had a "good" father (whatever that means), you must be careful not to compare Father God's love too closely with an earthly father's love or lack of love. There is a place in every human being's heart that only Father God can satisfy. No human father, mother, spouse, friend, or companion can match the love of Father God. It is also true that no human mistreatment, betrayal, or even abuse can keep you from receiving the love of Father God. Jesus is your Savior. Father is your Lover.

Do you desire to experience the love of God in a deeper way? I pray right now he takes you the next step to that place of knowing deeper love. The creative nature of God never stops making things better. These places are not just for *your* enjoyment. They are for God's entire creation. He not only wants to comfort you, but he wants to empower you to comfort others. He not only wants to love on you, but wants to empower you to love on others. Love considers the best interests of others. Let's keep the love ball rolling. Receive his love and give it away.

Remember the house illustration we discussed earlier in the book. In order for our hearts to be a place for God to dwell (Isaiah 57:15,

Ephesians 3:17), his renovations and reconstruction need to take place. In order for God's love to be welcomed in our hearts, and for us to extend his love to others, barriers may need to be removed and new structures built to facilitate this new love's activity. This often involves some degree of discomfort or pain. We are not entitled to a pain-free existence. Let's now look at some ways to view transformational challenges.

Trust Triumphs Through Trying Times

Like the constant drip of a leaky faucet is the reminder of human frailty when facing a chronic health condition, disability, or terminal illness. In situations like these, the definition of healing and wholeness seems to change as time moves on. Our perspective of God is key to removing our natural reactions of fear, and replacing them with supernatural responses of faith. Refuge and healing are more than the natural body can re-create, and are found in God, producing eternal value.

In 2019 we attended a celebration of life service for a good friend Carol Witmer. Her death followed a five-year progressive illness from a rare cancer. I am so impressed by her perspective in what she wrote before her death that I include it here.

> One morning while listening to God and praying for the healing of my body it seemed God was saying, "I have a bigger picture than simply healing your earthly body—trust me." So, I trusted God in his bewildering, puzzling, troubling but perfect plan even though I was not able to see it fully at that moment. During the past year and a half I had a deep sense that God's larger, grand, more complete plan was unfolding.
>
> The key for me was to trust! Whether I received answers to why things happened the way they did or not, I knew I needed Jesus far more than I needed understanding. I didn't understand, so I trusted!
>
> God sees and knows the bigger, more comprehensive plan for your life, too. Trust him!
>
> When I got the news that my lungs were cluttered with masses that didn't belong there, my first thought was friends that do

not have a relationship with Jesus. Is that you? My immediate silent prayer was, "Lord, let this journey with suffering that I am about to embrace lead them to you!"

I hope that my brief time on this earth inspired you to find your way back to relationship with God. Because Jesus' suffering on the cross gave me such life, it didn't seem too much if my suffering helped you find Christ!

Each of us are created to be in relationship with God, and that is what he longs for. He searches for ways to reach your soul.

Now I'm celebrating my new life with Jesus in Heaven! I'm finally seeing God, my Father, face to face! And now I am able to understand truths that, while on Earth, I could only believe in faith!

My earthly choices are now finished.
I chose Jesus, and I chose to trust.
You are still making your choices.
Choose Jesus!

Love,
Carol

Choosing Jesus in the midst of a difficult physical condition is similar to choosing Jesus with a mental or emotional struggle as well. We have a choice. We can choose to trust God and surrender to him the rights to be Judge in a situation that seems unjust, unfair, or unloving. Or we can allow ourselves to be overcome by bitterness, resentment, and hatred. Understanding does not bring complete freedom, but trusting God does. Trusting God to be big enough to make right even the greatest wrong that has been done to us, gives release to unwarranted demands for justice.

Forgiveness is God's way of making wrongs right. We have a choice to trust and cooperate with God's ways, or continue to rely on our own understanding in working things out (Proverbs 3:5-6). Even as a follower of Jesus, our choices to trust must continue beyond an initial born-again experience. Choosing Jesus is believing and trusting that he has accomplished all the forgiveness that is ever needed to take care of our offenses, and the offenses of others against us. Trusting and practicing forgiveness determines the condition of our core inner being. Refuge, healing, peace, and calm are truly known by choosing Jesus. Choose Jesus, each moment of each day.

Where Is God in Tragedy?

The answer seems simple, right? Since God doesn't change, he's the same place in the *presence* of tragedy as in the *absence* of tragedy. Although perhaps that explanation is too simplistic, it is certainly true that God is generally pinned (blamed) more quickly with the bad things that happen as compared to the good. Maybe the real question is, and it's perfectly okay to ask a question like, "How can a good God allow bad things to happen?" Since the beginning of time people have asked similar questions. However, I believe our human perspective is clouded by filters in things we sometimes forget or try to ignore. Let's look at a few important items to remember.

> Trusting God and practicing forgiveness determines the condition of our core inner being.

First and foremost is the inherent goodness of God. The nature and character of God as described throughout the Bible is holy, true, loving, kind, and faithful, and all things good beyond imagination. I talked about this briefly above. A number of great books have been written to help explain the awesome wonders of God. One that has helped me is called *Knowing God* by J.I. Packer. A.W. Tozer has some great books on this as well.

Secondly, God can be known as a personal being. He is all powerful and at the same time wholly personable. He is not just a paternal figurehead, but the most loving Father ever. His protection and provision cannot be matched by the best earthly fathers we have as our perception of "father." To get to know Father God in this most intimate of relationships is to get to know his Son Jesus first (John 14:6). We can each truly know God personally as Father by simply yielding to the truth, and way, Jesus made for us to come to him (John 3:16).

Another important thing to remember is that God's original design for the world did not include tragedy whatsoever. Humankind was designed to be sustained by what the Bible calls the "tree of life" (Genesis 3). Because humans chose to bear the burden of discerning good from evil (and rebelled against God's provision of bearing that burden on their behalf), we now have evil in the world, along with the good. "The Fall," as it is called, is responsible for the broken, hurtful, tragic, injurious, and evil circumstances of which humans are now born capable (by their own choosing, not God's choosing). Again, God does provide a way for this to be redeemed. The Christmas and Easter stories are real as they highlight the core of the gospel message of Jesus coming to earth to "seek and save that which was lost" (Luke 19:10).

God Is Our Refuge

God has made himself accessible. God does not impose himself on anyone, but is available for those who seek him. In a book called *Finding God*, author Larry Crabb writes, "You know you're finding God when you believe that God is good—no matter what happens." Psalm 46 begins, "God is our refuge and strength, an ever-present help in trouble." (NIV) From time to time in our world today, we hear of a mass shooter who causes much grief and loss for innocent bystanders. This reminds us of one who fits the description of a predator written about in Psalm 10 (which was penned several thousand years ago). Without space to unpack the treasures of Psalm 10 here, I encourage the reader to read Psalm 10 in its entirety and notice how the author ends the narrative. Good always triumphs over evil. For those who may be mourning a tragic loss at the moment, let me remind you of a transition verse in this Psalm 10, "but you, O God, *do* see trouble and grief; you consider it to take it in hand." (vs. 14) God himself grieves loss in tragedy.

One other important thing to remember is that our community is only as strong as the principle-centered behavior of its citizens.

Because of humankind's "fallen" condition, evil comes naturally for each person. Unless mores are taught and caught from one generation to the next, our "decent" society erodes, just like all great civilized peoples have crumbled in the past. We are doomed to repeat history if we do not learn from it. The godly principles upon which the United States was founded have largely been abandoned and even deemed unwelcomed. Our American society's thirst for violence, disrespect for chastity, obsession with death, and general intolerance for godly values (all promoted as "entertainment") weakens our moral resolve to conquer evil and do good. Incidents caused by violent perpetrators, at least in part, seem to exemplify an inescapable principle that "whatever is sown, will be reaped." Harboring and premeditating thoughts of destruction will end in destructive behavior. No amount of law-making and law enforcing will correct this sort of problem. As Emile Burkheim says, "When mores are sufficient, laws are unnecessary; when mores are insufficient, laws are unenforceable."

We explored very briefly a few truths to hold on to. God's nature and character defines "good." God is highly personal. God's original design for mankind did not include for him to know evil. God made himself accessible in spite of mankind's bad choices. God is still there even when we gang up against him in community. God is still available in spite of whatever other filters we erect that cloud our picture of God. Even with all this going for us, our spiritual eyes must be opened in order to believe the truth about God. Let us join our prayer with one of an early church leader. The Apostle Paul prayed for believers in the city of Ephesus, "I pray also that the eyes of your heart may be enlightened in order that you may know the hope to which he has called you, the riches of his glorious inheritance in the saints, which he exerted in Christ when he raised him from the dead and seated him at his right hand in the heavenly realms, far above all rule and authority, power and dominion, and every title that can be given, not only in the present age but also in the one to come. And God placed all things under his feet and appointed him to be head over everything for the church, which is his body, the fullness of him who fills everything in every way" (Ephesians 1:18-23). Our true hope is not in the physical (bodily) realm, but in the spiritual realm inspired by the Holy Spirit of God. Read Romans 8:18-39 to see how this works.

May I encourage the reader not to allow evil deeds, resulting from evil choices, made by people prone to evil, to rob you of experiencing the good deeds, resulting from good choices, made by an inherently good God, who empowers people to make good choices and demonstrate goodness in a broken world. Let's choose to overcome evil, rather than being overcome by it.

How Do You Handle Disappointment?

How a person responds to disappointments and failed expectations of self and other people greatly determines his or her outlook on life. Maybe we would rather allow our thoughts to focus on whatever brings us happiness or pleasure, but stopping to think about what creates unhappiness and displeasure may be exactly what we need for the problem to be solved.

Think about something in the last twenty-four hours that didn't quite go the way you would have liked. Do you think it's possible that your reaction, largely, or at least in a small way, had much to do with your initial feelings about the matter?

Disappointment is common to every human being alive. Because we live in a fallen, broken, and imperfect world, hurt feelings are inevitable. We become disappointed by peoples' mistakes, misunderstandings, mistreatments, betrayals, injustices, abuses, or even crimes. Disappointment is the entry point into a sometimes vicious cycle of complaining, blaming, justifying, and offending. Disappointment is the bait for the trap of defeat.

Disappointment piled on top of more disappointments can create stress, burnout, disorders, and even disease. Accumulated disappointments can be likened to a log jam. The logs of disappointment mount, constricting the flow of water and draining the life out of the stream.

The "king pin" of a log (disappointment) jam is *critical judgment*. When we wrongly judge others because of our skewed perspective, we needlessly carry bitterness and resentment in our heart. Jesus addresses this condition as recorded in the first book of the New Testament. Jesus uses the term hypocrite to describe someone who is quicker to point out the faulty actions of others than to correct his or her own attitudes and behaviors (see Matthew 7:1-5).

Because human nature defaults toward the familiar and resists change, finding fault with another (or critically judging) is often a diversion technique to avoid making the painful adjustments necessary to improve our character or behavior. The discomfort of restructuring our mind, will, and emotions must be overcome. As discussed in earlier chapters, our core belief systems must be examined and destructive thinking and feeling patterns must be replaced with constructive ones.

Changing Me, Changes the World

In an audio book called *Leadership From the Inside Out,* Kevin Cashman says, "Change is usually seen as something happening 'out there.'" The world changes, products change, competition changes, technology changes, people change .... All significant change begins with self-change. He continues, "Moving our concept of change for an outside-in paradigm to an inside-out paradigm has profound implications. When viewed from this perspective, we see change as an internal dynamic. An internal process of learning and development. Change is perceived as something to be mastered from within vs. something only going on 'outside.' Ultimately, people resist, adapt, or learn from it. In this regard, all change fundamentally takes place with the person."[21] If a person wishes to change the world, one must start by changing his or her "self."

---

21 Kevin Cashman, *Leadership From the Inside Out: Becoming a Leader for Life.* Narrated by Alan Sklar, Berrett-Koehler Publishers, 2017, Audiobook.

Organizational change follows the same principle of inner preceding outer change. Many leaders fail to make the connection between their own growth and transformation, and that of their organization. Transformation is not an event, but an ongoing process of knowing who we are, maintaining clear vision of who we want to create, and then going for it. Internal change precipitates marketplace change. Businesses, churches, and institutions of all types (particularly their leadership) will save themselves much time and money by recognizing this inside-out change dynamic.

So what are the steps one can implement to attain this kind of change? That's a great left-brained question, but unfortunately, step-by-step methodology doesn't work very well in this case. The three steps to unjamming the logs are as follows: 1) surrender, 2) surrender, and 3) surrender. Surrendering to God the rights to be judge uproots any bitterness jamming the flow of God's love. Changing your perspective on the people and events that created the disappointment jells the building blocks for lasting change.

Not all change is good change. Change for change's sake is not good change. Change that takes a person farther away from the ways of God is not good change. Good change is change of mind and heart that gives substance for hope. Romans 5:1-5 says, "Therefore, having been justified by faith, we have peace with God through our Lord Jesus Christ, through whom also we have obtained our introduction by faith into this grace in which we stand; and we exult in hope of the glory of God. And not only this, but we also exult in our tribulations, knowing that tribulation brings about perseverance; and perseverance, proven character; and proven character, hope; and hope does not disappoint, because the love of God has been poured out within our hearts through the Holy Spirit who was given to us." (NASB) Now that, is a formula for pacing to peace.

I believe there is a way to allow the opportunity in every difficulty to overcome the difficulty of the opportunity. Receiving the gift of God's Son Jesus to forgive our sins and shortcomings is the beginning of a process of surrender that can lead to a trust in Almighty God to embrace change (even change that involves trials and adversity) as a positive agent for victory. Even extreme disappointment and tragedy can be faced with a heart turned toward God as provider, protector, image bearer, companion, friend, comforter, caretaker, and teacher. "And His name will be called Wonderful Counselor, Mighty God, Eternal Father, Prince of Peace" (Isaiah 9:6 NASB). With all of our real needs met, what more could we ask for?

Some reading this may still be disappointed in the fact that disappointment is a normal expected part of the process. After all, doesn't following Christ mean adversity goes away? You may say, "I became a Christian to get rid of hard times." If that is your understanding of what it means to come to Christ, surrendering that expectation to God is a very good first-step entry point in beginning the change process!

Choose Love

I pray that the difficulties, hardships, adversity, setbacks, injustice, and suffering of any kind in the past or present will serve to draw you closer to God. Seeing God for who he *really* is, is at times best done by seeing him for what he is not. He is never the source of shame and condemnation. He is never the original source of suffering. God is altogether good, and his plans always are inspired by, and inspire, goodness. May you "lean into" your suffering. Read books on suffering. There is so much more I'd like to encourage you with about this topic, that maybe I'll write an entire book on it someday.

Above all, never, never, never blame God for bad things that happen. Remember, God is Judge of bad and good. Our judgments are only based on our perceptions, which are very limited and tainted. Even the worst injustices in the world will someday be made just (see Isaiah 61:2). Blaming God for the seemingly "bad" things that happen to us, and the pain they cause in our hearts, robs us of experiencing the love of God's true nature. Will we seek and embrace God's love, or allow the enemy to deceive into thinking it's not for us. I choose Love.

Especially when I'm not feeling it. I'm on a journey to find and hold on to God's love, no matter what.

Ability in Disability

The wisdom of Ecclesiastes 3:1-2 says, "There is a time for everything, and a season for every activity under the heavens; a time to be born and a time to die." (NIV) Boundaries are part of life. Every person is born with attributes which create mental and physical limitations for his or her activities. Limitations can be viewed as either negative or positive. Life hands us moments to depend on wisdom to change things that can be changed, and other moments to depend on grace to accept the things that cannot be changed. Whether self-imposed, or generated by others, each person's life story is written in great measure by how he or she responds to adverse surroundings. Here is one person's story.

On September 27, 1957, in Hanover, Pennsylvania, a healthy 8 lb. baby boy was born to teen parents. Sometime later this first-born son was diagnosed as having optic-atrophy, a severe deterioration of the optic nerve in both eyes. No explanation for the cause of this disorder was available except that it was congenital. The doctors informed the parents that the condition was not likely correctable with glasses. It would probably remain a serious limitation for life. The boy was termed legally blind and as such would need special magnification devices to read newspaper-sized print, never be eligible for a driver's license, and participation in competitive sports would be improbable. He would be considered disabled, and therefore, could become a burden to family, friends, or government.

Would it have been responsible medical practice for the doctors to try to prevent the birth of this child? By today's standards, through the use of ultrasound imaging and other medical data collection technologies, it could have been determined by the third month in his mother's womb that this baby had some sort of abnormality. If indeed that were the case, would it not be more responsible for the parents to abort this child and "try again," so to speak?

Well, I support the right to life for every human being from the moment of conception because I was that baby boy born in 1957. My blindness was most likely caused by an injury during the birth process. Whether it was the buildup of pressure from the long labor my mother experienced, or maybe the forceps used by the doctor, only God knows the cause. Regardless of whether someone can be blamed or whether an explanation can be found doesn't matter nearly as much as how I decide to respond to it. My faith and resolve are strengthened, knowing that God has ways of making good things happen out of situations in which we feel hopelessly lost. I can truly say that it is God's grace (his ability) that has overcome my inabilities.

Coping with a disability is not an easy matter. In my case I've had to work much harder to achieve the same level of success commonly enjoyed by others. Whatever I've been able to accomplish has been with less than 50% of the eyesight with which most people are equipped. I have no intentions of giving up or of being a burden on others for my livelihood. Through the prime years of my life, I lived in a single-income household with my income as the sole income. Although my wife spent a number of years teaching special education in the schools, after our first child was born, she was able to devote her time to our small children at home. I was employed as a computer programmer/analyst, having earned a Bachelor of Science degree in Computer Science from Millersville University.

First came a BA degree in German, a language which I speak fluently as a result of having studied at Marburg University in Germany my junior year. After a seventeen-year career in software development, I went back to school and earned an MA in Human Service Counseling. I was awarded the Outstanding Student in my program's class at Regent University. Academically, I missed a 4.0 GPA by an "A-" in one course with all the rest attaining an "A" grade. Prior to this a terminal degree was not even dreamed of, but in 2010 I finished a

Doctor of Religious Studies at Trinity Theological Seminary. My dissertation project was the basis for a book I published in 2011 called, *Escaping the Pain of Offense: Empowered to Forgive from the Heart.*

In 2002 we opened a bed-and-breakfast business and I now remain multi-vocational. I have been privileged to serve on various boards and committees in our community. In 2007 I became the founding President of a local affiliate of a national advocacy organization for blind and vision-impaired persons. I served with the Lancaster Abilities Coalition to promote dignity, opportunity, equality, and empowerment for persons with disabilities. Besides my education, employment, and community work, my wife and I married in 1980 and raised four wonderful, now adult, children together. Our entire family has been actively involved in church ministry over the years. I have done much to defy the societal stereotype of a blind person, but it is God to whom I give the chief credit for these accomplishments. If all this sounds exhausting, it is!

God is a Way Maker

Though severe limitations are not the fate for all of us, we all face things that remind us of our human frailty. It is our choice whether to become overwhelmed by the difficulties or energized by the opportunities. Perspective determines life experience. Napoleon Hill has said, "Strength and growth come only through continuous effort and struggle." It is my belief that in whatever circumstances we may find ourselves, God is more than willing and big enough not only to help us to overcome, but also to empower us to help those around us overcome.

Our shortcomings do not have to threaten our life's purposes from being accomplished. So whether we consider ourselves enabled or disabled, rich or poor, skilled or unskilled, part of the "in" crowd or not, a victim or victor, a divine purpose exists for each of our lives. Understanding the value the Creator places on each individual human life is essential to overcoming discouragement caused by infirmity and limitations based on bodily function. The concept of "normal" has no place when considering human value and worth. The value of an athlete's performance at the professional level is not necessarily greater than a high school athlete's. In team sports, the contribution to the team determines the value. The most gifted, well-trained athlete is not automatically the most valuable team member. I recently heard success defined as your journey of reaching your God-given potential in life. Each individual person is a member of the team of the human race.

I pray that each person reading this will find the courage to believe that meaning and purpose is forging a way to make a difference in the world. Each of us has a story being written with the details of our life. The final sentence of our story cannot be written without our final breath to be taken. It's never too late to get on track. Vision for destiny keeps us going. Both blind and deaf, Helen Keller said, "The most pathetic person in the world is someone who has sight, but has no vision."

May God grant us vision for our pace of peace!

Chapter 17

Apply Truth

In the Appendices, I include a diagram that I call the Cycle of Offense. Because we live in a broken world, all sorts of brokenness breaks hearts. The hurt we feel is often triggered by lies we believe about God, ourselves, and/or other people. Filling our minds and hearts with truth (as a preventative strategy) allows less opportunity for the lies to take hold.

In the midst of battling an offense, the truth that the Holy Spirit speaks to us can be applied to the lie to keep the freedom flowing. Thus, truth reverses this cycle, and frees us from the trap of the lies used as bait by our enemy.

Truth Transforms For Success

I attended a seminar recently where Andy Andrews was speaking. The thoughts expressed below are sparked by things he shared. Mr. Andrews has written some books you would find worth reading. One book called *The Traveler's Gift* is a motivating allegory presenting these seven principles of success:

1. The buck stops here. I am responsible for my past and my future.

2. I will seek wisdom. I will be a servant to others.

3. I am a person of action. I seize this moment. I choose now.

4. I have a decided heart. My destiny is assured.

5. Today I will choose to be happy. I am the possessor of a grateful spirit.

6. I will greet this day with a forgiving spirit. I will forgive myself.

7. I will persist without exception. I am a person of great faith.

Much of what Mr. Andrews shared centered around the theme that anything worth experiencing in life must be based on truth. There is great truth in each of these seven dynamic principles, but in order to find it, we must be transparent and completely honest with self. We all have garnered belief systems that get in the way of truth. Our ability to change inaccurate beliefs is limited because we don't know what we don't know. And what we don't know CAN hurt us!

Truth is always true whether you believe it or not.

Sometimes our application of what we believe to be true gets in the way of the real truth. For example, it is very true that diligence and hard work lead to success. However, workaholism or working to extreme without proper rest will lead to burnout and perhaps blowout. As another example, it is true that compassion and empathy are necessary in your relationships, but the truth is that any relationship without proper boundaries will lead to disappointment for one or both parties. A good question to ask ourselves sometimes is, "Am I falling short of the truth by holding on too tightly to something *partly* true?"

Another false assumption is that more knowledge makes things better. Knowledge and wisdom are quite different. Truth may be attained through knowledge, but truth can only be applied with wisdom. Wisdom exercises discernment which comes through a process of transforming the way we think and feel about things that shape our core belief systems. That explains why some people who are well-informed and educated can make serious errors of judgment. Education does not always translate into positive transformation. Remember the illustration of how a computer works (from an earlier chapter).

Success is something we all desire, but few are willing and able to submit to the process to attain it. Truth is always true whether you believe it or not. Your reality is based on your perception of truth which is shaped by your beliefs. But your beliefs never become reality unless you act on them. In that sense, you are in control of your own destiny. You can choose to be happy, to forgive, and to have faith by persisting even when success seems to have eluded you for the moment.

But it seems that many times we would rather choose an easier path than a harder path that living in the truth may demand. Here is a somewhat confounding question. If the truth sets us free from ignorance, error, and pain, why don't more of us want more truth in our lives more of the time?

If you are believing something that is not true, it may be limiting your path and faith for future success. If something you believe is obstructing the truth, do you really want to know what it is and how to get past it? Sometimes finding misbeliefs and falsehoods take you on what seems like a detour, but there are people ready to help you along the way. We all carry baggage that makes it harder to seek the truth.

Are you ready to take responsibility for clearing a path for truth to reveal itself in your life? Are you ready to apply the seven principles above to keep you moving in the right direction? Since human nature is rarely able to be honest with self, are you willing and able to truly hear what friends or colleagues may perceive in your speech and actions? I ask you these questions because they are some of the ones I use to try to keep my own journey on track. I wrestle with the challenges to be truthful with self, and I don't always win, but success is very rewarding. Give it a try. The truth is, only YOU can do what is true to the purpose for which you were created by the God who defines Truth. May truth be a blessing for your success today!

May Truth guide you in your PACE to peace!

Truth in Scripture

Over the past few years I have found the themes in this book more and more noticeable in Scripture. My reading and study of the Bible have topics of inner life change almost jumping off the pages at me. I share a few passages below as examples of familiar passages in which I have discovered new and constant life-changing messages. When we engage a life of inner change, we find God speaking ever new, though-provoking, behavior-altering responses to the Truth.

Sowing to Harvest

Until recently my reading the Parable of the Sower in Matthew 13, Mark 4, and Luke 8 left me thinking that because I had converted to Christ early in my life, I was automatically in the fourth (most fruitful) category of the four types of soils. May I encourage the reader to read Matthew 13 in the Bible before continuing. The reader may recall the four types of soil as hard, rocky, thorny, and fruitful (see Matthew 13:18-23 for the explanation of each). I have since come to understand that, in addition to a conversion experience, fruitfulness and harvest also apply to the on-going transformation and sanctification of our mind, spirit, soul, and body.

Harvesting is not merely an event, but it is process driven as well.

Our heart is the soil. The good soil produces a crop and becomes a harvest field. A fruitful harvest may be in the form of virtuous living fueled by godly character developed over time. The "fruits of the Spirit," as they are known from Galatians 5:22-23, are in this category of good fruit. But there are also three types of soil mentioned that produce nothing. One is a hard heart. A "heart of stone," as it is referred to in other parts of the Bible, is characterized by lack of teachability. When the seed (Word of God) falls on this kind of heart, unbelief, shallow beliefs, or distorted (destructive) patterns of thinking do not allow truth to take hold. A second soil type, the heart with too many rocks, does not allow the (Word of God) to take proper root. Truth cannot take hold because it has no root system to nourish the plants to life. A third soil, the thorny heart, has too many weeds that choke off the plant. Distractions, falsehoods, or mis-guided priorities overtake the truth (growing plant) so that it cannot produce and reproduce.

God is the farmer in the Parable of the Sower. God's seed always produces good fruit if it is allowed to flourish. God gives his creation choice in the matter. Our choices determine the soil content of the heart. Each day we are presented with opportunities to receive God's truth (seed) and give it the value it is due. We have the choice of allowing it to produce fruit or not. The "hard heart" choice rejects it outright. The "rocky heart" choice doesn't give it proper value to replace currently held misbeliefs and take root. The "thorny heart" choice considers it too great a cost to surrender its own perceptions of truth and yield to God's design. These choices come in the form of financial decisions, what we eat, how we spend our time, resisting vices, responding to authority, family relationships, neighbor relationships, church and other group relationships. Dr. Caroline Leaf's book, *Switch On Your Brain: The Key to Peak Happiness, Thinking, and Health,* does a great job at explaining how paying attention to your thoughts, making wise choices, and resulting behaviors (good or bad fruit) all work together.

Our heart soil becomes a field for harvesting good fruit in those areas where we allow God's truth to be our reality. God is a God of love. God gave his Son Jesus Christ to deliver us from the hard, rocky, and thorny conditions that became the reality of our broken world through sin. Surrendering to God, not just once, but as everyday practice, allows his love to become our expression and empowerment for living. In explaining the deeper meaning to his disciples, Jesus says, "But the seed on good soil stands for those with a noble and good heart, who hear the word, retain it, and by persevering produce a crop" (Luke 8:15 NIV). Jesus makes it clear that "persevering" in heart transformation is the way to restoration and healing.

We surrender our heart to God by confessing (acknowledging and verbalizing) and repenting (turning away from) the conditions identified as hard, rocky, and thorny soil. He makes our heart fertile with his love as he originally designed us to be. He changes us from the inside out so that we can share his love with others for the harvest of love to be made real in the lives of our fellow man. He is willing and able to receive with grace and mercy those parts of our heart (dark spots) not yet surrendered.

Soul Harvest

Jesus used the illustration of harvest often in his teaching. One such instance is in Matthew 9: "Then he said to his disciples, 'The harvest is plentiful but the workers are few. Ask the Lord of the harvest, therefore, to send out workers into his harvest field" (Matthew 9:37-38 NIV). Again, these verses are often interpreted by the reader to apply to conversion of souls to Christ. The context of these verses reveals the compassion of Jesus in his healing ministry. The physical healings Jesus performed were to demonstrate his power to redeem mankind from sin, thus healing their spiritually broken condition. I believe as well that these words show God's desire for the transformation and sanctification of people from the inside out. Harvest includes the on-going change of our innermost being.

In fact, as "workers" (leaders) in the harvest, an even stricter measure of attention must be given to the condition of the soil of our heart spoken of in the Parable of the Sower. A common principle of leadership is that a leader cannot take followers to places he/she hasn't gone himself. We cannot lead others into deeper transformation and healing of the inner life if we haven't experienced God's sanctification in deeper measure ourselves. That may be why Jesus says the laborers are few. It seems that very few people are willing to commit to deep transformation of the inner man.

So, what is the harvest spoken of by Jesus? The answer is getting a bigger and better picture of how much God loves you and has taken action on your behalf. Seeing and hearing him brings understanding to your heart. When Jesus taught this parable according to Matthew

13, Jesus quotes a Scripture from the prophet Isaiah, "Otherwise they might see with their eyes, hear with their ears, understand with their hearts and turn, and I would heal them" (Isaiah 6:10). Heart transformation is part of God's divine plan for release from struggles caused by our jaded perspectives. We have a choice. Do we choose to resist inner change and continue to struggle, or do we choose progressive surrender to God's ways for healing?

As for me, I want to experience more of God's love, and host maturing plants in the soil of my heart. I also want to esteem Jesus as the Lord of the harvest, and make his Name great wherever he is harvesting. Therefore, when I now read the Parable of the Sower, I ask myself questions like the following:

Where might my heart be "hard" to the truth of God?

How might I be trying to keep God on the sideline rather than allowing God's truth to take deeper root?

What might I be holding on to as a thorn choking out deeper revelation of God's truth and love?

What ugliness is a hindrance?

Do my priorities need a tune-up?

Can I look back (e.g., 1, 2, or 3 years) and see measurable growth in heart change?

Less disappointments? Less complaining? Less blaming? Less condemning judgment of self and others? Less unforgiveness? Less of whatever habit has bad fruit?

More love, joy, peace, forbearance, kindness, goodness, faithfulness, gentleness, and self-control? More habits producing these good fruits?

My prayer is that God, our Farmer, finds increasingly good soil in our hearts! May his peace find a resting place that paces us right into *our* peace.

Revelation 3:20

The last book of the Bible is called Revelation. As a Christian who has been around for a while, I've heard a verse from chapter 3 used in every evangelism training program I've studied. It reads like this, "Here I am! I stand at the door and knock. If anyone hears my voice and opens the door, I will come in and eat with that person, and they with me" (Revelation 3:20 NIV). In Bibles that use red ink, these words are printed in red, signifying that Jesus Christ himself actually speaks these words. When preachers or teachers quote this verse, they most often speak of this statement from Jesus as an invitation to the nonbeliever to take an initial step toward belief in Jesus as the Messiah who came to save all who believe and put their trust in him.

But there is so much more truth here to be grasped. This statement is a daily invitation to have an on-going personal relationship with God that transforms your life beyond initial conversion. Deeper love, greater peace, and unending happiness are not automatic for the Christ-follower. Allowing God to change our hearts from the inside out on a continual basis is the primary message of, "I stand at the door and knock." Our inner person is the door keeper. Our mind is used to hear his voice, and our heart is used to open the door. Our thoughts control what we focus on, and our will determines our actions.

In order to hear, we must learn how to listen. To hear God's voice, we must separate from distractions, and focus on listening (and not listen to other voices). Hearing the right voice can be a challenge of its own, but that isn't enough. We must "open the door." Opening the door always involves some degree of surrender. Surrendering thoughts, wishes, hopes, dreams, desires, judgments, etc., not begrudgingly, but as an exchange for the better food at the table of the Lord. The Lord will "eat with that person," who has heard his voice, and opened the door of welcome into his soul. The food is great at the Lord's table (see Psalm 23). Picture yourself eating at the table with a king in his palace. It doesn't compare to the feast of the Lord. No earthly feast can come close to what it means to eat in the presence of God. Life with God takes us beyond our natural experience.

Refining Gold

This understanding of Revelation 3:20 is made even clearer by reading several verses in context before it. "These are the words of the Amen, the faithful and true witness, the ruler of God's creation. I know your deeds, that you are neither cold nor hot. I wish you were either one or the other! So, because you are lukewarm—neither hot nor cold—I am about to spit you out of my mouth. You say, 'I am rich; I have acquired wealth and do not need a thing.' But you do not realize that you are wretched, pitiful, poor, blind and naked. I counsel you to buy from me gold refined in the fire, so you can become rich; and white clothes to wear, so you can cover your shameful nakedness; and salve to put on your eyes, so you can see. Those whom I love I rebuke and discipline. So be earnest and repent" (Revelation 3:14-19 NIV). Then Jesus invites, "Behold, I'm standing at the door, knocking. If your heart is open to hear my voice and you open the door *within*, I will come in to you and feast with you, and you will feast with me." (Revelation 3:20; TPT).

We have a stern warning here against thinking we are "rich." What is meant here is not so much in terms of rich in material resources, but the condition of mind and heart. Rich may mean a wealth of knowledge. Knowledge of the Bible, theology, and sound doctrine do not automatically equate to ability in hearing the voice of the Lord and opening one's heart to him. Hanging out with Christians or being raised in a Christian family also doesn't qualify as rich in the kingdom of heaven. Good works and community service also doesn't count. Nothing in terms of human effort with save us from our "wretched" condition. Our assurance of victory over this condition can only be based in the work of God's Son Jesus coming to earth as a man, dying on a Cross, ascending back into heaven, and leaving us with the Holy Spirit to live inside us. The Holy Spirit enables and empowers us to hear God's voice and open the door to nourishing meals of God's blessings.

God's counsel is to "buy from me gold." That is, we must "buy into" (as the saying goes) God's ways, and forsake our own. Becoming poor may mean giving up some long-held beliefs that simply aren't true. We all have blind spots to our own selfish ways. Continually surrendering our thoughts, emotions, and actions to God is a refining process that burns away the impurities and results in a life more deeply devoted to seeing God glorified in the world. Anything that keeps us from embracing this process of inner person change must be thrown into the fire. Surrender to the flames the demand to control our own fate.

Today, Jesus is saying, be honest and repent. "Look! I stand at the door and knock. If you hear my voice and open the door, I will come in, and we will share a meal together as friends." (Revelation 3:20; NLT).

The two verses following Revelation 3:20 read, "To the one who is victorious, I will give the right to sit with me on my throne, just as I was victorious and sat down with my Father on his throne. Whoever has ears, let them hear what the Spirit says to the churches" (Revelation 3:21-22 NIV). It may seem a little backwards, but surrender is actually the way to victory. And the more we surrender, the greater victory we have available.

Where might your "wealth" of knowledge, self-will, or accomplishments be keeping you from feasting more lavishly with God? Are you hearing God's voice? What might be keeping you from hearing his voice more clearly than you are right now? Have you opened the door? Are you willing to leave the door open for him and give him unlimited access? Do you want more of the King's food in your diet? My prayer is that you are able to feast and enjoy the table of the Lord in greater measure each day he has ordained for you on the earth.

Romans 8

Some of the verses in this chapter of the Bible are often quoted as favorites by many. For example, "And we know that God causes all things to work together for good to those who love God, to those who are called according to *His* purpose" (Romans 8:28 NASB 20). This is a wonderful reminder of God's sovereign provision and protection for all those whose hearts are fully committed to following God and his ways.

A closer look reveals how the Apostle Paul is advocating for the necessity of change from the inside out. This chapter is a description of how to resolve the classic struggle of the previous three chapters. It follows Paul discussing the tension of living in a sinful, earthly body with a personal spirit that has been awakened to the nature and power of God Almighty. "For I joyfully concur with the law of God in the inner man, but I see a different law in the members of my body, waging war against the law of my mind and making me a prisoner of the law of sin which is in my members. Wretched man that I am!" (Romans 7:22-24 NASB). So how do we free our imprisoned inner person from this wretched condition?

The answer is sanctification. That is, a process of allowing God's Holy Spirit to overtake our personal spirit, so that our inner being takes on the nature of how God originally designed it to be. More of God and less of me. God's will, not mine, be done. God's plans put ahead of my agenda. God's desires, ways, and outcomes sought regardless of whether it looks "good" for me or not. Trusting Romans 8:28 quoted above to be absolute truth. Embracing inner life change so I can believe the Truth without reservation. Focusing on being, ahead of doing.

Life is breathed into our spirit by God's Spirit. Believing in Jesus invites the process to begin. "But if the Spirit of Him who raised Jesus from the dead dwells in you, He who raised Christ Jesus from the dead will also give life to your mortal bodies through His Spirit who dwells in you." (Romans 8:11 NASB). A born-again experience initiates the new life. We become more and more alive to our purpose and destiny as we choose to yield more and more of our inner thoughts and feelings to God. The transformation and sanctification of our soul is necessary for increased growth and satisfaction in life. God's Holy Spirit living in our personal spirit overtakes more and more of our flesh as we grow with Christ. This is a progressive thing.

More and More

As our spirit grows, it has more control over our being and satisfies the dilemma of Romans chapter 7 (torn between doing what's right and dealing with the limitations of flesh). Romans 8 continues, "... for if you are living according to the flesh, you must die; but if by the Spirit you are putting to death the deeds of the body, you will live" (v. 13). Again, "putting" to death speaks of an ongoing process of progressive change. Our being becomes more and more alive, as the Holy Spirit takes control of us by expanding the function of our personal spirit to bring our body into submission and alignment with God. We get rid of things opposed to God, and take on new thoughts, actions, and habits pleasing to him.

Romans 8 continues, "For all who are being led by the Spirit of God, these are sons of God. For you have not received a spirit of slavery leading to fear again, but you have received a spirit of adoption as sons by which we cry out, 'Abba! Father!'" (Romans 8:14-15, NASB). Paul ties transformation and sanctification into sonship. Our identity is wrapped up in how willing we are to change from the inside out (not outside in). It's not about behavioral rules, but being "led by the Spirit" as sons is about personal relationship with Father God. We are adopted into a family relationship. We are not only legally adopted as sons, but we are also receiving (and must continue to receive) the "spirit" that goes with it. Our changing condition inside brings the peace, rest, and freedom from the fear of slavery.

Again, this all hinges on our willingness to change. Do we hold on to the familiar belief systems, patterns, habits, etc., or do we let God show us what freedom is really like?

Romans 8 continues, "The Spirit Himself testifies with our spirit that we are children of God, and if children, heirs also, heirs of God and fellow heirs with Christ, if indeed we suffer with Him so that we may also be glorified with Him." (Romans 8:16-17, NASB 20). The things that come with our freedom in Christ (our adoption, identity change, character change, sanctification, etc.) come at a price. You've probably heard it said, "Freedom is never free." The word "suffering" implies struggle. It requires giving up something (things), to gain something else. But whatever we are holding on to is really not worth much anyway. Without God we are broken, and the sooner we can admit it, the better off we'll be. There is no "quick fix" or "magic solution." It's a long-haul commitment. The good news is that Jesus Christ has done the work for us. It's not about doing the work of salvation, but cooperating with God to allow Christ's finished work to be worked out in our inner being.

Sanctification is the process of putting the pieces back together. Sanctification is how "God causes all things to work together for good to those who love God" (quoted above from Romans 8:28). Again, sanctification is the way back to the original design of our Creator. God makes our house into a wonderful dwelling. God makes our garden a productive resource.

God delivers us from the tyranny of the lies we believe. Allowing ourselves to feel, long enough to identify painful emotions hiding the lies, brings us out of denial. Confessing and repenting for the bitter root judgments releases us from the "right" the enemy has to hold us in bondage. Embracing the cleansing power of forgiveness refreshes our heart for each layer of unrest peeled off. Our lie-induced shame is traded for the truth-embraced identity. Each step of the way, Jesus is interceding (Romans 8:34), and cheering us on in our PACE to peace.

Chapter 18

PACE to Finish Line – Conclusions

The purpose of this book is to inspire the reader to take seriously the inner transformation call and journey. Hopefully you are inspired and better equipped for the journey. Transformation requires change through application of truth. Since we don't know what we don't know, we can only apply what we know. But we must apply. I encourage each reader, whether studying in a group or individually, to take the time to answer the study questions for each chapter. Progress in transformation can be measured by taking out the book again in a year and asking the questions again.

Progress is possible and guaranteed by the Lord. My journey is a testimony to God's mercy and grace in pacing to peace. By practicing the principles described in this book over the years, my wife and others have seen a radical change in my life. I am much less controlling and demanding. The fruits of the Spirit listed in Galatians 5 are more present in my thoughts and actions. Things that triggered a "tizzy fit" years ago, I now consider a stepping-stone in sanctification. It is easier for me not to see people as the problem. Instead of trying to change other people, I am much better off changing my ways of perceiving and responding. My wife, too, enjoys not being seen as the problem!

Of course, I'm still in process, and trying to surrender more and more to God's PACE for my journey.

Self-examination and setting a course for self-change is essential. Finding a community of people to help level and straighten the path is an important part of pacing as well. This usually takes the form of committing to a particular group as an expression of the Church meeting on a regular basis. But the most significant commitment to be made is deepening your relationship with the Maker of the soul. Lasting peace is only found in the presence of God. The most important activity in life is spending time with God—as Father, Son Jesus, and the Holy Spirit. Intimacy with Father, Son, and Spirit makes for an atmosphere in which his peaceful Kingdom comes to dwell in the heart.

In order to create the space for God to dwell in our heart, we must cycle through the four elements of the PACE—prepare the heart, accept our broken condition, cooperate with God in surrender, and engage inner transformation as a lifestyle. Hopefully, the reader finds some use for the tools included in the Appendices of this book as well.

Sometimes we run into blockages (see the earlier chapter). And sometimes we need help to make a breakthrough. If it seems like you are stuck somewhere, I encourage you to seek help. Seek help from someone who himself or herself understands and practices inner transformation and sanctification. Some counselors focus on merely managing symptoms rather than rooting out the problems. Painful feelings and emotions are usually part of the process, but that's okay. Jesus bore our pain for a reason. Anyone who tries to tell you that healing and character growth is painless is likely not qualified to help others. Avoid reducing transformation to "seven easy steps" or "four guaranteed principles." These are vain promises. Methodology is NOT the way to wholeness and lasting results. A counselor, who himself has a changed inner life through the power of the Holy Spirit, is the best choice for help.

I encourage the reader to take the next steps in your journey to inner life change. Write the next chapter. Apply the Truth you receive in your intimate times with God and secure your pace to peace.

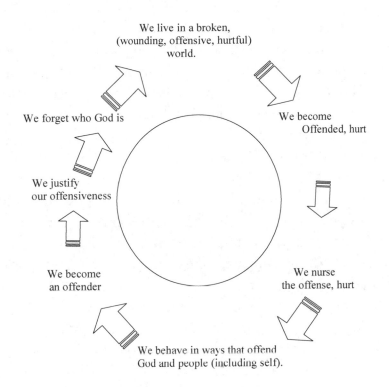

We live in a broken,
(wounding, offensive, hurtful)
world.

We forget who God is

We become
Offended, hurt

We justify
our offensiveness

We become
an offender

We nurse
the offense, hurt

We behave in ways that offend
God and people (including self).

We grumble and complain and wander in wilderness journey (Heb 3:7-18)
We behave in ways that offend God and people (including self); (1 Cor 10:1-13).
Misbeliefs & Expectations become Disappointment, Judgments, Discouragement, Confusion,
Depression, Loss of Vision, Disorientation, Withdrawal, Despair, Defeat

Appendix A

The Cycle of Defeat

Offense is at the core of the bitter root judgments that create most of our relationship problems. The diagram below is to illustrate how they form and become a trap of defeat unless we rely on God to break free.

This cycle is common to every human being alive. Because we live in a fallen, broken, and imperfect world, experiencing hurtful emotions is inevitable. We become disappointed (offended) by people's mistakes, misunderstandings, mistreatments, betrayals, injustices, abuses, or even crimes. We make critical judgments (nurse and amplify the offense) by rehearsing in our minds what coulda', woulda', shoulda' been done to avoid the pain. Many times our anger becomes directed at God for allowing bad things to happen to us. Some blame self, and become imprisoned by self-rejection.

We believe lies instead of God's truth and behave in ways that offend God, ourselves, and other people. Thus, we become an offender. Bitterness, resentment, and blame become an accepted way of life. Without God's help we try to rectify situations in many ways, including minimizing, revenge, obsessing for justice, forgetting, excusing, "moving on," self-inflicting condemnation, or finding some other way of replacing the negative feelings with positive ones. In our quest of human effort we may even find some relief and so we justify our offense. Unable to trust, surrender to God the sole right to judge the one(s) who disappointed us, we reject God's provision through Jesus to break the cycle. Having agreed with the lie that holding offense solves our problem, we become offensive to someone else who becomes offended, and the cycle spirals hopelessly on.

There is hope! Our hope is in Jesus and what God has done through him! Through God's Gift of forgiveness, we not only have hope to redeem this cycle in our own lives, but we can reverse this spiral in the lives of others as well. We do not have to be enslaved by this victim/predator cycle/spiral. Stress, anxiety, and depression no longer have to remain when we allow Christ Jesus into the deepest parts of our heart to break this cycle down.

The truth that the Holy Spirit speaks to us can be applied to the offense(s) to keep the freedom flowing. Thus, truth reverses this cycle, and frees us from the trap of the lies baited by our enemy.

Check out what the Bible says: Romans 12:1-2, Mark 7:20-23, Matthew 5:21-22, Matthew 7:1-3, Hebrews 3:12-13, Ephesians 1:7, 1 John 1:9, Matthew 18:21-35, Ephesians 4:32, John 20:23, 2 Corinthians 5:18-2

Appendix B

A Sample Prayer of Forgiveness

Lord Jesus, thank you for dying on the Cross and the work you completed in being the sacrifice for sin and paying the debt I owe for my wrongdoing. You accomplished forgiveness once and for all. I now receive the words of Psalm 32 which says, "Blessed is the one whose transgressions are forgiven, whose sins are covered." I wish to acknowledge, confess, and repent for any part of, and all guilt created by, the bitterness, resentment, and blame I have used to deny the hurt in my heart toward my offender(s). Thank you Lord for setting me free. I release the shame, and receive your mercy and grace.

I surrender to you the right to judge my offender(s). You alone are the Judge of their speech and actions. I give to you, Lord, the hurt I feel, whether they meant to hurt me or not. Whether the offense was real or just imagined on my part, I give it to you. I let go of the things I have used to control people and circumstances to meet my demands and expectations (list specific things if known) _____ .
I now trust you, Father God, to be strong in my weakness.

Lord, I forgive (specific person/s) _____ for (specific offense/s) _____.

By your ability (grace), Lord, I will no longer wrongly (condemningly) judge (list persons if known) _____ for their intentional or unintentional actions that hurt me. I trust you to be the righteous Judge, ruling with perfect justice and perfect mercy. I give up ruminating, blaming, justifying, complaining, and all forms of denying the truth about this situation(s).

Father God, where I have perceived you responsible for the pain I feel, forgive me for wrongly judging you. Where I have falsely blamed myself, condemned myself, or hated things about myself that you created me to be, forgive me.

Lord, heal my spirit, mind, soul, and body. Wash me clean as I break out of the debtor's prison. I declare myself whole, released from any torment in which my enemy would seek to imprison me. Christ has forgiven and I choose to receive his forgiveness. Therefore, I am forgiven, and I forgive as he has forgiven.

Amen

Appendix C

Emotions and Misbeliefs (Lies)

Identification List

Here are seven categories of emotions and accompanying lies (about self, other people, and God) producing bad feelings and pain. Remember, *naming* helps in the *reclaiming*. Use this list to help put some words to what you may be feeling and thinking. Renounce the lies and believe the Truth.

1. Abandonment (rejected, deserted, discarded, forgotten, left out, lost, don't belong ...)

"I am all alone. I have been overlooked. I will always be alone. They do not need me. I don't matter. No one even cares. They are not coming back. There is no one to protect me. God has forsaken me - too. No one will believe me. I cannot trust anyone. I am afraid they won't come back. I will never be as close to God as other people."

2. Shame (ashamed, depraved, failure, fault, stupid, trashy, unclean, unfit, unworthy ...)

"I am so stupid, ignorant, an idiot. I am not worthy to receive anything from God. I am the problem. When something is wrong, it is my fault. I am a bad person. If you knew the real me, you would reject me. I must wear a mask so that people won't find out how horrible I am and reject me. I have messed up so badly that I have missed God's best for me. I should have done something to have stopped it from happening. I allowed it. I was a participant. I should have known better. It was my fault. I should have told someone. I knew what was going to happen yet I stayed anyway. I felt pleasure so I must have wanted it. I was a participant. It happened because of my looks, my gender, my body, etc."

3. Fear (anxious, desperate, fearful, hysterical, nervous, scared, terror, untrusting ...)

"I am going to die, he/she is going to hurt me. I do not know what to do. If I tell, they will come back and hurt me. If I trust, I will die. He/she/they are coming back. It is just a matter of time before it happens again. If I let him/her/them into my life they will hurt me too. Something bad will happen if I tell, stop it, confront it. They are going to get me. Doom is just around the corner."

4. Powerless (confined, cornered, defenseless, frail, helpless, impotent, oppressed, weak ...)

"I cannot stop this. He/she/they are too strong to resist. There is no way out. I am too weak to resist. The pain is too great to bear. I cannot get away. I am going to die and I cannot do anything about it. I cannot get loose. I am overwhelmed. I don't know what to do. Everything is out of control. I am pulled from every direction. Not even God can help me. I am too small to do anything."

5. Tainted (crazy, careless, damaged, flawed, ruined, screwed up, wasted ...)

"I am dirty, shameful, evil, perverted, etc. because of what happened to me. My life is ruined. I will never feel clean again. Everyone can see my shame, filth, dirtiness, etc. I will always be hurt/ damaged/ broken because of what has happened. I will never be happy. I will always be unclean, filthy, etc. God could never want me after what has happened to me. My body parts are dirty. No one will ever really be able to love me."

6. Invalidation (belittled, betrayed, disgraced, inferior, insignificant, unappreciated, unloved ...)

"I am not loved, needed, wanted, cared for, or important. They do not need me. I am worthless, have no value. I was a mistake. I should have never been born. I am in the way; I am a burden. I was never liked by them because I was ____ . God could never love or accept me. I could never be as ____ as she/he. I could never jump high enough to please him/her. I am not acceptable. My feelings don't matter."

7. Hopeless (defeated, fatigued, despair, disoriented, need to isolate ...)

"It is never going to get any better. There is no way out. It will just happen again and again. There is no good thing for me. I have no reason to live. There are no options for me. I just want to die. Nothing good will ever come of this. I feel trapped."

Note: This list is adapted from p. 405 of Ed Smith's "Beyond Tolerable Recovery" manual. Adopted by Dr. Ed Hersh; see http://bluerockbnb.com/healing.

Sample Inner Vows

I will NEVER ...

... let anyone love me

... be weak

... trust anyone

... allow myself to feel

... allow myself to need

... let them take anything away from me

... allow anyone to touch me

... share what is mine

... allow anyone to give me money

... write, read, understand

... allow myself to be hit

... go out at night

... let you see who I am

... let anyone know I hurt

... tell a woman anything

... let a man control me

... be responsible for actions of others

... receive a compliment

... participate in life

... allow a woman in my heart

... be anything worthwhile

... be sick

... be violent or abusive ... grow up, mature

I will ALWAYS ...

... remain aloof, separate, independent, self-sufficient

... be logical

... be in control of my life

... be proud of _____

...stay away from people who _____

Bibliography

Amen, Daniel. *Healing the Hardware of the Soul: Enhance Your Brain to Improve Your Work, Love, and Spiritual Life.* New York, NY: Free Press, 2002.

Andrews, Andy. *The traveler's gift.* Nashville, TN: Thomas Nelson Publishing, 2012.

Augsburger, David. *The Freedom of Forgiveness: Seventy Times Seven.* Chicago, IL: Moody Press, 1988.

Barna, George. *American individualism shines through in people's self-image.* Barna Research Online. www.barna.org, 2007.

Boice, James M. *Foundations of the Christian Faith: A Comprehensive & Readable Theology.* Downers Grove, IL: InterVarsity Press, 1986.

Bridges, Jerry. *Trusting God.* Colorado Springs, CO: NavPress, 1988.

Brown, Brene. *The Gifts of Imperfection.* Center City, MA: Hazelden Publishing, 2010.

Bultmann, Rudolf. *Theology of the New Testament.* New York: Charles Scribner's Sons, 1955.

Cox, Paul. *Sacrifice the Leader: How to Cope When Others Shift Their Burdens Onto You.* Lake Mary, FL: Creation House, 2008.

DeMoss, Nancy. *Choosing Forgiveness: Your Journey to Freedom.* Chicago: Moody Publications, 2006.

Dial, Howard. *The Role of Suffering in the Life of the Christian* (study guide). Newburgh, IN: Trinity College and Seminary, 1999.

Ecker, Richard. *The stress myth:* Why the pressures of life don't have to get you down. Downers Grove, IL: Intervarsity Press, 1985.

Enright, R.D. *Choosing Forgiveness.* Washington, DC: American Psychological Association, 2001.

Fileta, Debra. *Are You Really Okay? Getting Real About Who You Are, How You're Doing, and Why It Matters.* Eugene, OR: Harvest House Publishers, 2021.

Friesen, J., E.J. Wilder, A. Bierling, R. Koepcke, and M. Poole. *The Life Model: Living From the Heart Jesus Gave You.* Pasadena, CA: Shepherd House, Inc, 2004.

Frost, Jack. *Experiencing Father's Embrace: Teacher's Manual.* Conway, SC: Shiloh Place Ministries, 2005.

Grudem, Wayne. *Systematic Theology: An Introduction to Biblical Doctrine.* Grand Rapids, MI: Inter-Varsity Press and Zondervan, 1994.

Hargrave, T. "The work of forgiveness: Miles to go before we sleep." *Marriage and Family: A Christian Journal,* 2(3) (1999): 315-323.

Hersh, Edward. *Christ-centered Forgiveness in Mental Health Treatment and Relational Conflict Resolution.* Dissertation, Trinity College and Theological Seminary, Newburgh, IN, 2010.

_____. *Escaping the Pain of Offense: Empowered to Forgive from the Heart.* Millersville, PA: Edward Hersh, 2013.

Hersh, E. and R. Hughes. "The Role of Suffering and Disability: Evidence from Scripture," *Journal of Religion, Disability and Health,* 9 3 (2005): 85-94.

Hodge, Charles. *Systematic Theology* (Vol. 2). Grand Rapids, MI: Eerdmans Publishing, 1997.

Holiday, Ryan. *Ego is the Enemy.* New York: Penguin Random House, 2006.

Jeffress, Robert. *When Forgiveness Doesn't Make Sense.* Colorado Springs, CO: Waterbrook Press, 2000.

Jennings, Timothy R. *The God-Shaped Brain: How Changing Your View of God Transforms Your Life.* Downers Grove, IL: IVP Press, 2017.

_____. *The God-Shaped Heart: How Correctly Understanding God's Love Transforms Us.* Grand Rapids, MI: Baker Books, 2017.

Jersak, Brad. *Can You Hear Me? Tuning in to the God who Speaks.* Abbotsford, BC: Fresh Wind Press, 2008.

Jordan, James. *Sonship: A Journey into Father's Heart.* Taupo, New Zealand: Tree of Life Media, 2012.

Kendall, R. T. *Total Forgiveness.* Lake Mary, FL: Charisma House, 2007.

Kraybill, D., S. Nolt, and D. Weaver-Zercher. *Amish Grace: How Forgiveness Transcended Tragedy.* San Francisco, CA: Jossey-Bass Inc., 2007.

Kurath, Ed. *I Will Give You Rest.* Post Falls, ID: DivinelyDesigned.com 2003.

Kylstra, Chester. *Restoring the Foundations: An Integrated Approach to Healing Ministry.* Santa Rosa Beach, FL: Proclaiming His Word Publications, 2003.

Leaf, Caroline. *Switch On Your Brain: The Key to Peak Happiness, Thinking, and Health.* Grand Rapids, MI: Baker Books, 2013.

_____. *The Perfect You: A Blueprint for Identity.* Grand Rapids, MI: Baker Books, 2017.

McCullough, M. E., E.J. Worthington, Jr., and K.C. Rachal. "Interpersonal forgiving in close relationships," *Journal of Personality and Social Psychology,* 73 (1997). 321-336.

McDowell, Josh. *Beyond Belief to Convictions.* Wheaton, IL: Tyndale House Publishers, 2002.

McMinn, Mark. and K. Meeks. *Psychology, Theology, and Spirituality in Christian Counseling* (Forgiveness: pp. 203-236). Wheaton, IL: Tyndale House Publishers, 1996.

Powlison, D. "Idols of the Heart: and 'Vanity Fair'," *Journal of Biblical Counseling,* 2 (1995): 35-50.

Richards, Janet Keller. *Unlocking Our Inheritance.* Anabaptist Reconciliation Planning Committee, Lancaster, PA, 2005.

Ripley, J. S. and E.L. Worthington, Jr. "Comparison of Hope-focused Communication and Empathy-based Forgiveness Group Interventions to Promote Marital Enrichment." *Journal of Counseling and Development,* 50 (2002): 452-463.

Rothschild, Babette. *The Body Remembers, Vol 2, Revolutionizing Trauma Treatment* . New York: W. W. Norton & Company, 2017.

Ruth, John L. *Forgiveness: A Legacy of the West Nickel Mines Amish School.* Scottdale, PA: Herald Press, 2007.

Sande Ken. *Peacemaking for Families: A Biblical Guide to Managing Conflict in Your Home.* Wheaton, IL: Tyndale House Publishers, 2002.

Sandford, John & Paula. *Transformation of the Inner Man.* Tulsa, OK: Victory House, 1982.

Sandford, J. & P. and l. Bowman. *Choosing Forgiveness.* Arlington, TX: Clear Stream Publishing, 1999.

Scazzero, Peter. *Emotionally Healthy Spirituality: Unleash a Revolution in Your Life in Christ.* Nashville, TN: Thomas Nelson Publishing, 2006.

Seamands, Stephen. *Wounds that Heal: Bringing Our Hurts to the Cross.* Downers Grove, IL: InterVarsity Press, 2003.

Smalley, Gary & John Trent. *The Blessing.* Nashville, TN: Thomas Nelson Publishing. 1986.

Smedes, Lewis B. *Forgive and Forget: Healing the Hurts We Don't Deserve.* San Francisco: Harper & Row Publishers, 1984.

Smedes, Lewis B. *The Art of Forgiving.* Nashville, TN: Moorings, 1996.

Smith, Edward M. *Healing Life's Deepest Hurts: Let the Light of Christ Dispel the Darkness in Your Soul.* Ventura, CA: Regal Books, 2002.

The Holy Bible (New International Version). Grand Rapids, MI: Zondervan, 1985. Note: NIV is the version referenced mostly. Other translations are referenced also.

Thompson, Curt. *Anatomy of the Soul.* Wheaton, IL: Tyndale House Publishing, 2010.

_____. *The Soul of Shame.* Downers Grove, IL: InterVarsity Press, 2015.

Van der Kolk, Bessel. *The Body Keeps the Score: Brain, Mind, and Body in the Healing of Trauma*. New York: Penguin Publishing Group, 2015.

Viola, Frank. *Hang On, Let Go*. Brentwood, TN: Tyndale Momentum, 2021.

Wade, N.G. and E.L. Worthington, Jr. "Overcoming Interpersonal Offenses: Is Forgiveness the Only Way to Deal with Unforgiveness?" *Journal of Counseling and Development*, 81 (2003): 343-353.

Worthington, E.L., Jr. *Handbook of Forgiveness*. New York: Brunner-Routledge. Yalom, ID. Theory and Practice of Group Psychotherapy. New York: Basic Books, 2005.

_____. *Five Steps to Forgiveness: The Art and Science of Forgiving*. New York: Crown House Publishing, 2001.

_____. *Forgiveness and Reconciliation*. Downers Grove, IL: InterVarsity Press, 2004.

Wright, Henry W. *A More Excellent Way: Be in health*. Thomaston, GA: Pleasant Valley Publications, 2005.

Yancey, Philip. *Disappointment with God*. Grand Rapids, MI: Zondervan, 1988.

About the Author

Dr. Edward Hersh is a Board Certified Christian Counselor (BCCC). In 2010 he completed a Doctor of Religious Studies program in Conflict Management at Trinity Theological Seminary in Newburgh, Indiana, and in 2001 earned a Master of Arts in Human Service Counseling from Regent University in Virginia Beach, Virginia. Pastor Ed has completed advanced level training in techniques for healing of the inner person. As an ordained minister he provides chaplain services and pastoral counseling to individuals, couples, and families. His counseling, writing, and teaching ministry have helped thousands around the world grow in reclaiming their God-given purpose in life. He maintains membership in American Association of Christian Counselors (AACC), Christian Association of Psychological Studies (CAPS), and other professional and ministry organizations.

Past employment experiences have included seventeen years in software development and a variety of jobs in foreign language teaching, social services, and adaptive technology training. Ed's volunteer Board service has included the VisionCorps, Bethany Christian Services, Virginia Beach Mayor's Committee on Persons with Disabilities, Breath of Life Ministries, and Pennsylvania Council of the Blind. Ed and Stephanie co-founded a group called Respect Young America (advocating for teens and pre-born children), and Ed is the founding President of Red Rose Council of the Blind.

Since transitioning to pastoral and counseling ministry in 2000, Ed has worked with a number of churches and ministries including Light of Hope Community Service Organization in Lancaster, Pennsylvania. Dr. Hersh's desire is to see professional and para-professional services connected for mental health and addictions treatment to care for the whole person—spirit, soul, mind, and body.

Ed and his wife Stephanie, married since 1980, are the parents of four adult children and have grandchildren. They are active in community service and church ministry. They are Innkeepers at Blue Rock Bed and Breakfast near Lancaster. They host many who come to the popular Pennsylvania Dutch Country for vacation. See more at https://bluerockbnb.com.

Besides the lodging hospitality services, Ed and Stephanie also offer counseling, debriefing, guided retreat, and respite through the BnB Healing Ministry. For ministry information see https://bluerockbnb.com/healing.

Ed has also authored the book *Escaping the Pain of Offense: Empowered to Forgive from the Heart*

Visit the author's blog at: https://edwardhersh.com

Invitation:

We would welcome your stay at the Blue Rock Bed and Breakfast. We also welcome those who wish to dive into deeper ministry around the themes of this book. Especially helpful is a model of personal debriefing for Christian missionaries, pastors, and church leaders to help find new vitality and meaning for their ministry. This model is a proven method of assessing events of life and ministry in a safe and supportive environment. It is a five-day structured progression through stressors, associated losses, adjustments, and recovery of hopes and dreams. The result is fresh vision and energy for reengagement.

We would also welcome an opportunity to join your venue to share around the themes of this book. Please contact the author to share with your group, in person or online.

Questions For Each Chapter To Help Apply

Below are questions to accompany the content of each chapter. These questions are designed to help the reader apply the themes of inner transformation to their own personal journey. Faith without deeds is dead, right (James 2:14)? It does no one good to know about transformation without wholeheartedly surrendering to the process. I encourage taking each question before the Lord and asking him for the answer. Sit with it, pray about it, rephrase it, and personalize it. May God meet you in a mighty, Spirit-led, transforming, life-affirming way.

Chapter 1 – Housing Peace in the Heart

Where might there be some unbelief in my life?

What specific lie(s) might I be believing?

What is the truth that will turn me toward God?

What might I be holding on to (or hiding) in my house, hoping that God's reconstruction won't come to (expose) this closet/cabinet/room?

What am I thankful for that God already began (or completed) to make my house a better place to live?

Am I giving God praise for the good works he is doing? How so?

What is Proverbs 4:23 ("guard your heart") speaking to me in specific situations of my life?

What are the ANTS (automatic negative thoughts) that need to be exterminated in my life?

What needs to happen to guarantee that consuming more "pure spiritual milk" becomes a reality?

Where might my demands to understand be getting in the way of trusting God? In what ways might I be more prone to trying to find peace on my own rather than asking God for peace?

Chapter 2 – Knowing Is Not Enough

How is knowing about transformation different from surrendering to the process of change? What are some personal applications for me?

What aspects of the workings of the computer illustration stand out to me?

What specific Scriptures show the words of Jesus identifying the heart as the source of behaviors? What are these verses speaking to me?

Explain the idea that "bad roots" produce "bad fruits"?

True or False: All people are born with a virus of sin. Explain.

What are your thoughts on the statement, "Knowing the truth will set you free?" Explain John 8:32 in context of verse 31 preceding it.

What examples can I identify in my life that show how I might have missed a degree of Christ's freedom because of my disobedience? What are some examples of the obedience side of things, and resulting freedom?

What lies might I be believing that are influencing my self-concept? What is the truth with which to replace these lies?

Chapter 3 – Trade the Will for the Well

To what degree overall might I be relying on will over well? In what specific areas of my life?

What might I need to surrender in order to show willingness to engage the process of transformation from willpower to well power?

Do I need more well power to forgive (a person, group, or situation)?

How might I be a more devoted worshiper in spirit and truth?

Is there something(s) in my life I need to give up that is in the way of gaining access to God (the Well)?

What is the next step I need to take in surrendering it to God?

Part 2

Chapter 4 - Spiritual Laws that Govern Life

How would you explain the statement, "The spiritual realm is just as relevant as the physical realm in placing boundaries on how life works?"

What are some examples of workings of spiritual laws in my life? When, where, how have they worked? Are working?

Keeping Romans 7:15 in mind, list those things that you don't want to do, but keep finding yourself doing anyway. Be specific.

Then list the good things that you would like to do, but somehow never are able to do. Again, be specific.

What past struggles in my life have been applications (or maybe are still applications) of Romans 7:24-25? Things that made (are making) you miserable and desperate for God to redeem?

Chapter 5 – Bitter Root Judgments

What is the difference between "good" judging and "bad" judging?

Describe a "root of bitterness" referred to in Hebrews 12:15.

What instances of bad judging am I aware of? That I am guilty of? That someone might be guilty of judging me?

In what relationships, or in what situations, might I be trying to be judge instead of allowing God to be Judge?

Has condemning judgment of myself been a problem for me (past or present)? How so?

What Inner Vow(s) might I have made that come to mind reading this chapter? (See Appendix D for examples.)

Now ask your HEART the last few questions, not just your intellect.

Our heart contains both bad roots and good roots at the same time. Explain. Why is this important to remember?

Chapter 6 – Emotional Trunk

How is what I read about emotions in this chapter different from what I thought about emotion before?

Where might I have been (or right now be) denying or numbing a sounding alarm?

What are the emotions and what are the messages? If I cannot determine the message(s), to whom (where) can I go for help?

Using the Misbeliefs/Emotional Identification list in Appendix C, what emotions do you most closely identify with? Try to think of additional words/phrases that describe how you feel/think. How might these connect to the roots revealed in the previous chapter?

How is Emotional Capacity (EC) different from Emotional Intelligence (EI)?

What are some ways to increase EC?

Explain why/how self-concept drives EC?

Chapter 7 – Identity and Shame

What do I think about having light and dark living inside together at the same time? What evidence do I see?

Do I "love" God? How so? How not?

Do I "love" myself? How so? How not?

How big of an issue in my life is self-rejection? Explain why.

What did I learn here about shame that surprises me? May not completely agree with? Am puzzled by? Thankful for?

Questions in the text:

What do I think about vulnerability?

Do I allow myself to feel?

Am I afraid to be honest with myself? What do I fear?

Am I honest with myself about my mental and emotional condition?

What positive expressions would I like to see more of in my life (e.g., love, joy, peace …)?

How could I, being more honest with myself about my emotional condition, produce better results?

Are any of my activities/behaviors numbing pain?

If so, what kind of help do I need to address the problem?

Am I truly willing to make the adjustments necessary for lasting transformation?

What is the next step for improvement?

Can/will I do it now? What is the date/time the step will be taken by?

Chapter 8 - Trauma

As I read this chapter, what Type A traumas come to mine? Type B traumas? What might this mean for seeking or applying more healing in my life?

How well, and in what areas, have I received The Blessing growing up?

What effects of a Type C trauma have I encountered?

What tangible and intangible losses can I identify during the last year or so?

How is my adjustment to these losses going? Have I "grieved" sufficiently? How so? How not?

Part 3

Chapter 9 – Give Away the House

What is the #1 "take away" for me in this chapter? How do I plan to apply it?

How does the author define forgiveness?

How do I define forgiveness (based on what the Bible says)?

What does it mean to be "born from above"? Am I "born again"? Am I continuing to allow God to do his rebirth in my thinking, feeling, and acting? How so? How not so?

What does surrender look like? How difficult is surrender for me? What holds me back from more complete surrender?

What might I have been falsely believing from the list of things that forgiveness is not?

Do I have symptoms of bitterness? What bad judging might be at the root?

(Again, ask your HEART this question, and not just your intellect).

What might I be holding against God? Am I willing to release it?

What guilt might I be falsely directing at myself? Am I willing to ask God's forgiveness for this self-condemnation?

Chapter 10 – Clean Up the House

How would I explain sanctification to a new believer?

How is change from the inside out different from merely trying to change behaviors?

How would I explain being "transformed by the renewal of your mind" in Romans 12:1-2? How is this being practiced in my own life?

How would I rate my self-honesty (in relation to the condition of my inner being)? Would my closest friend(s) consider me to be honest with myself? Why or why not?

How would I rate my humility (in relation to needed change in my inner being)? Would my closest friend(s) consider me to be humble in regard to openness to transformation and sanctification? Why or why not?

What myths about forgiveness might I still be believing?

If you haven't worked through the "unforgiveness examination exercise" in this chapter, do so now.

What might I be experiencing from the list of "common effects of unforgiveness"?

How might the practice of the healing prayer model (discussed here) help with adding more rest to my soul? How can I apply it (practice it more)?

Chapter 11 – Care for the Neighborhood

Describe the difference between forgiveness and reconciliation.

Is it easy for me to believe "people are not the enemy" when I feel hurt? Who is the real enemy, and what is the grand scheme (John 10:10)?

What does it mean to become an enemy of self?

Where in the Bible does the author identify the "Great Commission to Forgive"? How does this Commission to Forgive guide me/us as a Christ-follower?

What is the difference between guilt and shame?

How can I be a better reconciler?

Part 4

Chapter 12 – Remove Blockages to Peace

Which of the blockages mentioned do I identify with the most at this point in my life? How so? How would you have answered this ten years ago?

What role has "sin" played in slowing down my pace to peace?

What role has "unmet needs" played in limiting my pace to peace?

What role has "false beliefs" played in blocking my pace to peace?

What role has emotional "pain" played in robbing my inner peace?

In what ways might I have chosen religion over true relationship with God?

Which of the cognitive distortions mentioned here do I identify with most? Explain how they manifest in me.

Are so-called "mental health disorders" (labels) a concern for me or those I live with or closely work with? How might they be helping or hurting the healing process?

Am I trusting God as my primary caretaker and "doctor"?

Is there anything I do or say that contributes to stigmatizing mental health concerns?

Chapter 13 – Garden the Soul

What are some parallels between growing vegetables in a garden and spiritual growth?

In what ways might I not be allowing (and am I allowing) God to be the Gardener of my soul?

In what ways am I prepared (and preparing) for the harvest of souls in God's garden? Is my view of evangelism in line with God's transformational healing work?

Does my life show evidence of esteeming Jesus? How might I esteem him more?

Is there "pain" in my life that indicates an area of loss (not yet found and healed by Jesus)? Is there a part of my soul not yet "evangelized" (as talked about in this chapter)?

Consider the answers to the questions posed at the end of the section about living as a champion. Take time to rejoice in your strengths, and let God be strong in your weakness.

Chapter 14 – Lead with Transformational Living

Have you thought about, and answered, the questions posed in the text of this chapter? If not, go ahead and do so for a good start to applying transformation.

"Are you tired, worn out, burned out on religion ..." (Matthew 11:28 Message)?

What are you doing to "guard your heart" (Proverb 4:23)? Daily? Short term? Longer term?

What are your thoughts about "dry dock"? How do you plan to apply this?

How can you be more intentional about psychological rest, building emotional stamina, and transformational renewing of the mind and heart?

Chapter 15 - Choose God Daily

What things make people not want to embrace change? What makes me resistant to change?

Answer the questions for each of the eleven parts of the definition of "sanctify."

Are you willing to take the challenge of studying these topics deeper for a period of time?

How can I apply the idea of "baptism of repentance" in my own journey?

How can more of the Holy Spirit's presence in my life make a difference for the better? Be specific with thoughts, feelings, and actions being transformed.

Am I allowing God to be Judge in all situations? Where might surrendering to God the full rights of judgment be necessary to apply?

Chapter 16 - God Is Altogether Good

What things have happened in my life that have caused me to question God's goodness? What beliefs about God do I hold on to that make me think God is to blame for bad things?

How difficult is it for me to believe in the absolute, unequivocal goodness of God? Has it always been this way? What may have changed my perspective?

John's Gospel records many reminders of God's peace that Jesus gave to his disciples in the final hours of his time with them on earth. Why might this be so?

How easy/difficult is it for me to trust God in trying times? Has there been a time when it was easier/more difficult? What changed, or why hasn't it changed?

What is my attitude toward disappointment/adversity/"suffering"/difficulty in general? What might be good to surrender to God for change (to make this more like what the Bible says)?

How could I be better prepared to help others in their struggles with trying times?

Chapter 17 - Apply Truth

Answer the questions posed throughout the text of this chapter.

What are some additional Scripture texts that might have inner transformational themes (that you might now notice more easily with the themes of this book in mind)?

I encourage the reader to be on the lookout for new Bible revelation, and continue to allow the Lord to speak to your heart about these "heart messages."

Engage the throne of God for his guidance. Seek him each day, and sometimes every hour. What is HE wanting to transform, right now, in this moment of discomfort, disappointment, or some pain-based thoughts or feelings? Am I willing to apply the process in order to pace to peace? If yes, God's richest blessings await. Trust the process and celebrate the miracles. Receive your Gift of peace today!